"This book is a long-overdue and unique. It is a treasure-tro[...]
from thousands of pages of scholarship and research on sel[...]
can be immediately used by anyone in sales to drive growth and improve [...]
These are not just anecdotes and 'war stories', but genuine insights based on high-quality
scientific research, but presented in a way that any sales professional can take action on. A
fantastic book, and a phenomenal achievement".

Professor Dr. Nick Lee, *Professor of Marketing, Research Environment Lead*
(Marketing), Warwick Business School

"There are many sales books that will tell you that their model or latest fad will be the
magic bullet that changes your sales game. Anderson makes no such promise. What is on
offer with Anderson is evidence based, pragmatic ways of thinking and working that will
change the way you approach, plan, deliver and follow up sales. Every chapter gives insight
into what works in real life and encourages you to develop your own practice in a way your
customers will appreciate".

Karen Bailey, *Head of Competence Development, Volvo Trucks, UK*

"We were already an established, profitable and fast growing B2B SME when we first met
Anderson.
Every conversation was relevant, realistic and refreshing. Just as is every chapter in this
book, and the information within. Detailed, insightful and transformative. We benefited
beyond any reasonable expectation, by making these oft overlooked processes, part of the
culture of our business".

Barry Cooper, *founder and owner, Cooper Solutions Limited, 2001–2019*

"In 'B2B Sales Management for Start-ups and SMEs,' Anderson Hirst brilliantly encapsu-
lates the essence of digital transformation in sales, offering invaluable insights and methodologies that are indispensable in today's rapidly evolving market. I highly recommend this
book to educational institutions for courses in sales, sales management, entrepreneurship,
and marketing. Its practical, research-led approach demystifies the complexities of sales,
making it an essential guide for future leaders and innovators".

Johannes Habel, *Associate Professor, University of Houston,*
C.T. Bauer College of Business

"Small and Medium businesses make up half of the (UK) economy. Our research shows that
most struggle with sales. This book fills a void, providing excellent explanations of all the
aspects that make for an effective sales function. If you are serious about building a sales
function that will grow your business, this is a must read."

Guy Lloyd, *Director, Institute of Sales Professionals*

Sales Management for Start-ups and SMEs

Managers and entrepreneurs know they have a great product or service – but they may not know how best to sell it.

Useful for nearly any sector or industry, this book is a thoroughly practical guide on how to build an excellent sales organisation, brick by brick. Creating an effective sales organisation is a challenge for many businesses, and it's easy to waste resources on ineffective approaches. Many MBA and executive education programmes do not cover sales management in any depth. Filling this knowledge gap, this guide will help readers create their own unique, high-performing sales organisation that fits their product and market environment. Evidence-based and field-tested, it will give answers to critical questions, including:

- Which sales process should we use?
- How do we recruit, retain and inspire our sales team?
- What should we measure, and how should we manage it?
- What do great sales managers do?

Rich with case studies from the author's 25 years of sales consulting experience, this book will appeal to a wide variety of managers and entrepreneurs who wrestle with the question "How do I grow my business?" from sales directors to start-up founders to MBA students.

Anderson Hirst has worked with over 300 international clients over 25 years as a consultant and trainer in sales. With an MBA focusing on sales, behaviour and change themes, he brings a unique evidence-based discipline to his work, demystifying the black box of sales for clients. Today, he is actively involved in working with start-ups and SMEs to help them design and implement effective B2B sales strategies for growth.

Sales Management for Start-ups and SMEs

Building an Effective Scalable Sales Organisation

Anderson Hirst

Routledge
Taylor & Francis Group

NEW YORK AND LONDON

Designed cover image: Getty

First published 2025
by Routledge
605 Third Avenue, New York, NY 10158

and by Routledge
4 Park Square, Milton Park, Abingdon, Oxon, OX14 4RN

Routledge is an imprint of the Taylor & Francis Group, an informa business

© 2025 Anderson Hirst

ISBN: 9781032583273 (hbk)
ISBN: 9781032583259 (pbk)
ISBN: 9781003449614 (ebk)

DOI: 10.4324/9781003449614

Typeset in Sabon
by codeMantra

For Helen, Lorna & Alastair

Contents

Acknowledgements

This book is a perfect example of Isaac Newton's quote:

"If I have seen further, it is by standing on the shoulders of giants".

There have been so many giants that have inspired and educated me to make this book a reality. Here are a few of them:

Meredith Norwich at Routledge for seeing the potential in my book, championing the cause, and enabling its publication. Her endorsement of the project has given me massive motivation to get it completed.

Bethany Nelson at Routledge for being ruthlessly efficient in answering my endless stream of newbie questions during the writing process.

Lauren Purser for taking my dull PowerPoint images and turning them into the wonderful diagrams you will see throughout the text.

In terms of my sales and consulting career:

Alan Sweet, my first sales manager and the best coach I could ask for, to get me excited about sales. I have wonderful memories of covering South Wales and doing joint visits with him. He was very encouraging and set me up for success with my first ever ink-written purchase order!

Chris McBean, at Unilever, who saw my potential to be a key account manager and recruited me to be part of an excellent sales team. He is a highly intelligent, driven sales leader who took me to the next level of strategic thinking.

George van Evert at Krauthammer International, who recruited me for my first training consultant role, and taught me the importance of the highest standards when working with clients and showed me how we can most effectively change behaviour through training and coaching.

Francesc Fabregas and Santiago Fernández at GEC SA, true leviathans in the consulting world, who helped me understand knowledge management in sales, complex consulting projects, scope and business management.

The many academics and teaching staff at Warwick Business School who taught me to think critically and to use existing research to define best practices. Through the MBA programme, I had time to deeply explore evidence-based sales literature.

Professor Mike Bresnan, my dissertation supervisor, who guided me through my research project on sales process adoption in the automotive sector. He opened my eyes to the commercial value of my work, culminating in me founding Selling Interactions to help clients develop their sales organisations.

Professor Nick Lee and Associate Professor Johannes Habel, two giants of the sales research world (quoted in this book), not only inspired me but are also brilliant role models for practical academic research in sales.

Sarah Jackson and Monica Garcia-Romero of the Careers Plus team at Warwick, who put me in front of MBA students to run many workshops, sharpening my approach to sales organisation development.

Steven Adjei, a Warwick MBA alum and author of the excellent book "Pay the Price". His encouragement to get me started on writing this book was invaluable.

Clients have played a massive role in this book. I have worked with some truly inspirational sales leaders from whom I have learnt so much.

The training and consulting community: There are simply too many to name, but so much of what I have learnt about organisational improvement has been from experienced and generous consultants I've worked with.

My wife Helen has continually encouraged me in my career and supported me unstintingly in the writing of this book. She is also an excellent role model for continuous learning and my very best friend.

My daughter Lorna and son Alastair constantly challenge me to be a better human, and as the next generation and digital natives, their insights into problem solving and learning have greatly inspired me as to how technology is shaping sales.

The last thanks go to you, the readers, because without you, what is the point of a book like this? I have tried in every sentence I wrote to think about the men and women around the world, putting their heart and soul into growing their businesses.

I sincerely hope it helps you do that.

Introduction

Let's keep this introduction short. I am guessing you'd like to get on and read the things that will help you grow your business!

Why is this book on sales management different?

There are plenty of "When I...". books, that is stories from ex-VP of sales leaders. who have 'been there and done it'.

These can be extremely valuable when they have worked in the same context as you, but the methods are not always transferable to all contexts.

Then there are the academic textbooks. These are solid and well-researched, but extracting wisdom from them can be time-consuming.

I had a conversation with an entrepreneur in 2023 who said, "It would be great if someone could objectively summarise trusted best practices and research in sales management, to save me doing it myself".

That is pretty much the entire design concept of this book.

It is based upon a principle I call *research-led sales excellence*. What does this mean? You would not expect your doctor/physician to try 'quack' treatments on you. You would expect them to diagnose your personal situation carefully and then make a recommendation based on evidence-based medical practice. This book uses a similar approach. The content is based on:

- My work with around 300 clients internationally as a *consultant* and *sales trainer*, over 25 years. This has given me exposure to a wide range of business improvement tools and processes to aid growth. Importantly, I have worked with many start-ups and SMEs across multiple sectors and geographies.
- A review of 2,500+ research papers and sales/marketing books to identify *evidence-based* best practices. There has been a huge increase in high-quality academic research into sales over the last 20 years, shining a light on an area that is sometimes seen as a 'black box' or 'dark art'.
- Thirty years' personal frontline experience, selling a variety of products and services (I am still active in selling as I write this book) from industrial chemicals to e-learning. The continual involvement in selling every day hopefully keeps my feet firmly on the ground!

I believe the combination of these three perspectives is unique and provides you with a highly practical, solid and researched approach to driving growth in your own start-up SME, which translates across sectors: I've done the hard work of identifying best practices in sales, so you don't have to.

It is a direct application of Kurt Lewin's quote: *Nothing is as practical as a good theory.*[1]

Who is this book for?

This book is for you if:

- You work in a start-up, a small to medium-sized enterprise (SME), or in a smaller division of a larger organisation.
- You want to grow your sales.
- You sell to other businesses (B2B).
- Your go-to-market approach requires an element of *personal selling*; that is, your customers want to have a conversation with you before buying.

It is very much written to help make your organisation *scalable* by making your sales approach visible with clear processes that can be trained, explained and delegated.

It aims to help you create a sales organisation that has *sustainable* and *predictable* growth. For sure, predictability of revenue growth is a hallmark of a great sales organisation.[2]

How to use this book

This book is written a little bit like a car maintenance guide: You can dip into the section you need to, to address the problem you want to solve. If you are already an experienced sales manager with some gaps in your knowledge, this approach will save you time.

For start-ups looking to figure out their basic sales approach, reading the chapters in order will help you put the essential building bricks in place in a logical sequence. For example, it makes sense to have a rough sense of your sales strategy (Chapter 2) before you design your sales process (Chapter 3).

If you do not have any personal sales experience, Chapter 4 will give you the essential elements of a typical B2B sales process to work from. If you have your first sales meeting tomorrow – start here!

As the approaches in this book are built upon a wide variety of excellent sources of sales best practices, these are signposted in the main text and listed at the end of each chapter, so you can go deeper into a topic if you want to.

You will also find more sales-related content at www.sellinginteractions.com.

A word on sales technology

The whole buy-sell paradigm is undergoing existential changes at the moment, thanks to a relentless stream of new technological innovations. At the time of writing, there are well over 1,200 companies providing different types of sales technology. As you read this book, I strongly urge you to look at all aspects of how you sell today and tomorrow, to consider how it might be better enabled by technology.

Learn by doing

One thing I have learnt from working with some truly excellent sales directors and strategists over the years is that it is very hard to design the perfect go-to-market approach up front. Only by trying sales strategies with customers can we truly learn.

As an example, this book will help you design your sales process. Once you start really using your sales process with customers, I am certain you will find ways to improve it quite quickly. This is normal and to be encouraged.

So, the best way to get maximum value from this book is to build *your* sales process, *your* sales methodology and *your* sales approach as you go along. Try them out. Make mistakes, make corrections, make improvements, but most of all, make them happen.

Sales management is a really dynamic, exciting and challenging profession. With the rapid advances in technology, it is set to become even more so.

I hope you enjoy using this book as much as I have enjoyed writing it.

Notes

1 D.J. Greenwood & M. Levin *Introduction to action research: Social research for social change* American Psychological Association Sage Publications 1998
2 A. Ross & J. Lemkin *From impossible to inevitable – How hyper-growth companies create predictable revenue* Wiley 2016

Chapter 1

The scalable sales organisation

What are the key elements we can define to make our sales organisation scalable?

There are two fundamental questions to ask up front if you are responsible for growth. Firstly, "Do you want to grow your sales?" If the answer is yes, then the second question is, "Do you have a plan on how to do that?". As the author Antoine de Saint-Exupéry once said, "A goal without a plan is just a wish". If we do want growth, then we need to put the building blocks in place to achieve it.

This book is designed to help you, brick by brick, build an excellent sales organisation (or tune an existing one) that delivers sustainable, predictable growth. Firstly, let's look at the building blocks we can use to build a sales organisation. They will form the basis of the individual chapters.

Sales as a system

Even a few moments of reflection would generate a long list of components that can be designed and improved in a sales organisation: the people we recruit, the job specification, training, coaching, targets, technology, incentives and so on. Andris Zoltners, the founder of global consultancy ZS Associates and his colleagues[1] recognised this in their *Sales Force Effectiveness Framework*. They argue the performance of a sales organisation is based on various *definers, shapers, exciters, enlighteners and controllers*. By paying attention to the parts, we can influence the output of the whole.

Imagine for a moment if the component parts do not align. For example, our product/solution requires a team sell, but we offer individual commission to the lead salesperson. How motivated is the team in this situation? Or if we expect to sell a complex, high investment solution with one sales call: In this situation, there is a clear disconnect between our sales process (way of selling) and the customer decision-making process (way of buying).

The systems thinking approach to sales is reinforced by other sales specialists: Dr. Christian Homburg and colleagues express it as "We are convinced that preoccupation with isolated solutions in sales cannot ultimately succeed".[2]

Paying attention to the building blocks of a sales organisation and their alignment is like having a team of Olympic rowers synchronised in their stroke. Ultimately, the result is a faster boat.

Defining the system makes it easier to scale

If you were leading a manufacturing organisation, you would be well used to *standard operating procedures*. You would be used to precisely defining layout and flow. How else

DOI: 10.4324/9781003449614-1

would you manage and control your output? Why, then, should sales be any different? The myth of *sales as an art* still persists, even though an army of researchers is systematically shining a light on just about every aspect of the profession.

In their very personal and wide experience of scaling start-ups, Aaron Ross and Jason Lemkin state this very clearly in their book *Impossible to Inevitable*: "Your ability to scale a sales team depends on making everything a system".[3] If we truly want to grow, we need to be able to see what good selling and sales management look like. It needs to be visible, defined and communicable.

Continuing the factory analogy, knowing intimately how the operation runs and how to manage it means we can build another successful factory in another location. We can recruit new team members and rapidly train and coach them to deploy the successful approach.

What are the basic building blocks of an effective sales organisation?

Before we get into the question of what defines a sales organisation, we need to talk about the boundaries of marketing. The relationship between sales and marketing has evolved substantially over time. The title of the seminal paper, *Ending the war between sales & marketing* by two giants of sales and marketing, Neil Rackham and Philip Kotler,[4] written in 2006, says a lot about the history of these two functions, which were often siloed and conflictual in their relations.

With the advent of digital marketing, technology and a shift to inbound marketing, the relationship is evolving in very different directions, with much more integrated 'revenue generating' arrangements emerging. Consultants McKinsey have argued the case for a more integrated technological approach in their whitepaper, *Six governing considerations to modernise marketing*.[5]

For the purposes of this book, activities like product marketing, brand management and content development are treated as marketing activities, whilst lead generation is shown inside the sales organisation, even though it is often part of marketing. In some ways, it doesn't matter which 'departments' activities fall under; it matters more that they get done and get done well.

Figure 1.1 outlines the core building blocks of an effective sales organisation that need to be in place and fit together well so that they can generate sustainable growth.

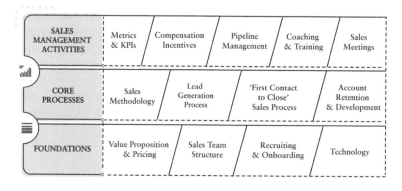

Figure 1.1 The core elements of a scalable sales organisation

The core processes

The key processes of an effective sales organisation are:

- Lead generation
- The first contact to close sales process
- Sales methodology: Our way of selling
- Account retention and development

Fundamentally, these four processes cover how we find opportunities and convert them into happy customers who stay with us and grow. Along with effective pricing,[6] the effectiveness of these processes will have a huge impact on an organisation's profit.

If we understand these processes really well, we can build structures and processes around them to sustain them.

Of course, these processes will only work if the value proposition we are offering is attractive to customers. If you are working in a start-up, you might not have proven your value proposition, and so we effectively have to 'learn by doing' and iterate our product/service based on customer feedback.

In this book, we will go through how to assess and design which processes will work best for your setting and how to embed them in your organisation so they become habits.

The sales methodology that we will cover in Chapter 5 is the detailed 'how' of selling. It will set out the attitudes, behaviours, skills, knowledge and routines that salespeople need to bring the sales process to life. Without them, anything we create in the way of processes will be 'paper tigers', which are nice ideas that are never lived into our daily behaviour.

Once the central processes are clear, we can measure them, train them, support them, incentivise them and improve them over time.

The supporting foundations

For the core processes to succeed, they need firm foundations. In a sales organisation, the foundations we will pay particular attention to are:

- Value proposition and pricing
- Organisational structure
- Recruitment and onboarding
- Technology

The value proposition is a way of answering the question, "Why should customers buy from you?" If there is not a compelling reason to buy, then any amount of organisational improvement is not likely to fix that problem. We will go into detail on how to do that in Chapter 7. As was already hinted at, pricing is a critical lever for growth and profits and sets the foundation for what is possible in terms of funding further investment and growth.

Alfred D Chandler is famously quoted with the line, "Structure follows strategy",[7] making the simple point that we need the structures in place to execute the strategy we have in mind. Surprisingly, few organisations actually seem to achieve this. Research quoted by Carucci and Shappell in 2022 estimated that only 10% of organisations achieve this.[8]

It's no different in sales organisations: We have to put the right people in the right roles to make the core processes work. This also means figuring out what types of roles we will need to support our sales process, a topic we will discuss in some detail in Chapter 8.

Similarly, once organisations start to grow, they need effective processes to recruit good people who can fill these roles and train them to competence as quickly as possible. Start-ups and SMEs may not have experience or the mechanisms to do this well, as they go from survival phases to maturity, and yet good recruitment is pretty much universally agreed to be a vital element of good sales management. Trish Bertuzzi argues that "Focus on recruiting needs to be upgraded from important to urgent"[9] while Cuevas et al. state that "A major determinant of sales performance is the quality of those recruited to the job".[10]

Technology hardly needs any introduction for business. At the time of writing, the headline article on saleshacker.com, an online community for salespeople, was "How to use AI for sales coaching: A sales manager's guide".[11] Choosing and deploying the correct technology is a challenge for many large organisations, let alone SMEs, that often have much restricted budgets and teams to work on them. Nonetheless, technology can clearly increase the efficiency and effectiveness of human operators and, if used well, can make a real difference to a sales team.

The management activities

The top row of the sales system model outlines the activities effective sales managers do on a daily basis to drive the central sales processes. The attitude, "A good plan violently executed now, is better than a perfect plan next week", attributed to General George S Patton,[12] generally serves us well in running sales organisations. This is because sales managers operate in a fast-changing, turbulent world where competitors often try to win our business. Setting a high-tempo pace based on execution and learning is generally thought to be more effective in this type of environment.[13]

What are the key activities sales managers should put in place?

- Coaching and training
- Setting and measuring KPIs
- Sales meetings
- Pipeline/opportunity management
- Designing and deploying compensation and incentives

These activities can be seen as accelerators to help the core processes flow with speed and efficiency.

How do we know what should be on the list of key sales management activities? Whilst there is unlikely to be a single model of success, two key studies have provided strong evidence for the most useful activities sales managers can perform to drive results. The first of these *An assessment of needed sales management skills* by Thomas Powers and his colleagues[14] provides a detailed list of 15 key activities. These include "*Provides effective verbal feedback*" and "*understands salesperson evaluation metrics*", two of our five core activities.

The second study, by Karen Peesker and her colleagues, published in 2019,[15] summarised the activities of effective sales managers into four categories: *Coaching, collaborating, customer engaging and championing*. This work reveals the importance of bringing together salespeople to solve problems, build morale and drive progress, which is why sales meetings and pipeline/opportunity management are on the list.

Finally, compensation and incentives are 'table stakes' for most sales organisations: Recruiting the best people is very difficult when we compete with our competitors for talent. Therefore, having motivating, appealing compensation and incentives in place is very important.

Mark Roberg sets out the importance of adapting the compensation and incentives programme according to the growth stage of the organisation,[16] and we will look at ways to structure your incentives so they do actually incentivise the behaviour that supports your core processes in Chapter 15.

Compensation and incentives provide us with a great example of how a sales system works: what we pay for sends a strong message about what management is looking to achieve, and so aligning this element with the structure, the sales process and the key performance indicators (KPIs) is important.

Adaptability and agility

Isn't there a risk of rigidity if we install too much process, structure and methodology? Entrepreneurship, agility and speed are often recognised as competitive advantages and benefits of start-ups and Small and medium sized enterprises (SMEs), versus large, bureaucratic organisations.

Poorly designed and implemented sales processes and sales methodology *can* stifle agility. Perhaps you have experienced this already in your career if you were sent on a training course with prescriptive sales techniques that you didn't feel were appropriate for your customers. Indeed, as sales is often a job done solo, mostly away from the scrutiny of management, salespeople often completely disregard rigid processes.

If designed well, a good sales process and structure can aid adaptability. If we have a sales team well used to implementing a way of selling that works and that they believe in, we have a team used to following processes! We can then adapt the process and, with good training and coaching, set the team in a different direction.

Understanding the building blocks of your sales organisation and having them codified and visible means we can also change them. This also enables us to go from being 'good' to 'great'.[17] Let's understand why.

Building a world-class sales organisation

What makes a 'great' sales organisation? 'Good' sales organisations achieve their target and 'make their number' at the year end. Everyone celebrates and breathes a sigh of relief: "We hit target!". But did they actually execute the strategy for the organisation? For example, what if one of the goals was to "achieve X sales of a new product" or "find 10% new customers?" Sometimes these 'secondary' goals get lost in the noise of the target achievement party.

A truly great sales organisation can:

- Sell the chosen product
- To the chosen segment
- At the agreed time
- At the target price

A truly great sales organisation can effectively "do what it has decided to do" and execute its chosen strategy. This is a compelling theme developed in detail by authors Jason Jordan and Michelle Vazzana in their excellent book *Cracking the sales management code*,[18] and we will look at the processes and KPIs we need in place to effectively refocus a sales organisation to align it with organisational strategy in Chapter 10.

For now, if we define, optimise and align the building blocks of our sales organisation, we can start on the path towards *predictable* and *sustainable* growth, targeting the *right product* to the *right customers* at the *right price* and *time*.

These are the hallmarks of a world-class sales organisation.

Into action

To assess your sales organisation's scalability, complete the diagnostic below to see where your development gaps are. You can either go directly to the indicated chapter or work through the book to see how the components fit together. Each chapter has an action plan to help you apply the ideas to your context.

Component		Score: 3 Strong point 2 In progress 1 Weak area	For more information, go to chapter...
Sales strategy	Our sales strategy is written down and used regularly		2
Value proposition	We have a clearly defined value proposition		7
Pricing	We have optimised our pricing for profit generation		7
Sales team structure	Our sales structure supports our strategy		8
Recruiting and onboarding	We have good processes in place for this		16
Technology	Our technology supports our selling activities effectively		12
Sales methodology	We have defined our best way to sell		4,5
Lead generation	We generate an acceptable number of new opportunities		6
First contact to close	We have a clear way to do this		3
Account retention and development	We have active account retention plans in place		14
Targets, metrics and KPIs	Our KPIs helps us measure and manage sales growth		10
Compensation and incentives	Our team is motivated by the current incentives		15
Pipeline management	We have an effective, regular process for this		9,11
Sales training and coaching	The sales team receives regular training and coaching		9,13
Sales meeting	We have regular productive, motivating sales meetings		9

Expert view: Building a scalable sales organisation Cooper Solutions automotive software

In the field of automotive dealer software, Cooper Solutions is seen as a market leader. Their innovative, highly specific products enable dealers to manage the unique operational and financial challenges of buying and selling cars.

Having worked in the sector for some time, founder Barry Cooper knew exactly what those challenges were and was quickly able to address them with a suite of six products. For example, FullCover helped dealers manage the insurance aspects of courtesy and loan cars, while FullAuction enabled dealers to get the best prices for disposal of trade-in cars. While the company was growing, Barry believed things could be better, so started working with an external consultancy, Selling Interactions, to explore options.

"When we first involved an external consultancy, we were a well-established, profitable business, with consistently good growth of over 10% pa. We had excellent, long term customer relationships, a proven suite of quality products, and a great team of senior managers and staff.

But we weren't scaling as fast as we'd envisaged or as fast as our products, people and performance deserved. Our products were complementary and while some customers took all or most of the full suite, many only used that which they'd started. Our cash cow product was the simplest to sell, install and support, so the team handling it had little interest in promoting other products.

By the second meeting with Selling Interactions, our seasoned senior team were looking sideways at each other, as the penny dropped that we'd achieved a good degree of success in spite of our lack of a defined sales process!"

The start-point in building a scalable sales organisation was to define Cooper's sales process from first contact with a dealer to a happy advocate.

"As we understood more about what a sales process for our business could be, we remembered many instances over the years when we'd not followed what we now knew to be good practice and consequently not secured new business.

We'd fallen into the trap of thinking our continuously developed products were what every customer needed and once they'd seen them, new business would follow. To an extent that worked, but it didn't produce optimal results and we failed with several new opportunities.

So, while business was good, we'd never experienced that 'light the blue touch paper' moment. When we reviewed our current sales process, it became clear that we were emphasising what we had to offer much more than spending time truly understanding the situation of the prospective client.

This was particularly true of our more complex products where we were looking to replace financial management products that were embedded in the systems and processes of a business.

We learnt to slow everything down, spend far more time asking questions and listening to the answers. We found that the casual, 'show us what you've got' request by a client at a sales meeting was one to be handled with care and to be managed until the time was right to do just that.

We worked with Selling Interactions to design what we believed to be the sales DNA of our company, bespoke to us, our situation, products, client relationships and people. We all bought in and all customer facing staff were involved in the roll out.

We didn't just talk it. It became the most discussed, reviewed and acted upon programme we'd ever introduced.

The results were impressive: A defined sales process and culture of using it became the most valuable tool we had, and our success rates consistently improved. Sales of our leading product doubled in just over 4 years, from a level that had taken more than 11 years to achieve".

Notes

1 A. Zoltners et al "Sales force effectiveness: A framework for researchers and practitioners" *Journal of Personal Selling & Sales Management* vol. 28, no. 2 (2008), 116–120.
2 C. Homberg et al *Sales excellence – Systematic sales management* Springer Verlag 2012
3 A. Ross & J. Lemkin *From impossible to inevitable* John Wiley & Sons 2016
4 Kotler et al "Ending the war between sales and marketing" *Harvard Business Review* Jul-Aug 2006
5 Guggenberger et al *Six governing factors to modernise marketing* McKinsey June 2019
6 P. Hill *Pricing for profit* p41 Kogan Page 2013
7 Alfred duPont Chandler was a professor of business history at Harvard 1962
8 Carucci & Shappell "Design your organisation to match your strategy" *Harvard Business Review* digital article June 2022
9 Bertuzzi *The sales development playbook* p56 Moore-Lake 2016
10 J. M. Cuevas et al *Sales management: Strategy, process and practice* p201 Palgrave 2016
11 R. Cossar "How to use AI for sales coaching: A sales manager's guide" www.saleshacker.com 2023 May
12 Quote from G. Patton as noted by www.brainyquote.com
13 D. Snowden & M. Boone "A leader's framework for decision making" *Harvard Business Review* Nov 2007
14 T. Powers et al "An assessment of needed sales management skills" *Journal of Personal Selling & Sales Management* vol. 34 (2014), 207–208.
15 K. Peesker et al "A qualitative study of leaders behaviours perceived to enable salesperson performance" *Journal of Personal Selling & Sales Management* vol. 39 (2019), 323.
16 M. Roberg "The right way to use compensation" *Harvard Business Review* April 2015
17 J. Collins *Good to great: Why some companies make the leap and others don't* Dewey Decimal 2001
18 Jordan & Vazanna *Cracking the sales management code: The secrets to measuring and managing sales performance* Vantage Point Performance 2012

Chapter 2

Your sales strategy and growth model

How exactly are you going to grow your revenues?

Indira Gandhi is quoted as saying "The power to question is the basis of all human progress". For Small and medium enterprises (SMEs) and start-ups, a very important question to ask is, "Where will growth come from?". Sometimes, the instinctual answer is "sell more stuff", but closer inspection reveals that we can be more specific about where growth can come from. Understanding what these *sources of growth* or *levers of growth* are and the relative importance of each for our business forms the basis of an organisation's *growth model*.

Understanding the growth model is a vital ingredient to put in the pot when we build an effective sales strategy, since it defines the kind of sales activities that need to take place. Since nearly all organisations are under pressure to grow, answering this question helps us figure out how we will practically do that.

When we use the term *growth* here, we simply mean to increase the revenues or top line of an organisation.

The six levers of growth

If you imagine being a growth consultant and looking at a wide range of businesses and figuring out how to help them grow, it would be helpful if there was a tool kit to help. Fortunately, there is one. If we make a list of all the ways we can grow a business, they tend to fall into one of six categories, as shown in Figure 2.1. We will call them the *six levers of growth*, because if we put effort into them, they should help us grow revenues.

Each start-up and SME will use the different levers with differing levels of emphasis. This will depend on the product/service/market context, whether you are at the start of the start-up journey or simply trying to up the performance of your established sales organisation.

The six levers help us to effectively prioritise where to invest valuable time and resources to drive maximum growth. In this sense, growth model thinking is a kind of portfolio/prioritisation method similar to *strategic customer relationship management (CRM)*, as outlined by Francis Buttle and Stan Maklan in *CRM – Concepts and Technologies*.[1]

Let's consider each growth lever in more detail.

Lever 1: Sell more volume to existing customers

Definition: The first lever is simply selling more of your existing product/service to your existing customers.

Imagine an organisation that sells translation services to the US regional office of an international company. Today, most work is commissioned by this office translating US English

DOI: 10.4324/9781003449614-2

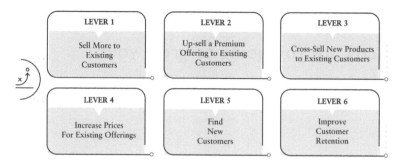

Figure 2.1 The six levers of growth

into other languages. One option for growth would be to sell the same service to other regional offices, this time translating from the local language, say German, into other languages. It's the same service to the same customer, just more volume.

Sometimes, this growth lever is called increasing *share of wallet (SOW)*[2] and can be an easy win because:

- We have a relationship already with the customer
- We don't need to design a new product
- The customer understands precisely the value of our offering

Indeed, SOW is often used by organisations as a measure of account management success. It's also known as *penetration*. This lever makes sense if we already have a foothold with customers and there is clear potential for more sales of our existing product/solution.

Lever 2: Up-sell a premium version of your product

Definition: This lever involves selling a higher-value product to existing customers and is often called up-selling.

If you've ever booked a flight or ordered a meal from a fast-food restaurant, you have mostly likely seen this approach in action. As you complete your purchase, you are offered all kinds of upgrades/premium versions that are supposed to enrich your experience. It simply means that we try to sell a better, more expensive version to a customer. Note that customers don't buy any more airline flights or meals; they simply pay more for a better version of what they consume.

This lever is an excellent growth tool, as Peter Hill explains in Pricing for Profit, noting that providing "alternative price options affect the perception of value of all options".[3] One way to imagine this is to think of how you might feel if you bought the entry-level model of a very premium car brand: Seeing that it is part of a family of premium products gives you the feeling that you are buying a high-quality product.

Selling premium products makes sense because:

- We don't need to develop new customer relationships.
- Premium products are nearly always more profitable.
- There are always some customers who appreciate premium products and are willing to pay for them.

Level 3: Cross-sell other products to existing customers

Definition: Cross-selling involves selling different product lines or services to an existing customer that already purchases one line from us today.

Like the first two levers, this approach is attractive in that we don't need to find and win new customers, which is typically harder than selling to existing ones.

Cross-selling is ubiquitous in daily life, "Would you like fries with that?" is a classic example. Again, the airline industry is a consummate practitioner, offering hotels, hire cars, travel insurance and other products alongside their core 'seat on a flight' product.

When *bundling* (offering a basket of products and services at a special offer price) is used to cross-sell, for example, selling cars with service packages, paintwork protection and break-down insurance, this can have a material effect on profit. Again, Peter Hill's excellent book provides detailed calculations on how this can work.[4]

In B2B situations, cross-selling has another advantage: it creates a degree of stickiness or *customer lock-in*, as it becomes more convenient for busy organisational buyers to use just one supplier for several product/service needs.

Provided we have products to sell, cross-selling is a good lever because:

- We have an existing relationship to build from.
- We can help customers to satisfy multiple needs with one supplier.
- We can increase customer retention through 'convenience purchasing'.

Lever 4: Increase prices for existing offerings

Definition: This simply means charging more for the exact same products customers already buy.

For some reason, when managers are asked what ways organisations could increase growth, the idea of increasing prices rarely comes up. And yet, it is one of the simplest and most powerful ways to get growth. No new products required, no new customers, no cross-selling, just some careful communication and training for the sales team, and growth can be instant. Furthermore, price rises often translate directly to the bottom line.

Both Christian Homburg[5] and Peter Hill[6] are strong advocates of effective pricing in sales organisations. Homburg calls it a "fundamental line of attack", and Hill talks about "the remarkable benefits of getting pricing right".

We will speak more about this fundamental growth lever in Chapter 7, when we begin to develop effective value propositions.

Pricing is an effective for growth because:

- It requires relatively little effort.
- It almost always increases profit, which can drive further growth.
- If your product and services are good, it reinforces a premium image.

Lever 5: Find new customers

Definition: This simply means winning sales with organisations we don't yet do business with.

Jeb Blount, named one of the top 50 most influential leaders in sales and marketing, makes the case for finding new customers very simply; he says it's "*the secret that separates superstars from everyone else"*.[7] One way to grow is to consistently find and win new customers. Indeed, many salespeople instinctively go for this option as the most obvious route to growth.

Clearly, if we can win new customers, then they bring in new revenues. For some industries that are based on 'one-off project-based sales', for example, solar panel installation, this way to grow is very important. After all, there are only so many sets of solar panels you can sell to the same household!

Unless we keep all our existing customers forever finding new ones is an inevitable and essential part of any growth plan. Our customers' businesses fail; they don't need our services any more, or they start to buy less. For these reasons, an important part of any growth plan is nearly always to keep a steady flow of new customers coming in.

Two important considerations to bear in mind for this lever are the *customer acquisition cost* (CAC) and the *customer lifetime value* (LTV). For a business to be scalable, the LTV must be greater than the CAC. In their article, *The Hybrid Start-up*, Nathan Furr and Kate O'Keefe recommend the LTV be at least three times the CAC.[8]

This growth lever helps growth because:

- It plants new seeds to grow into future loyal customers.
- It enables us try out new products, prices and approaches.
- It fundamentally increases our options for further growth through up-sell and cross-sell.

Lever 6: Improve customer retention

Definition: Ensuring current customers stay with us year after year.

The analogy of filling a bucket with a hole in it is often given as an argument for why customer retention is important. Winning new customers is hard work, and if we lose the ones we have, we end up on an unremitting treadmill of sales misery.

Strictly speaking, retaining customers may not actually increase revenues, but it is an essential part of the mix to 'hold the fort', while growth can be found in other areas.

For subscription-based industries, customer retention is of the utmost importance, as anyone who has tried to cancel a monthly streaming or telecom payment plan can attest. Valuations of subscription-based businesses are highly sensitive to retention rates.

Loyalty schemes are a very visible manifestation of the need for customer retention. Air Canada was quoted as generating anReturn on investment (ROI) of 500% on their *Earn your wings* gamified loyalty programme.[9]

Customer retention is an important lever of growth because:

- If we lose too many customers, we have to put double the effort into finding new customers.
- It is closely linked to customer satisfaction. Happy customers stay and recommend you.
- Retained customers are opportunities for up-sell and cross-sell.

How do we assess the relative emphasis to put on each growth lever?

Let's start with two truisms: Every organisation is different, and no organisation has infinite resources. Because of this, the relative importance of each growth lever will vary based on your product/service context and the organisational resources available to you (typically

Table 2.1 Three growth stages of start-ups

Stage of growth	Description	Approximate timescale
Exploration	The company tests hypotheses about how it will deliver value to customers until it achieves 'product-market fit'.	Three months to three years
Extrapolation	Demand rises rapidly, and the company strives to bring in additional revenue while decreasing marginal costs until it achieves a 'profit-market' fit	One to three years
Exploitation	Revenue growth begins to level off, and the company fine-tunes its business model.	Indefinite

people, cash and time). For example, as already stated, a solar panel installation firm will put greater emphasis on finding new customers than on customer retention.

The mix will also depend on the stage of development your SME/start-up is at. Jeffrey Rayport and his team define three helpful growth stages to guide us,[10] as shown in Table 2.1.

The authors make the important point that many start-ups fail because they don't put enough effort into the 'extrapolation' phase, that is, growing sales *and* profit.

Companies in the exploration phase generally do well to test their offering with enough customers to prove the *product-market* fit. Jason Lemkin recommends the '20 interview rule'[11] as a way of meeting enough customers to validate a start-up's offering.

By contrast, SMEs in the exploitation phase may have plenty of customers and need to focus more on retention, cross-selling, up-selling, and pricing.

To find out what the most effective growth levers to focus on are, we can work through the ten questions below.

For start-ups, this can often be done by common sense/expert judgement of your context (for example, if you only have one customer, then finding new ones is normally a top priority).

For more mature SMEs, it's advisable to look at some key data to draw meaningful conclusions and be more objective, for example retention rates, new customer acquisition and profitability.

Here are ten key questions to work through:

1 Which growth lever has the best potential to deliver results?
2 If we focused on it, how much extra revenue could it realistically deliver?
3 What other growth levers have good potential to deliver?
4 What percentage increase could we expect from them?
5 Are there any of the levers that we don't use today and could add to growth?
6 What revenue uplift could we expect from them?
7 Which growth levers should we spend less time on to free up time/resource?
8 What therefore is the most logical emphasis of each lever to get growth?
9 What needs to change to achieve this?
10 How realistic is it to make the shift?

The process then involves assessing each lever systematically to establish which ones offer the most promise. It also necessarily involves considering where *not* to invest so much time/money. If we don't free up time/resource from one area, it is difficult to invest them in another area, unless you have a bottomless pit of time and money.

As stated, if you have sales practice and trading history, it makes sense to use data to work through the ten questions. Typical measures that organisations use to assess progress on each lever are shown in Table 2.2. There are also some 'ballpark' figures to assess your own operation, along with some questions to ask to dig deeper. Generalised figures have to be interpreted with caution, as every industry is different.

Value trees

As you work through your options for growth, you might want to consider building a value tree to visualise your chosen options. Value trees are used in various guises to make the levers of growth very explicit, so a management team can stay focused on doing the right activities. They also allow for the visualisation of cost inputs, as shown in Figure 2.2.

Table 2.2 Typical growth lever metrics

Growth lever	Typical quantitative indicators	Benchmark figures Questions to ask
Sell more volume to existing customers	Share of wallet % of our sales to a customer/ total customer purchases in our category	100% may be unrealistic, as sensible buyers try to have more than one supplier if possible. If you have one competitor, then 50% S.O.W. is a good starting point. If you sell less than this figure, then why is that?
Upselling	Upselling profile % of customers buying premium/Total number of customers	Using the Pareto rule of thumb, at least 20 customers ought to be buying premium. How often are premium options presented to customers? If not often, why not?
Cross-selling	Cross-sales index Average number of our product and service lines sold per customer	An organisation with ten product lines should typically aim for a cross-sell index of at least 2, otherwise there is little cross-selling occurring. How often are other service/product lines presented?
Price increase	Price development Average % increase over three to five years	How many customers have you lost because of the price? Around 5–10% is okay. If the figure is less than this, maybe your prices are too low. Are you 'proud of your price'?
Find new customers	New customers gained % of new customers this year/ Total number of customers	This varies enormously. A minimum of 5% could work for businesses with high customer retention rates. For one-off sales companies, it needs to be much higher, maybe 60% to 70%. Is the sales team setting aside enough time to win new customers?
Customer retention	Raw retention rate % of customers retained this year/No. of customers retained last year (excluding new customers)	For subscription-based businesses, retention needs to be above 85% for a business to be viable. The best B2B organisations achieve 95%.

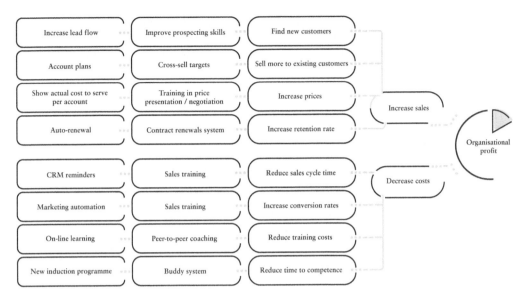

Figure 2.2 A typical value tree

Building a value tree forces us to be clear about which activities we need to do to 'pull the levers' of growth. We can also explicitly track these activities as 'lead measures', so we can check we are on track to meet the growth plan. Chapter 10 explains more about deriving your key measures.

With a sense of where you are in the development of your organisation and a clearer view of where you can obtain growth, it's time to build a sales strategy.

What is a strategy?

This is not an easy question! Whole chapters have been dedicated to defining what a strategy is. John McGee and his colleagues do this very thoroughly in their book *Strategy: Analysis and Practice*,[12] quoting Alfred Chandler's 1963 definition as a starting point: "the determination of the basic long-term goals and objective of an enterprise". A long-term plan is a great starting point for our definition.

Henry Mintzberg and his colleagues add to the debate of what strategy is, outlining the 5Ps of a strategy in *Strategy Safari*.[13] They speak of strategy as a *plan, pattern, position, perspective,* or *ploy.* This enriched view of strategy is helpful because it gives us some sales-focused options to consider. For example, establishing a 'position' as the highest quality supplier in an industry is a great place to be for sales. Also, the idea of strategy being a 'pattern', rather than a pre-determined plan, reminds us that 'structured long-term plans' often become outdated in the face of dynamic, rapidly changing marketplaces.

Structured long-term plans are often called *deliberate strategies,* while 'adapt as you go' approaches are called *emergent strategies.*

Emergent strategies are particularly important for start-ups, where the perfect way of selling is yet to be established. When we design a start-up sales strategy, it should include planned checkpoints to review learning and adapt accordingly.

The choice of deliberate versus emergent strategies depends on the *predictability* and *malleability* of your sector. For example, industries like pharmaceuticals and banking tend to be predictable and difficult to change, whereas software and SaaS businesses can be much less predictable. Martin Reeves and others set this out extremely well in their HBR article *Your Strategy Needs a Strategy*,[14] and this is well worth reading to assess your context.

With these caveats in mind, let's use a practical working definition for your sales strategy: *The mid- to long-term series of actions and resources to secure your growth model*

Now let's turn to the essential components of the strategy.

Five key questions that a sales strategy should answer

If your CEO asks you to write a *sales strategy*, what should be in the document? Because of the aforementioned debate on strategy, there probably is no single right answer! Thankfully, because of years of painstaking work and experience by practitioners and researchers, many of the component parts of effective sales strategy are known, and they can be grouped into five key areas, defined by these essential questions:

1 Who are we selling to?
2 What are we selling?
3 How will we reach them?
4 How will we measure progress?
5 What resources do we need to enable the strategy?

Figure 2.3 shows the component parts that help us to answer each question. By systematically working through each of these, we can arrive at a robust, well-thought-out sales strategy. Let's explore these in turn. It will help you to build your strategy if you make notes after reaching each component based on two key questions:

• How does this component relate to our business?
• What should we consider for our own business in the future?

Once you have a set of notes based on the components, figuring out your options for the overall strategy will be easier.

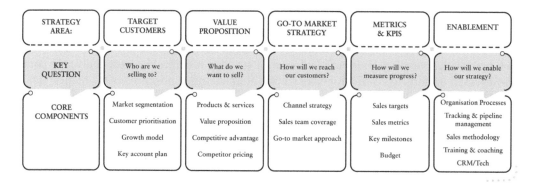

Figure 2.3 Elements of a sales strategy

Question 1: Who are we selling to?

The first important step in defining our sales strategy is to figure out who our ideal customers are to work with. This initial focus is built on four key areas: *segmentation, prioritisation, growth model* and *key accounts.*

Segmentation The idea of some customers being better customers than others is not new. Dr. Christian Homburg dedicates a chapter on *"Farewell to the standard customer"*[15] based on this idea. Darrell Amy, an experienced growth architect, advises us to *"Define your ideal clients".*[16]

Having an *'ideal customer profile'* is vital in so many areas. It enables us to look for more of the same. Working with this type of customer means we are more likely to build profitable, effective working relationships which endure over time.

Ideally, we want to have many customers with these characteristics. If we can identify more *ideal customers*, we have defined an attractive *market segment. Segmentation* is a very common marketing approach to grouping ideal customers so that they can be targeted effectively.[17] With the advent of machine learning and real-time sentiment technologies,[18] it's likely that more and more organisations will employ dynamic segmentation in their selling approach.

Effective market segmentation is based on groups of ideal customers with the following characteristics:

- Homogenous in terms of their needs.
- Substantial enough to merit investment.
- Actionable and accessible: It is possible to reach these customers.
- Measurable: There is a way to identify the segment.
- Profitable.

It is a really useful exercise to map out who your ideal clients are and what their common characteristics are. Once you know this, you can establish whether this customer represents a larger segment. If we can identify such a segment, we have a strong foundation for growth.

Customer prioritisation: As stated, not all customers are equal. Within each segment of potential customers, there will be some who are more attractive than others. Relative attractiveness will be based on several factors, including:

- Size
- Profit potential
- Value of brand to future marketing
- Company fit
- Willingness to test new products
- Relationships

As most organisations don't have unlimited resources, deciding where to invest valuable time and money is a key decision in effective strategy. Many organisations use a scoring system to categorise and rank their customers according to their attractiveness. Dr Christian Homburg has shown this to be a major lever to increase growth and profit[19] as have Mark Johnston and Greg Marshall. Who cites the example of Shell Oil, who saw "selling costs reduced, sales increased, and profits soared".[20]

Growth model: The six levers of growth approach from earlier in the chapter generates insights into who we are selling to. For example, are we looking to sell to more new customers? Or are we looking to sell new products to existing customers? For most organisations, it will be a mix. The sales strategy document is the place to commit to the relative efforts for each lever and derive sales targets for each aspect of growth. We will go into more target settings in Chapter 10. For now, it helps to have some provisional values, so we can see the overall projected growth.

Key accounts: If you have large accounts of significant value, your sales strategy should include the targets and plans for these. Chapter 14 gives more details of what should be in a key account strategy. By definition, they are large chunks of your revenue, so they need special treatment.

Question 2: What are we selling?

Once we establish who we are selling to, the second question relates to what we actually sell to them. Again, this question breaks down into a number of subsections: *Products and services, value proposition, competitive advantage, competitors* and *pricing.*

Products and services At the simplest level, our sales strategy defines the products/services we'd like to sell to customers and prospects. In Chapter 1, a 'world class sales organisation' was defined as one that choses, which products it sells to which target customers. This is an important part of strategy execution, and if you can deliver on these goals, you will truly be in a strong position.

Value proposition The discipline of articulating your value proposition answers the question, "Why should customers buy from you?". This topic will be explored in greater depth in Chapter 7.

Competitive advantage Returning to John McGee's excellent book on strategy,[21] a definition of competitive advantage is *"Delivering superior value to customers and in doing so earning an above average return for the company".*

In practical sales terms, start-ups and SMEs without a competitive advantage will have continual price pressure, difficulties in retaining customers, and endless negotiations or disinterest from buyers. Indeed, such unlucky firms are often called *'price-takers'* because they are not in a position to set a price.

Your sales strategy, therefore, really needs to build and maintain a competitive advantage. In simple terms, this could come from one or more of these sources:

- Unique products/services
- Being the lowest costs
- Unique processes
- Specialist, difficult to copy expertise
- Geographical location
- Unrivalled number of users or network effects
- Access to product/service data in use

Bear in mind that in an established market, there can only be one *'lowest cost'* provider, and this source of competitive advantage relies on relentless attention to cost control. Start-ups do have the advantage sometimes that they can redefine a market and establish a competitive advantage through new business models.

The options to secure a competitive advantage will be explored in more depth in Chapter 7.

Competitors A closely linked concept to competitiveness is a good understanding of your competitors. The art of beating the competition is a large topic and relates to how we position ourselves in a segment. If we do not have a distinctive positioning, then we will find it difficult to answer a customer's question when they ask, "Why should I buy from you, and not your competitor?". It will also make it difficult to respond when they say, "We already have a good supplier".

A simple practical approach is to build a table, as shown in Table 2.3.

Seeing the big picture helps us see how we can play to win. In this example, we would need to prepare our sales team to handle objections related to price and product performance, but we could also train them on how to demonstrate the advantages of better service. We could train them on how to uncover dissatisfaction with other suppliers.

All these elements will feed into our sales strategy.

Pricing As set out in the *growth model* section, pricing is both a valuable lever of growth and can be used in multiple ways to enhance start-ups and SMEs. For example, off-peak pricing in service industries can be used to help efficiency, and subscriptions on auto-renewal remove the need to close deals each year.[22] Chapter 7 explores pricing in more depth.

Targets having established in detail what you are selling, a closely linked question is: how much do you want to sell?

Setting the target price levels and quantities to be sold is essential to coming up with an overall revenue number, profits, and derived budgets. Chapter 10 outlines the various methods you can use to do this.

Question 3: How will we reach them?

The third question to answer is about the route to market. Incubators are full of start-ups with genius ideas, but if they do not get in front of customers, unfortunately, they wither on the vine. This question is built up of three decisions based on *channel strategy*, *sales team coverage* and *go-to-market strategy*.

Channel strategy There are a number of ways customers can potentially buy products:

- Direct from our sales team.
- Via a distributor, wholesaler or sales agent.
- Self-service on the internet.
- From a sub-contracted sales force.

Table 2.3 An example of competitive analysis

Competitor	Competitor X	Competitor Y	Competitor Z	Us
Strengths	Long running business	Cheap prices	Product A is very much appreciated	Strong service ethos
Weaknesses	Lacks innovation	Service can be hit and miss	Product range weak	Highest prices

Our channel strategy depends on figuring out which route or mixture of routes is best for our business. To guide this decision, we could consider:

- How much human interaction is required to sell the product?
- The transaction cost of each sale and profitability.
- The potential for technology to augment/automate the sale.
- The value of direct customer contact to learn about their needs.
- The sales networks of potential distributors.
- The profit we have to forego by using an intermediary.
- The geographical advantage of distribution partners.

Thus, there are many factors that could influence our choice. *Sales and marketing channels*, written by Julian Dent and Michael White, is a very thorough guide to channel selection and management, and if distribution is a large part of your sales strategy, this book will be very beneficial.[23]

For start-ups, it is worth remembering the enormous value of having close contact with your early customers so you can learn about their needs and your product/service in use. Yes, this approach is initially time consuming, but the learning is normally invaluable and enables you to refine, improve and standardise many aspects of your sales system.

Sales team coverage Once you have identified the customer segments you are going after, if a personal selling approach is mandated, it's a logical decision to decide how many sales-people are needed and where geographically they should be established.

Darrell Amy, referred to earlier, has a clear explanation of this: "The goal of outbound marketing is 100% coverage: Every decision maker and influencer in your ideal prospect account hears from your business on a regular basis".[24]

Clearly, for SMEs and start-ups, budgets might not exist for this scale of coverage, but the underlying principle is still important.

Go-to-market strategy Having established who our ideal customers are, what we would like to sell them, and which channels to reach them through, we need to think about *how* to actually do that. Whole textbooks have been written about this area. After all, it is a core component of marketing as a discipline. For practical purposes, the areas to think about are:

- Is our product service best suited to personal selling or internet marketing?
- Are we B2B or B2C?
- What sales process should I use? (Chapter 3)
- What sales methodology will be needed? (Chapter 4)
- What digital marketing and social media are needed to support our growth model?
- What promotions and campaigns can help us achieve our growth ambitions?

Two good sources of books to explore further if you want to sharpen up your go-to-marketing are *Digital Marketing* by Dave Chaffey and Fiona Ellis-Chadwick[25] and, for more general marketing principles, *Marketing Management* by Philip Kotler and colleagues.[26]

Question 4: How will we measure progress?

To avoid creating a *paper tiger*, which is a document that looks good but never gets used, we must pay attention to the 'what' and the 'how' of strategy. We must pay as much attention to implementation and execution as we do to direction and targets. Having clear measures in place for our strategy means we can apply the useful adage, "What gets inspected gets respected".

The four areas we have to consider for this question are: *key performance indicators (KPIs), targets, budgets and milestones*. These are key operational aspects of the sales strategy.

Sales targets Why have sales targets? Lewis Carroll was quoted as saying, "If you don't know where you are going, any road will take you there". So it is with targets; if we don't have an objective in mind, it's pretty hard to judge progress. Javier Marcos Cuevas, in his book *Sales Management*,[27] lists four key reasons:

- To evaluate sales performance.
- As an incentive for salespeople.
- To calculate remuneration.
- To control activities.

One of the first areas CEOs or investors are likely to discuss in the sales strategy is the sales target, as it will affect many other aspects of business planning, such as budgets, staffing and investment.

You may well be working towards a target already. This topic will be explored in more depth in Chapter 10.

Sales metrics: In the context of sales strategy, good KPIs help us stay on track to hit our targets. They are like GPS checks on a long journey. Chapter 10 covers the details of how to decide on the right KPIs for your sales strategy. You will need to think about which *activity measures* and *sales objectives* are most useful.

Key milestones This is a catch-all topic to think about any major activities or goals that need to take place to enable your strategy. It could include things like:

- Implementation of a CRM system
- Recruiting a new hire
- Completing a major customer project
- Launching a campaign

Milestones are useful because they enable us to think about and execute key stages in strategy development. For example, ensuring your lead generation campaign is in place by the end of Q1 gives you three quarters to reap the rewards.

Budget Sales organisations are not cheap. An essential part of any financially viable strategy is visibility of cost and profit. For SMEs, this is probably an established routine for you already. For start-ups, even if you only have one or two salespeople (maybe you personally!), it is still good discipline to cost up your sales organisation costs against your revenue projections. For a definitive explanation of this area, *Sales Force Management* is the go-to book.[28]

Question 5: What resources will be needed to enable the strategy?

If you set yourself the goal to walk to the North Pole, you would be very sure to pay close attention to the logistics. You would be very careful to make sure you have everything you need to make the arduous journey.

We can apply the same logic to sales strategy: if we really want to achieve the target, we had better think carefully upfront about the resources we will need to achieve it. There are six underpinning components: *Organisation, processes, tracking and pipeline management, sales methodology, training and coaching and CRM/technology.*

Organisation: An African proverb states, "If you want to go fast, go alone. If you want to go far, go together". Having the right organisation in place is a big help in sales, even if that is you plus one other in a start-up. Chapter 8 explores the options we have, and it should support the sales strategy we have chosen. For example, we might need to strengthen our account management resources if retention is a large part of our growth model.

Processes: Chapters 3, 9, 13 and 14 will look at some of the essential processes that we need in a scalable sales organisation. We need to make sure our processes are well defined and in place to support effective sales. If winning new customers is a big focus for your strategy, then having good lead generation in place will be vital.

Tracking and pipeline management: McKinsey's book *Sales Growth*[29] shows how the best sales organisations "set the tempo of performance" via weekly pipeline management calls. To really enable a sales strategy, it is a good idea to set out how you will drive it! This vital topic is explored in Chapter 11.

Sales methodology: Think of this as "the way we sell". For an organisation to be truly scalable, it must know what good selling looks like. This should be written down, for example, in a 'playbook'. In the context of sales strategy, we need to figure out what kind of selling will support the ambitions we have for growth. For example, if cross-selling is required, what does that look like? Do we need to provide training to enable the strategy?

Training and coaching: Another key finding in McKinsey's book is that star organisations invest time and money to improve the performance of their salespeople.[30] Large corporations tend to have very well-defined coaching routines and metrics for sales managers, respecting how important they are for performance.

For start-ups, this can mean acknowledging that you, as the growth leader, may need to invest time in your own sales development to be effective. Either way, it is wise to consider what skills and attitudes are required to enable your strategy and plan for them.

CRM/Technology: Once organisations have more than about 10 to 20 customers, investing in CRM technology is almost essential. For start-ups and SMEs, this area can be particularly challenging because of budgets and technical know-how.

This topic will be explored in Chapter 12 to help you make an informed choice. Technology can be a massively useful enabler of sales strategies. It is a very fast-developing field, with a huge number of options to help automate or enrich various activities in sales organisations.

Bringing the components together

You might be forgiven for asking, "Does my start-up actually need all this to make a strategy?". Possibly not. Like all good recipes, what you have here is a list of ingredients, and a good chef can decide which to include, which to miss out on, and how important each ingredient is according to what they need.

The five questions follow a logical order, so it normally makes sense to work through them in turn. By asking "Who are we selling to?" first, we focus on the customer and their needs upfront before deciding what to sell next. However, you might develop a fantastic new product or service and then figure out who to sell it to afterwards.

Therefore, the process of strategy development can be messy and non-linear.

This brings us to the topic of mindset. Good entrepreneurs and sales managers are often 'action orientated', and sales strategy development can sometimes feel frustrating. It can help to consciously choose a mindset for the task at hand. Good strategy development and execution depend on three distinct modes of thinking, as shown in Table 2.4.

As you develop your sales strategy, it's worth understanding your own preferences and strengths. If analysis is not your thing, maybe someone else in your organisation can help. If you find creative thinking a challenge, discuss the analysis work with a colleague who can see things from a different angle.

Inspiration cannot be forced. Research into problem solving has shown that sometimes we need a period of 'incubation' to arrive at answers.[31] In this regard, it helps to keep a journal or strategy document live and update it periodically as you have time to think through each component while at the same time noting down any inspirations or creative ideas you have.

By discussing your ideas with a colleague and hearing their constructive criticism, you can use the 'refiner's fire' principle, which is to make your gold purer by burning off the impurities. Over time, you will develop a thorough, intelligent, actionable plan that stands a strong chance of meeting your growth objectives.

Typical strategic plays

What overarching sales strategies might we use? Whilst every organisation and context is unique, Table 2.5 presents some 'generic strategies' that might help you shape your approach.

Table 2.4 Strategic thinking modes

Stage of strategy process	Description	Mindset
Analysis	Accurately assessing the current situation	Granular analysis of data Into details Objectivity Resist early conclusions
Strategy	Figuring out direction and courses of action	Creativity/Inspiration Following logically from analysis Consider options
Execution	Making sure the strategy is delivered	Just do it What gets inspected gets respected

Table 2.5 Typical strategic plays

Strategy	Description	When to use
New customer focus	Heavy focus on winning as many new customers as possible	To make a start-up with a transactional sale viable. To go for 'network effects' where you lock out competition through high market share.
Develop existing customers	Focus on retention, up-sell and cross-sell	Where you have a good customer base with low SOW or cross-sell index.

(Continued)

Table 2.5 (Continued)

Strategy	Description	When to use
Defensive strategy	Provision of loyalty programmes, offers and discounts	If you face a strong competitor.
Offensive strategy	Proactively targeting a competitor's account	Where a competitor has become weak
Foothold strategy	Focus on selling a specific product that enables you to 'land and expand'	If your product suite lends itself to this approach.
Learning strategy	Working closely with key customers, even if it is not profitable in the short term	To test/develop a new product/service
Premium brand marketing	Doing your best to win some large corporate clients that will aid your marketing	For start-ups wanting to create good marketing collateral

Into action

Start a journal or an active document on your PC, making notes about each component of the sales strategy. Build the picture over several weeks.

What is written down about your sales strategy today?

What data can help you analyse your current situation?

What options do you have for growth?

What is the most sensible emphasis for each growth lever?

What are realistic targets?

What would be required to enable your chosen strategy?

How much would it cost?

How practical is it to execute?

What could be the key milestones over a one-to-two-year time schedule?

Remember to allow some 'incubation time' to allow your natural intelligence to do its thing!

Expert view: Stone's throw media

The world of videomaking is both popular and competitive. Started by two university friends, Matt and Mike, who met in 2008, Stone's Throw Media (STM) is now a fast-growing business offering video production, animation and live-streaming services with an impressive list of clients.

Working through the five-question sales strategy method revealed that the business needed more customers to grow, as its retention and account development practices were already strong.

Furthermore, Matt and Mike could add a lot of value once they were in front of customers where creativity and direction were needed.

Therefore, if lead generation was strengthened, the ball could be passed to them, and they could close the deal.

Accordingly, STM hired a digital marketer, whose main responsibility was to generate leads and hand them on to Matt and Mike to finish off the sales process.

Matt comments on the process of defining a growth strategy:

"I likened our sales situation to having a bucket with a number of holes in. Once they were fixed, we had more confidence to pull the lever on attracting new leads knowing we would be more prepared than ever to give them great results and build a strong relationship without letting anyone down.

I feel that getting those solid foundations in place has been critical to the growth of Stone's Throw and is something worth investing time into for anyone serious about growing an organisation".

Notes

1 F. Buttle & S. Maklan *Customer relationship management – Concepts and technologies* p119 Routledge 2015
2 Ibid., p44
3 P. Hill *Pricing for profit* p85 Kogan Page 2015
4 Ibid., p80
5 C. Homburg et al *Sales excellence* p62 Springer 2012
6 P. Hill p35 Kogan Page 2015
7 J. Blount *Fanatical prospecting* p3 Wiley 2015
8 N. Furr & K. O'Keefe "The hybrid start-up" *Harvard Business Review* Mar 2023
9 F. Buttle & S. Maklan p104 Routledge 2015
10 J. Rayport et al "The overlooked key to a successful scale-up" *Harvard Business Review* Jan 2023
11 A. Ross & J. Lemkin *From impossible to inevitable* p37 Wiley 2016
12 J. McGee et al *Strategy: Analysis and practice* p7 McGraw Hill 2005
13 H. Mintzberg et al *Strategy safari* p9 FT Prentice Hall 1998
14 M. Reeves et al "Your strategy needs a strategy" *Harvard Business Review* Sep 2012
15 C. Homburg et al p31 Springer 2012
16 D. Amy *Revenue growth engine* p51 Darrell Amy 2020
17 R. Lilien & R. Grewal "andbook of business-to-business marketing* p182 Edward Elgar Publishing 2012
18 https://emarsys.com/learn/glossary/dynamic-segmentation/#:~:text=Dynamic%20segmentation%20is%20a%20marketing,based%20on%20key%20customer%20behaviors
19 C. Homburg et al p34 Springer 2012
20 M. Johnson & G. Marshall *Sales force management* 13th ed Routledge 2021
21 J. McGee et al p165 McGraw Hill 2005
22 R. Mohammed "Expand your pricing paradigm" *Harvard Business Review* Jan 2023
23 J. Dent & M. White *Sales and marketing channels* Kogan Page 2018
24 D. Amy p144 Darrell Amy 2020
25 D. Chaffey & F. Ellis-Chadwick *Digital marketing* Pearson 2016
26 P. Kotler *Marketing management* 16th ed Pearson 2021
27 J. Marcos Ceuvas *Sales management* Palgrave 2015
28 M. Johnson & G. Marshall 13th ed p373 Routledge 2021
29 T. Baumgartner et al *Sales growth* p214 Wiley 2016
30 Ibid., p217
31 S. Brodt et al "Incubation, not sleep, aids problem solving" *Sleep Research Society* vol. 41, no.10 (Oct 2018), 7–9.

Chapter 3

Defining your sales process and customer journey

How can you best develop potential customers into loyal advocates?

What is the sales process?

What is the sales process you have in place for motivating potential customers to become actual customers?

I've heard all these answers:

- We don't have one.
- Everyone does it differently.
- We have one, but it's not used.
- We have one, but we are not sure if it is right.
- We have one; it's perfect, and everyone uses it.

Your *core sales process* is a vital piece of 'sales DNA' that affects just about every other aspect of your sales organisation. So, what exactly do we mean by a *core sales process*? I am very convinced by my consulting work that no universal definition exists. To further complicate matters, organisations might have many individual sub-processes related to the processing of customer orders and so on.

Javier Marcos Cuevas offers this insight: "For many years, the seven steps of selling (Moncrief & Marshall 2005) have underpinned the thinking behind professional selling".[1] Indeed, there are many examples of the 'n-step sales process' that can be sourced on the internet or presented by sales trainers.

The basic idea of a core sales process is to lead a customer through a journey that increases the chances they will buy from us. Typically, the steps salespeople follow include:

- Research
- Needs discovery
- Presenting a solution
- Closing the deal
- Account management

The big problem with these generic 'n-step' sales processes is that they are, well generic. Clearly, there is a big difference between selling stationery to an individual manager and selling a bespoke software solution that is enterprise wide. Applying the same sales process to every situation without taking care of the context is like using a screwdriver for every DIY job in your house, which is successful in a few cases but not in many others.

DOI: 10.4324/9781003449614-3

Added to this, a very important question to ask is: do we actually need any personal selling at all? More and more organisations are finding ways to automate their sales processes, which gives them an advantage through lower costs.

This chapter, therefore, is going to help you work out and design what your core sales process should be like so it fits your context. Therefore, the definition of a 'core sales process' that we shall use is:

> The series of stages we aim to lead a potential customer through, from first contact to a loyal happy customer

By *first contact*, we mean the first actual conversation we have with a potential customer. Of course, we must find a customer and motivate them to make this first contact in the first place. This topic will be covered in greater depth in Chapter 6 concerning *lead generation*.

Why do we need a core sales process?

For many tasks in life, there are often good and bad ways to approach them. Imagine something as simple as painting a wall. Preparing the surface well, applying even coats of paint, sanding down any imperfections and allowing each coat to dry thoroughly will likely lead to better results than simply picking up the tin and plastering the paint on. So it is with sales; some ways to engage with customers are more likely to be successful than others.

Furthermore, if we can define a process, we can standardise activities, automate sections, improve it and, very importantly, train others on how to follow the process. Operations gurus Nigel Slack, Stuart Chambers and Robert Johnston state it like this: "One significant advantage of mapping processes is that each activity can be systematically challenged in an attempt to improve the process".[2]

Your sales process is essentially a visualisation of what good selling looks like for your product/service/sector combination. Once this is clear, then you can:

- Train new people to use it.
- Coach those using it to be better.
- Use it to understand what type of salesperson is best to recruit.
- Measure the progress of your opportunities through the process.
- Manage your pipeline accordingly.
- Optimise organisational structures to fulfil it.

For start-ups, figuring out what good selling looks like can be challenging, as you might not have enough sales encounters under your belt to know it yet.

Fortunately, help is at hand in this chapter, as it is possible to derive a first draft sales process for most types of sales by analysing the context and product/service.

Criticisms of sales process

There is a school of thought that says sales processes are redundant. David Meerman-Scott, for example, says, "It is no longer a selling process. The buyer is in charge".[3] The fact that buyers often do substantial research before engaging with salespeople and come armed with information and questions is most vital to acknowledge. This is a view echoed by Brent

Adamson, Matthew Dixon and Nicholas Toman in their Harvard Business Review article, *Dismantling the Sales machine*. They say, "Recently sales has been caught off guard by a dramatic shift in customers' buying behaviour".[4]

The fact that customers can contact you at any moment is definitely something we need to be ready for. Using meta-analysis, the gold standard of academic studies, *adaptive selling* (the ability to adapt behaviour in the moment according to customer cues) has been shown to be an effective driver of sales performance.[5]

With these caveats in mind, we can design a sales process that is both adaptive and flexible and still guides best practices. After all, whenever a customer makes contact with us, we want them to have an excellent experience that motivates them to buy.

A very simple practical example can demonstrate this: If you want to buy a new car and you have already done extensive research before you go to a dealership to test drive the car, you expect to be treated very differently than if you just walked in off the street because you saw a car you liked in the window.

How can we build an effective sales process?

To build your sales process, it will really help if you can get several people working on the project. For SMEs, ideally, you can form a project team consisting of:

- Head of sales
- Sales manager
- Two to three good sales reps
- A senior marketer

Working in a small project group like this has several benefits:

- Involvement of key stakeholders is a good change management practice.
- Sales and marketing activities will be better integrated.
- More diversity and debate to arrive at the best solution.
- Better implementation of the new process by the sales team because you will create 'champions' as part of the exercise.

For start-ups and solopreneurs, having even just one other person to sense-check your thinking will be a huge asset.

You can use a workshop format where you work through the key steps over two to six weeks to arrive at a unified sales process that everyone buys into.

The basic process you can use to design your sales process is shown in Table 3.1.

You can think of steps 1 to 7 as ingredients to throw into the casserole pot. The order you put them in is not so important. They are included so that you can make a wonderful meal at step 8. You might, for example, stumble across a new technology that could materially change the way you sell and then start designing your sales process. Or you might have a better understanding of your customer's buying process, and that will influence your sales process design.

What is important is to take the various perspectives onboard when you design your first draft at the final stage.

Table 3.1 Steps to build your sales process

Step	Description
1	Map your customer's buying journey
2	Do a win/loss analysis
3	Surface your sales best practices
4	Assess your 'type of sale'
5	Consider the role of sales technology
6	Align your core sales process and lead generation
7	List any compliance/operational requirements
8	Build a 'first draft sales process'

If you are brand new to selling, you might find it helpful to read Chapter 4 first, where the nature of B2B selling is examined in more detail. This will make it easier to understand what the routines and activities in your sales process could look like.

Step 1: Map your customers' buying journey

A customer-centric view of your buyer behaviour has been at the forefront of marketing for some time now. Simon Hall, the author of *Innovative B2B Marketing*, lists five main stages buyers typically go through to purchase,[6] *need recognition, need quantification and research, vendor review, purchase* and *post purchase.*

Logically, if you can understand how your customers develop a need (or desire) for your product and how they search for and evaluate suppliers, you can design a sales process to make it both easy for them to buy from you and influence them positively on the journey.

Putting yourself in the shoes of your customers and thinking clearly about how they might buy a service like yours offers valuable insights into what you need to do to help them. For example, do they need approval for the budget? Who would need to be involved in the purchase? What obstacles might they face?

Brown paper and post-its or virtual whiteboards are really useful for building this type of process, as they allow input from all the project team and can be reorganised into categories. As much as possible, try to map your customer buying process using as much objective, anecdotal evidence as you can.

Pay close attention to how they research solutions and find you online. There are some tricky decisions to be made between how much you allow customers to do their own investigation of your capabilities and how much you control that, with, for example, signposting to arrange a meeting. Today, buyers often expect to find out as much as they can without human contact. There are pros and cons to this, because your solution might require human intervention, expertise and assertiveness to help customers find what is best for them. Buying journeys can be automated, which potentially reduces costs and has the potential to supply you with leads that are already qualified. On the other hand, meeting with customers early in their buying journey gives you the potential to influence their thinking more effectively.

Output: This stage should yield a process map of the typical stages that your customers go through to buy your product/service.

Step 2: Do a win/loss analysis

If you have been trading or trying to sell for more than a few months, you can probably learn a lot by reviewing your progress so far. Think about three to five opportunities that you won and three to five opportunities that you lost or never came to fruition. For SMEs, you can invite each person that joins the workshop to list their own examples of won/lost opportunities.

Then, try to extract the common threads:

- What you did that made you successful?
- What went wrong where you did not win the opportunity?

Beware of *attribution error*[7] when you do win/loss analysis. Salespeople will often protect themselves by arguing that opportunities were lost for reasons beyond their control, not because of omissions on their part. This is human nature, and if you create a climate of psychological safety in the workshops, it can be minimised.

Output: A list of activities that seem to help you win customers and anything that needs to be managed to avoid opportunities dropping out.

Step 3: Surface your sales best practices

These often arise as part of win/loss analysis. The idea here is to reflect on those activities you did that helped you advance your progress with opportunities. Some examples may help:

- A customer visit to your impressive offices.
- A customised demonstration of your product.
- Meeting with a valued technical expert.
- Workshops during the sales process that help customers gain valuable insights into their businesses.
- A well-presented proposal that offers clarity.
- A sequence of high-quality content that you send between meetings.

These 'space-dust' activities will be the things that differentiate your sales process from others. By revealing them, including them in your sales process, and doing them repeatedly, you will likely increase your conversion rates immediately.

Output: A list of routines and activities that salespeople can repeat to increase chances of success.

Step 4: Assess your type of sale

As already discussed, not all sales involve the same kind of activities. You may have heard the phrases *transactional sale* and *consultative sale*. These are definitions that try to capture the very different types of sales[8] that exist. A transactional purchase involves little thought and organisational involvement. It could be the purchase of a ream of paper already alluded to. A consultative sale would apply if we sold the bespoke software option. The budget would be much higher, and more people would necessarily be involved in approving the decision.

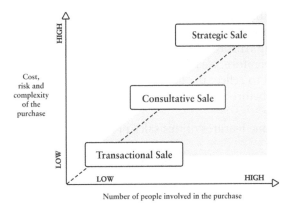

Figure 3.1 Sales typologies

Table 3.2 Some of the design criteria for your sales process

Characteristics of your sale	Implications for design	Product service example

High value OR
Complex or highly bespoke
  product/service delivery OR
Important risky purchase
	Multi-step process unfolding over
	  several weeks and months.
	High-quality personal selling approach
	Emphasis on precise understanding of
	  needs and building trust over multiple
	  interactions
		Bespoke software
		Consulting services
		Industrial equipment

Low value transaction
Simple product
Low risk
	Standardise or automate.
	Single 'one and done' sales call
	  (telephone, virtual or in-person)
	Reduce cost to serve.
	Challenge the use of personal selling
		Software as a Service
		  (SaaS)
		Consumables
		Parts and spares

Figure 3.1 shows one typology of sales that helps to conceptualise these types of sales. What kind of product or service are you offering the market? Your insights from mapping your customer's buying process should help you decide (Table 3.2).

The other design criteria to consider are the conclusions from your *growth model* and *sales strategy* work. To make sure a sales process is fit for purpose, it's vital that you can answer the first two questions of the sales strategy development process:

1 Who are we selling to?
2 What are we selling?

This is because sales process design effectively answers the third question, "how will we reach them?" For example, if customer retention is big on your agenda, your sales process should ensure that not only do you 'close the deal', but that you set up excellent account management. Similarly, if cross-selling is big on your agenda, then your sales process should sow the seeds for it.

Before we turn to the next step in the sales process, let's look at some examples to see what we are aiming for.

Table 3.3 shows an abridged sales process used by an SME selling physical education services to schools. In this sector, it takes several meetings to truly understand the needs of schools and build enough trust to introduce change. The budgets also have to be approved by several influencers; therefore, we have a multi-step process unfolding over several weeks. The term 'phase' is used to reflect the fact that we might have several contacts with a customer within one phase before moving on to the next. Equally, we might deal with a couple of phases in one meeting.

Note some of the unique features of this sales process:

- *Researching the Ofsted report before meeting.* In the UK, schools are audited by Ofsted, a government body, to drive up standards. Schools must comply with its findings, which include looking at physical education. This was found to be a 'sales best practice' during workshops and is therefore done before all sales meetings.
- *Networking and cross-selling.* By quickly working on selling other services, the risk of losing a school to the competition is greatly reduced, aiding retention, which was a key part of the growth strategy.

By contrast, Table 3.4 shows a more transactional sales process, used by a call centre that receives incoming calls from consumers wanting to invest in precious metals. (This case is featured at the end of this chapter.) This is an example of a *one-and-done* sales process, where all activities are typically handled in one call. The differences here are:

- Less phases, some of them quick, to facilitate short, effective telephone calls
- Highly specific elements related to compliance, for example, checking the source of funds
- The importance of offering insights about precious metals to build trust with potential customers

Thus, at step 4, you are going to make a call about what type of sales process will suit your product/service/market combination. At this stage, it makes sense to order the insights you gained from steps 1 to 3 into a process with some approximate headline phases (e.g. connect, discover and negotiate).

This 'first draft' process will get iterated over time.

Step 5: Consider the role of sales technology

Chapter 12 will look at sales technology in greater depth. We will see there is a staggering number of possibilities to enhance sales processes, and so ideally, it's best to read that chapter before hard baking the sales process you might create from this exercise.

It's something of a 'chicken and egg' challenge in which it's difficult to see what technologies might help your type of sales without a basic sales process to work from. And, on the other hand, you might design your sales process quite differently if you had insight into all of the technology you could use.

If you sense you are closer to a transactional sales model with little customisation required in your product, then could you dispense with personal selling altogether? Could the whole sales process be automated? If yes, then it would substantially reduce personnel costs, but you would need to shift emphasis to digital marketing to reach, attract, engage and retain customers.

Table 3.3 Multi-stage sales process

Phase	Contact	Meet	Propose	Finalise	Deliver	Care
Description	Contact the school based on excellent preparation	Make an excellent first impression and discover influencers	Suggest intelligent next steps and keep the sales process active	Stay in contact to cross the line	Over deliver our service promise, network and cross-sell	Keep good customers and lock out competitors
Routines	Visit school website. Check Ofsted report Check if part of school network Prepare first meeting	Top quality meeting management Active listening and smart questions Offer useful insights to position as a school physical education expert Dig the pain Discover influencers	Present proposal in person Take control of next steps	Contact creatively Stay close to contacts Confirm decision Discuss and confirm the next steps	Ensure our promise is delivered and surpassed Network in the school and develop our influence map Plan for the next best service	Renew SLAs in good time Demonstrate added value Carry out feedback meeting

Table 3.4 A transactional sales process

Phase	Connect	Listen and lead	Investment options	Conclude
Headline	Ensure a positive and trustworthy first impression	Assess buying motives and lead conversation appropriately	Confirm/explain advantages of our offer	Confirm the transaction and ensure the next steps are clear
Routines	Audible smile Personal intro for credibility Use names/titles How can I help you? Agenda setting	Focused questions to discover needs/requirements Adapt the call according to the customer type Explain the WHY behind questions before asking Offer precious metal insights Six attitudes of persuasion Be alert to fraud	Explain options and pros/cons of each Help to buy attitude Proud of price attitude Check if the client wants to go ahead and finalise the transaction Sow seeds for future investment ideas	Explain what happens next Plan next contact moments according to customer type Create an account and/or send lead pack
Essential checks	? Investment amount ? Which product	>Motives and investment known >Source of funds known	>Spreads discussed >Flexibility requirements	>Client aware of checks/process/timelines

For now, it's a good idea to make a note of:

- Any repetitive, time-consuming sales tasks that could potentially be automated.
- Any areas where technology might help your customer experience.
- Any ideas on how technology might increase your effectiveness in selling.
- Any marketing automation/CRM you might be using that will generate leads needs to be joined up to your core sales process (e.g. Hubspot)

Once you've read Chapter 12, you might well make some changes to your sales process.

Output: A list of potential ideas on how to use sales technology to enhance your sales process.

Step 6: Align your core sales process with lead generation

Since we defined the core sales process as the *first contact to happy customer*, we need to spend some time thinking about how we get those *first contacts* and how best to manage incoming leads. This is where having a marketing representative in your workshops is invaluable, as you can co-create the best way to hand over any marketing-generated leads.

The choices to make have already been alluded to when looking at your customers' journey: Should we allow potential customers to do their own research about our solution, or should we control it? Your technology decisions will also have an impact on how this works.

Imagine being a customer for a moment and making an enquiry via a supplier's website. What happens next will immediately influence your perception of the quality of the organisation you are dealing with. Work done by Marketo has shown that a response to your enquiry within five minutes is four times more likely to qualify than a follow-up time of ten minutes.[9] Whatever time frame you work in, having a high-quality handover from marketing to sales is essential for success. After all, how would you feel if you filled out a comprehensive form on the website and then the salesperson that calls you starts by asking, "How can I help you?" forcing you to explain all over again what you'd already written?

You can hard-wire the procedure for handling incoming leads into your core sales process. This discussion will raise many questions about how best to align sales and marketing activities and which technology could support the process. This may not be easy, but ultimately, it will lead to a much better customer experience and higher conversion rates.

Output: Definition of the handover process from marketing to sales and the routines and checks to be done when leads come into the core sales process.

Step 7: List any compliance/operational requirements

Certain types of sales are regulated by legislation and demand that we explain customer rights and obligations, for example, financial services and telecoms/utilities. These 'non-negotiable' elements should be written into the sales process at the appropriate stage.

Similarly, if you are selling a complex product with long lead times or one that demands significant internal resources, you may need to build these elements in too. An example would be submitting the scope of a potential consultancy assignment to your operations manager early in the sales process to see if it can be resourced before committing a delivery date to a customer.

Output: A list of 'must-dos' to be added to the final version.

Step 8: Build a first-draft sales process

Having worked through steps 1–7 (i.e. put the ingredients into the casserole), it's time to have a go at designing your first draft sales process (let the ingredients blend for a perfect flavour).

It should incorporate the insights you discovered on the journey, and as a group, you should have the feeling that you've produced a good approach worthy of sharing with others.

Iteration of the first draft can then be done asynchronously by e-mail or shared drive.

Circulate the nascent sales process within the project team and potentially with other stakeholders, asking the following five questions:

- Does this feel really tailored to our business?
- Is this a useful daily guide that reminds us of what to do in the heat of sales action?
- What is missing from the process?
- How does it guarantee an excellent customer experience?
- Can we improve it?

There will be a process of 'wordsmithing' to get the language, clarity and conciseness right. At a certain point, you should arrive at a sales process that you feel excited about and believe in.

At this point, the beta version is ready for testing. As boxer Mike Tyson was famously quoted, "Everyone has a plan until they are punched in the face". By actually using your sales process over several months, you will be able to adapt and improve it based on real customer interactions.

Indeed, all sales processes need refreshing regularly to adapt to internal and external changes.

Output: A sales process you feel proud of and that is ready to be implemented.

Embedding your sales process

It's one thing to design a great sales process; it's another thing altogether for a sales team to live it every day. Now the hard work starts! If your sales team is not used to working in a process-led way, then it is wise to recognise the challenge of embedding a sales process as an exercise in good change management. *The secret sauce for leading transformational change* by Ian Ziskin is a good resource to help you in this regard.[10]

In the following chapters, several reinforcing mechanisms will be introduced that will help to embed your sales process, specifically:

- Your sales methodology
- KPIs/metrics
- Pipeline review meetings
- Sales management routines
- Coaching and training
- Technology and CRM

When all these components are based on and align with your core sales process, then the reinforcement effect is strong.

What else can we do to support the implementation of a sales process? The working group method introduced here means you have 'champions' in the sales team who helped design and hopefully support it. Make their work visible and empower them to coach/train others in the sales team. Peer-to-peer influence can be very strong in sales teams if used well.

Presenting your core sales process as a 'coaching guide' rather than a non-negotiable 'straitjacket' will help with the common resistance we all feel when forced to comply with a process. We employ salespeople to use their common sense and adaptive selling skills, and so we have to trust them to deviate occasionally from the process if it helps (a) improve the customer experience or (b) increases our chances of success.

Your sales process as a culture shift

In business, there is an expression that states, "An amateur hopes for a good result, a professional plans for one". This gives us a clue as to how to think about sales processes. We want to encourage a spirit in the sales team where excellent preparation and high-quality management of opportunities are the norm. There is no better example of this than *The Checklist Manifesto*, written by Atul Gawande.[11] It tells the story of how Atul transformed surgery worldwide by borrowing the 'checklist principle', used to good effect by airline pilots for some time now.

For each and every flight, pilots go through a printed checklist to make sure everything is safely set up for the journey (e.g. Do we have enough fuel? Do we know our route?). He introduced this approach into hospitals, to use before each surgical procedure, greatly reducing the error rate (e.g. Do we know exactly which procedure we are doing? Do we have the patient's blood type in store in case it's needed?).

The method of going through a checklist before every procedure initially created a lot of resistance among highly educated surgeons, but in time, they came to see the powerful results it achieved. Using a process consistently like this effectively changes the culture from a 'wing it' sales approach to a 'let's plan for success at every step'.

Thus, with careful messaging, you can appeal to your sales team's desire to 'be the best' when you introduce your sales process.

Into action

Before building your sales process, ensure you can answer the initial two questions for your sales strategy:

Who are we selling to?

What are we selling?

Next, pull together your working group and work through the sales process design approach.

Map your customer's typical buying journey
Do a win/loss analysis of recent opportunities
Inventorise your sales best practices
Assess your 'type of sale' to select the design format for your sales process
Consider technology options to automate/augment the process
Integrate lead generation/marketing activities
Integrate any compliance/operational requirements
Trial your first draft sales process

Expert view: Sales process at Volvo Truck

Volvo Truck is a brand that needs no introduction. Awarded the truck of the year for 2024, with its new FH Electric model, Volvo Truck is a world leader in transport and haulage. With a long history of innovation and a reputation for high quality and safety, the brand supplies transport solutions to the widest range of operators globally.

For many years, Volvo Truck has used a sales process to guide the activities of its sales teams. Why do large, successful brands like Volvo use sales processes, and what can start-ups and SMEs learn from them? Martin Foley, Director, sales excellence UK, explains:

Why do you think it is useful for salespeople to follow a sales process?

First and foremost, it's habit-forming, which gives us efficiency and effectiveness. It gives us quality and consistency in what we do. For truck selling, there are a number of things we need to do because of the relative complexity of what we sell. If we do them at the right times and do them properly, they act as safety nets. Our sales process provides important checks along the way and, accordingly, supports customer satisfaction.

It forces us to ask if we are doing the right thing when we are building a specification for a haulier, for example, taking care of driver comfort or fuel economy. It helps to ensure that we've met all the expectations of the customer before we present a proposal to them. It means that when we present the quote, we should be 95% of the way there. Any further discussion with the customer after that should just be fine tuning; for example, do we have the right cab colours and make of tyres in place?

A sales process should save us time, because if we do it over and over again, it becomes an unconscious habit. We know it's robust, and it will deliver what customers expect from a blue-chip firm. We are selling a high-value product that needs to be right for every customer. They don't just give us their money for fun; they need a result to run their business effectively. And the truck must be road legal as well. Five minutes of work at the start of a sales process to get the truck specification right can save weeks of rework if we get it wrong.

Our sales process is beautifully simple in some ways. We find a customer. We do a needs analysis. We know what they need. We prepare a quotation and present it to the customer. We negotiate the final order. Then we plan the delivery and then manage the handover.

It's like cooking a recipe, isn't it? It's six easy steps. You break some eggs and put some flour in, but you have to do it well and in the right order if you want to end up with a good cake.

What is your advice for embedding a sales process?

Firstly, I think you've got to take a step back and look at what you did today. That's the starting point. We often find a sales process shortens the sales cycle and access to customers, and by doing so, increases profitability. A good sales process will likely reduce costly stock days, for example. It will also give clarity on what a customer is going to do, enabling our dealers to measure and manage their sales more effectively.

It's important that senior managers understand these kinds of benefits, because without their support, it's very difficult to implement a sales process. It's very much a case of monkey see, monkey do. Implementation of any sales process for me requires discipline, and that's hard to instil in those who don't have a disciplined mindset. Some salespeople seem to enjoy chaos. They somehow thrive on the 'busyness' that is caused by this chaos.

It's the same as a sausage roll manufacturer; they make their sausage rolls the same way every day, all day, every day, don't they? They don't deviate from the recipe. And the product's always of good quality because of this. That would be the one big thing for me – to have the right discipline for success in sales. It's absolutely critical.

Notes

1 J.M. Cuevas et al *Sales management* 4th ed p100 Palgrave 2016
2 N. Slack et al *Operations management* 4th ed FT Prentice Hall 2004
3 D. Meerman Scott *The new rules of sales and service* p102 Wiley 2014
4 B. Adamson et al "Dismantling the sales machine" *Harvard Business Review* Nov 2013
5 G. Franke & J.E. Park "Salesperson adaptive selling behaviour and customer orientation: A meta-analysis" *Journal of Marketing Research* vol. 43 no. 4 (2006), 693–702
6 S. Hall *Innovative B2B marketing* p36 Kogan Page 2017
7 D. Buchanan & A. Huczynski *Organisational behaviour* 5th ed p230 FT Prentice Hall 2005
8 J.M. Cuevas et al 4th ed p105 2016
9 An article by Jon Miller https://business.adobe.com/uk/resources/guides/sales-lead-qualification-and-sales-development.html
10 I. Ziskin *The secret sauce for leading transformational change* Routledge 2022
11 A. Gawande *The checklist manifesto* Metropolitan Books 2011

Chapter 4

B2B personal selling under the microscope

What are the essential elements of typical B2B selling?

The purpose of this chapter

It's difficult to scale a sales organisation if we don't know what good selling looks like. Many start-ups are founded by individuals with a brilliant idea and the drive to make it happen. And yet, just by the law of numbers, not many founders have prior sales experience, so selling their idea can be challenging. Similarly, many of those responsible for growth in Small and medium enterprises (SMEs) may have had limited exposure to excellent sales approaches.

For this reason, this chapter lays out the essential basics of B2B selling to help you get started if you feel this is an area to develop. It is also here to help you build and refine your sales process/sales methodology by examining good sales routines, behaviours and attitudes.

The core characteristics of B2B selling

In Chapter 3, the idea of *transactional* and *consultative* sales was introduced. Upfront, it is worth recalling that not all B2B sales are the same. We need to bear this in mind when considering which B2B selling approach to adopt.

In this chapter, consultative selling-type environments will be used to explore B2B selling skills, as they typically involve a wider range of activities and actions than transactional sales. With that in mind, you should carefully consider what elements will really help you and what elements you can safely leave out.

There has been a lot of good work done on what makes for effective B2B selling, and it is big business. Perhaps the most famous approach of all is 'SPIN[1] selling', pioneered by Dr Neil Rackham,[2] described as *"The world's leading sales methodology"*,[3] which focuses on highly effective questioning to set up sales processes for success. Similarly, *The Challenger Sale* approach by Matthew Dixon and Brent Adamson[4] has sold over 500,000 copies worldwide.[5] Here, the focus is on challenging customers to find great solutions, thereby improving the profile of the supplier.

Other points of view on B2B selling are *High Performance Sales Strategies* by Russell Ward, which explores multiple aspects of sales processes,[6] and *The Qualified Sales Leader* by John McMahon.[7] This last book is a great choice for technology companies. McMahon was chief revenue officer at five leading tech firms.

There are in fact many viewpoints on exactly what good B2B sales look like, so this chapter presents a curated, 'big picture view', drawn from a broad range of sources like these and experience of implementing programmes on the ground.[8]

DOI: 10.4324/9781003449614-4

So, what are some essential hallmarks of B2B sales?

- Purchase values can be large, requiring sign-off by a budget holder.
- Many people can be involved in influencing and making a decision to purchase.
- The selling process can take weeks, months or years.[9]
- The importance of the purchase means that approval criteria and trials might be required.
- Professional buyers may be involved in the decision-making process, meaning you have to go through various supplier screening processes (e.g. request for proposals) and price negotiations.
- The process can involve multiple meetings and extensive work in the background to close a single deal.

Because of these factors, B2B selling often mandates a *multi-stage sales process*, as discussed in Chapter 3. It is simply not realistic or desirable to achieve everything in one call/meeting.

Let's now consider some typical phases of B2B sales processes, respecting the fact that as stated in Chapter 3, every product/service/market combination demands its own specific approach. Experience shows that there are some common themes across industries, and this general approach will help to explain typical attitudes, routines and behaviours. You can then assess how your process is different and which of these are going to help you the most.

Typical phases in a B2B sales process

Recall from Chapter 3 that the word 'phases' is used because it may take several customer interactions to complete one phase. Or indeed, several phases might happen in one interaction. For example, negotiating and closing often take place in one single meeting to 'agree terms'.

Let's now go into each phase in more detail (Table 4.1).

Prospecting

Without a steady stream of new customers, most sales organisations struggle to grow revenues. Prospecting is an activity that often gets shared/split between sales and marketing, according to the way organisations are set up. Chapter 6 will go into more detail about how we generate a stream of leads to feed into our core sales process.

Most organisations today use a mix of inbound and outbound marketing. The exact mix will depend on many factors, and this will be explored in Chapter 6.

Table 4.1 Typical phases in B2B selling and their objectives

Phase	Description
Prospecting	Finding a potential customer using a variety of lead generation methods
Discovering	Making the first contact to understand needs and build trust/confidence
Engaging	Educating and motivating customers to carry on discussions with you
Proposing	Proposing a tailored commercial offer to meet the customer's needs
Closing	Negotiating the final terms and getting the go-ahead
Securing	Ensuring your product/service delivers on its promise
Nurturing	Looking after your new customers and growing sales

Key work to be done in this phase: Ensure you put regular time and resources into prospecting every week to generate a steady flow of potential sales.

Discovering

Did you ever feel when meeting with a salesperson, "I wish they would try to understand what I am looking for a bit better"? If you did, it's their needs exploration skills that were lacking. Even if you only have one solution to offer, customers still want to be heard and acknowledged. It's a basic human need. If you have more than one solution, understanding your customers' needs precisely is absolutely essential for effective B2B selling.

This attitude is backed up by research done by the tech company Gong.io. By analysing 500,000 sales conversations, they found that, "consistent with past research, the data shows a strong connection between the number of questions a salesperson asks and his or her conversion rate".[10] Discovering involves asking precise questions to understand what a customer wants or needs. This enables us to present a product/ service that is tailored very well to their needs. It is the behavioural manifestation of *customer-centricity*.

The twin sister of good questioning is *active listening*. Much has been written about the importance of good listening in the context of personal selling, for example, Roy Whitten and Scott Roy call it *precision listening*.[11] Good salespeople listen fully, are genuinely interested in customers, and don't interrupt them mid-sentence. This attitude, in itself, is a powerful positive influence mechanism. After all, how do we feel when people fully listen to us like this?

Discovering then means asking a lot of questions upfront to see if the customer has a need, for example:

"What issues are you experiencing that you think we might help with?"

"What are your ambitions for next year?"

Note the use of open questions in these examples. Often starting with *what, when, how, why, which, where* and *who*, open questions are particularly useful to discover information.[12] Questions can also be used to help customers look at their situation in new ways, thereby offering valuable new insights.

Armed with answers to these questions, the salesperson can then adapt their communication to cover the points that are relevant to a customer. Indeed, if we present a 'benefit' to a customer who has no need for it, it becomes an annoyance. Maybe you have experienced this when a poor salesperson has bored you senseless with a long list of irrelevant information about their offer.

Thus, discovering involves asking a set of focused questions to understand a customer's situation, needs and motivations, and listening very carefully to the answers so that they can be addressed in our solution.

Key work to be done in this phase: For every sales meeting with a new customer or opportunity, write down a list of open questions to fully discover their needs. Ensure you listen fully to their answers to allow you to advocate for a fully relevant solution.

Engaging

You can imagine that a first meeting with a potential customer that only includes a long list of questions might well feel like an interrogation. A conversational approach has been found to be more effective,[13] with questions interspersed as part of an information exchange.

Early on in the sales process, we normally need to provide some motivation for a customer to carry on interacting with us. There are a number of things we can do to facilitate this. First, building trust is very important. Would you buy from someone you don't trust?

Research done by Aaron Arndt and his colleagues identified that trust can be built by showing *benevolence* and *competence*.[14] Benevolence is setting out upfront how you will ensure you have your customers best interests at heart. Competence means showing that customers are in *safe hands* with someone who knows their subject area well. This could include statements like:

Benevolence: "If ok with you, what we will do today is go through your requirements thoroughly, and then I can come back to you with some ideas for you to evaluate. How does that sound?"

Competence: "Your project reminds me of a similar one we are working on right now for customer X. They have the same challenge that you do with increasing efficiency".

What is also happening during the engaging phase is that we are *sowing seeds* for future interactions. It is normally wise to hold back some information or offers so that we can create motivation for future meetings. Recall that for many sales processes, we want to encourage a multistep process, so we can:

- Take time to fully understand customer needs.
- Have time to think about and prepare a customised, valuable solution.
- Demonstrate our reliability and organisation's professionalism by *doing what we say we will do*.

Engaging serves the role of motivating a customer to 'stay with us', while we arrive at a solution. Start-ups and SMEs can do this in several ways:

- Organise a follow-up meeting to survey, assess, measure or double-check needs.
- Arrange a workshop with key individuals to explore insights and solutions together.
- Trial a product over a specific time frame.
- Arrange a follow-up meeting to present a proposal.
- Invite your customers to your office to meet your team/see a product demonstration.

Creativity is your friend here. Every organisation has unique 'space dust' they can add to engage customers.

Key work to be done: Keep your potential customers motivated to stay in conversation with you.

Product trials and demonstrations

For some organisations, the engagement phase may involve product trials or demos. Many industrial products will need to be validated before the sales process can move on. Similarly, Software as a Service (SaaS) businesses often demo their product to potential customers to gain traction and move towards a sale. If done well, trials and demos can really draw a customer in. If done badly, it can be the end of the road for an opportunity.

Here are some guidelines to help make these activities productive:

- Ensure customers' needs are fully understood before entering into any demonstration of your product, so that you can select and emphasise the key features of your offer that will be valuable.

- Beware of 'autopilot demo behaviour' i.e., boring customers with irrelevant information about all the quirky, unique features you have. If they don't need/want it, don't talk about it.
- If possible, let your customer use/try the product/service/software. It's the same principle as test driving a car: It's not much fun watching someone else drive!
- Make the demo interactive by asking questions regularly, e.g., "How would you see this working in your organisation?" or "Could this help you?". Good demos are discussions, not monologues, enabling you to adapt as you go.
- For industrial products requiring production validation, it is wise to agree on the evaluation criteria upfront before a trial. This serves both as an important qualification mechanism and ensures everyone is clear about what success looks like.
- Where multiple decision-makers are involved in product/service selection, try to have them all attend the trial/demo, so you can manage the internal discussions about your offering.
- For organisations that are strongly procurement-led, it may be necessary to agree on pricing ahead of a trial.
- If practicable, be with your customer when they trial your offering to iron out any problems immediately. Where this is not practical, make sure you have review points booked in the calendar to check progress.

Key work to be done in this phase: Understand precisely what customers need/wants and motivate them to move on to the next stage in the sales process by creating interest and excitement about the future.

Proposing

Having a clear understanding of what customers are looking for means we can come back with a solution that is precisely tailored to their needs. It will cover in detail the formulation of your unique value proposition, including the benefits it will bring to potential clients.

Your proposal essentially answers your potential customer's question, "How will your offering help my business?" so it should link back to the needs/wants/ambitions you picked up in the discovering phase.

A common mistake made by many start-ups and SMEs is to have a discovering/engaging initial meeting and then promise to send a quote proposal by email or post. For sales opportunities of any significant value, it is better to personally present your proposal/quote, either face-to-face or using virtual meeting software, for time efficiency.

By agreeing to a follow-up session to present your proposal, several things happen:

- You have a chance to think about and prepare a top-quality solution.
- Your customer has time to adapt to the idea of actually buying from you.
- You have a chance to prove your reliability and professionalism by being on time and providing a well-thought-out, personalised solution.
- You can handle any concerns/objections they have when they see your proposal.
- You can adjust your proposal based on any new information that arises.

When building a written proposal, many supplier proposals start with a long introduction about their own company, history, capabilities, etc. This sends a very clear message about who is the most important party! As a benchmark, Russell Ward, in his book *High Performance Sales Strategies* says, "around 60 to 70% of an effective sales value proposition will be customer focused".[15]

A better structure for a 'proposal document' is:

1 Your customer's ambitions/requirements
2 Your solution to meet these ambitions
3 The benefits and value your solution offers
4 The investment/fees/figures
5 Information about your organisation (your organisation in brief, your team, evidence of competence and results, customer testimonials)

Using this structure and presenting the proposal personally means you can sequentially confirm each section before moving on to the next. This is sometimes known as the *3 yes approach*, as it involves the deliberate use of three key closed confirmation questions, as shown in Table 4.2:

Key work to be done in this phase: Agreeing on a solution that works well for your potential customer.

Closing

Often people associate the sleazy side of sales with *closing*, especially high-pressure selling. There are many 'closing techniques' trained, and they are occasionally used clumsily by salespeople. Russell Ward lists 70 different variants[16] (e.g. the *courtship close, the now-or-never close, the puppy close*), qualifying them as, "some of the techniques of closing are a bit crass".

One definition of closing is *agreeing on concrete next steps*. If you have conducted your sales process well, then it is natural for the discussion to move on to "how do we get started?". Therefore, a very logical thing to do after you present your proposal is to ask, "Would you like to go ahead?" or similar.

In my consulting experience working with organisations, when a training request for 'closing skills' comes up, it is nearly always because the early parts of the sales process are

Table 4.2 The 3 yes approach to proposal presentation

Step	Example question	Our response
Present your customer's needs (Obtain a 'Yes to the needs')	"Did we understand your needs precisely?"	If you understood the needs perfectly, move to 'Present solution', otherwise, note the edits and decide whether substantial rework is required or not
Present your solution and its benefits (Obtain a 'Yes to the solution')	"Do you feel this is the right solution for you?"	If your solution is good, move to 'present fees'. If not, agree on what solution would work better and decide if you need to rework the proposal or carry on the meeting with minor edits
Present the fees/investment (Obtain a 'Yes to the sale')	"Do you want to go ahead?"	If the customer is happy to go ahead, agree on concrete next steps in the diary. If no, understand why, and what needs to be done to make it a 'yes'.

done poorly. For example, not understanding customer needs well enough before presenting a proposal. Yes, there are a significant proportion of people who are uncomfortable asking for commitment, as it feels 'pushy'. If you are one of these individuals, it helps to remember the assistant in the shoe shop, who, when you smile and say, "these are perfect!" very naturally asks, "Shall I take them to the till for you?". Imagine how awkward it would be if they *did not* ask that question! A salesperson who cannot recognise when a customer is ready to buy is frustrating.

If your customer is willing to go ahead, closing implies making the next steps very concrete, so everyone knows what will happen next and when.

Key work to be done in this phase: Ask if your customer is ready to go ahead/sign-up, and manage any objections if not (objection handling will be covered in this chapter).

Securing

When we buy something new and significant, it's natural to experience a certain amount of anxiety as to whether we made a good decision or not. The sales organisation's behaviour at this stage makes a huge impact on how that feeling evolves. If we have frequent contact and maybe some pleasant surprises from a supplier (delivery ahead of schedule, a welcome pack, a phone call from a senior executive to thank us for the business), then we are likely to be both reassured and to recommend them to others. And the reverse is also true!

A good sales process systematises routines and behaviours that kick in at the closing stage to secure customer satisfaction and advocacy. Indeed, the closing phase of your sales process should include any routines that set up success for the future (professional handover to your service/customer success team, detailed agreement of implementation and training activities).

Over the last few years, there has been a large increase in *customer success teams* as a way to structurally guarantee customer satisfaction post-close.[17] This model is especially prevalent in SaaS organisations that rely on the recurring revenue model. The option of restructuring to facilitate this activity is considered in Chapter 8.

Key work to be done in this phase: Deliver on your sales promise to ensure your new customer is happy enough to recommend you to others.

Nurturing

Once you have made your initial sale a success, your focus shifts to activities such as customer retention, cross-selling, up-selling and networking. In this phase, the work shifts to looking after our customers, building strong relationships, locking out the competition and finding ways to grow revenues if such opportunities exist.

Complacency among salespeople is more common than we might imagine. Research carried out by Scott Friend and Jeff Johnston identified 20 types of 'misbehaviour' that B2B buyers identified.[18]

Many large organisations use *marketing automation* and *account-based marketing* to support this phase. For some great examples of how this can be done, *Data-driven Sales* published by Clearbit,[19] is a good read. For SMEs and start-ups, you might need a manual process to get started.

Key work to be done in this phase: Build relationships and networks with your new customer so they don't have a reason to leave, and you can develop new sources of revenue through cross-selling and up-selling.

Overarching themes in B2B sales

Each phase in a B2B sales process has its own specific routines and objectives. Beyond these, there are other key themes that we need to pay attention to when interacting with customers to increase our chances of success.

Theme 1: Professionalism, trust and integrity

What is professionalism in sales? As stated in Chapter 3, "An amateur hopes for a good result, a professional plans for one". How is this manifested in sales? Eminent psychologist Paul Watzlawick was quoted as saying, "One cannot not communicate".[20] In other words, we always influence. This means paying attention so that we make a positive impression during every customer interaction, for example, by:

- Always being on time
- Preparing well for every meeting
- Paying attention to personal appearance and documents
- Managing meetings with customers effectively to stay on time and achieve valuable outcomes

Much has been written about *conformation bias*, where we form opinions based on limited information (*Thinking, Fast and Slow* by Daniel Kahneman is an excellent place to start[21]). If we make a poor first impression through little preparation or being late/unreliable, it is quite difficult to undo a customer's perception. Therefore, paying attention to the little things is essential to maintaining our professional image.

Also, for customers to be willing to do business with us, trust is essential. This topic has already been introduced in the *engaging* phase. Erin Meyer argues that an important aspect of trust is cognitive,[22] that is, the confidence customers feel in your accomplishments, skills and reliability. "To do as we say we will" is an essential component of this. Too many salespeople promise next steps but don't follow through, thus eroding trust. Having concrete actions at the end of each customer interaction and actually following through on them shows our professionalism and reliability.

As alluded to already, sales call preparation is an essential component of good B2B selling. Things to prepare include:

- Researching your customer's business online (website, blogs and news articles)
- Agreeing on the agenda in advance with your customer
- Specific questions to ask during the meeting
- Useful insights to bring
- Products, software and documents to show/demonstrate
- Ideal next steps after the meeting

Theme 2: Attitude and ethics

Have you ever said to yourself, "I don't want to be salesy"? Or do you find the whole idea of being involved in sales quite off-putting? Don't worry, you are not alone! It's really normal for start-up founders and 'technical' sales specialists to be uncomfortable with sales as a profession. Stories in the media of unethical, high-pressure selling do not help.[23] Authors and specialists in this area, Suzanne Dudley and Trelitha Bryant, refer to this as *call reluctance,* or the *fear of self-promotion*.[24] In their book *Relentless*, they identify "16 faces of call reluctance", more than enough reasons not to pursue sales activities! This book is an excellent read to help you identify specific sales mindsets that might block you and strategies to overcome them.

One way to help with this common problem is to redefine buying and selling. Who 'decides' if a purchase goes ahead? Is it the salesperson? Can we 'decide' if a customer buys? Clearly not! Therefore, our role can instead be to '*help customers buy*', through our positive influence, meaning to:

- Precisely understand their needs, so we can recommend solutions that meet their needs.
- Help them objectively evaluate options to move forward, including the option *not* to use our solution.
- Work alongside them, as you would a good friend, to make good decisions.
- Help them move forward when they are indecisive, busy and losing focus.
- Help them work through any objections.
- Do not put pressure on them to make a decision unless there is an open, transparent reason to do so.

When we approach selling as *helping to buy*, it helps us take a more ethical approach. Researchers Moon and Choi showed that customer satisfaction does increase, as we might expect, with sales behaviours perceived as ethical.[25]

Theme 3: High-quality communication

Active listening and precise questions have already been alluded to in the *discovering* stage of B2B sales. These two attitudes are vital throughout all customer interactions. When looking at interactions between buyers and sellers over a longer time period, Susie Pryor and her colleagues have shown there is a link between a "salesperson's listening, and impressions of affective and cognitive empathy".[26] Thus, good questions and active listening are just as important during contract negotiation, post-sale customer management and complaints as they are in the early phases of a sales process. When people listen fully to us, we feel it.

Theme 4: Objection handling

Another stumbling block that sometimes rattles entrepreneurs and salespeople is when customers raise objections or concerns during sales meetings, for example:
"Your solution is too difficult to implement"
"You are more expensive than our current supplier"
It can be tempting to respond with:
"Yes, but we can help you with that"

"Yes, but we offer more than your current supplier does"

When reading these responses, it's clear that they are ineffective. Our "yes, but…" attitude is a sign of our defensiveness and rarely helps. So why do objections surface, and how should we manage them?

Firstly, it is worth noting that salespeople can actually create objections! Neil Rackham discovered that "in the average sales team, there's usually one salesperson who receives ten times as many objections per selling hour as another person in the same team".[27] This happens because the salesperson simply presents feature after feature without checking if the customer needs or wants any of them.

Therefore, it is important that we do not propose solutions before we fully understand a customer's needs. It's the equivalent of a 'good friend' offering us advice on how to solve a complex personal problem with an overly simplistic, unhelpful approach. We reject it and may even resent the friend for 'lecturing us'.

Customers raise objections or concerns when they have a doubt or a worry. It's totally normal. Imagine you go to choose a new television that costs a month's wages. The picture quality is stunning, but for a month's wages, wow, that's quite an investment. You might say:

"I love the picture quality, but it's quite expensive"

Internally, you are a bit nervous about committing so much household budget to a TV (doubt). If the salesperson responds with:

"Yes, but the quality is great, isn't it?"

It does not really help you. It doesn't address your concern about budget. A better approach for them would be as follows:

"Ok, it's a good idea to talk about budget so we can help you make a good choice. What is your ideal budget?"

They could also respond with:

"This model is one of the higher quality ones. To help you make a good choice, what do you typically use your TV for?"

You can imagine that, armed with your views on your desired budget and your needs, the salesperson has a better chance of helping you buy the right TV. If they had asked these questions upfront, then, as Neil Rackham advocates, this objection might never have arisen. Instead, they could have recommended the right TV for you, based on your individual circumstances.

If we do have to manage concerns and objections, a good approach is to:

1 Listen actively to the concern/objection without interruption.
2 Acknowledge it (e.g. "Thanks for bringing this to my attention…").
3 Ask questions to understand the concern more fully (e.g. "what exactly is your concern?").
4 Respond with a well-thought-out answer/next step.

Being able to deal with objections is an essential component of *helping to buy*, because if we gloss over customer objections, we are not really helping them make a good decision.

It's the same as a good friend saying, "I don't feel like going to the gym today". If we really want to be good friends, we help them unpack the objection to make a good decision, as there could be several reasons for making this objection. If we went deeper with the questions, they might say:

"I think I have a cold coming" (In which case, encouraging them to avoid the gym makes sense) or

"I find it boring" (In which case encouraging them to change their programme and go anyway might serve their interests better in the long run)

Objections can arise at multiple points during B2B selling, so being ready for them is a useful skill.

Often, we can foresee them in advance and prepare fully to manage them, which is a great confidence booster when they arise.

Theme 5: Staying in control of your sales process

If we accept that having a multi-stage process makes sense for B2B sales, then it implies multiple meetings with customers spread over time. Who leads the process? Another critical insight from Neil Rackham's work is the different outcomes salespeople achieve at the end of each customer meeting.

He defined four categories[28]:

- Orders – we get the go-ahead
- Advance – we get closer to a decision
- Continuations – there is a follow up meeting, but we are no closer to a decision
- No sales – customer says an outright 'no'

In particular, he warns against *continuations,* that is, follow-up meetings with customers, that add no value for either side. Worse still is when salespeople arrange no follow-up. In other words, they say something like:

"I'll leave this with you, and just get back to me if it looks interesting"

Who then has control of the sales process? It's up to us to figure out in advance what the next step and explicitly ask for it.

By way of example, imagine you are in the *discovery phase* of your sales process. Having asked lots of questions to understand your customers' needs, it's time to prepare a proposal for them. One option is to say:

"Give me a couple of days, and I'll send you a quote through"

If we do this, who is in control of the next step? Not us! Better to set up the *proposing* phase accordingly:

"When is convenient for us to meet, so I can present our proposal? How does next Thursday at 1400 look in your diary?"

By agreeing on a concrete next step and fixing it in your mutual diaries, we take control of the next step. This example serves to demonstrate why we should never send a proposal, as already mentioned during the proposing phase description.

Ideally, all sales meetings should have a *commitment objective*, defined as follows:

- Concrete: It is clear whether it has been achieved or not.
- It advances the sales process, that is, gets us closer to a decision.
- We can explicitly ask a customer to agree to it during the meeting.

The implication of this approach is that we need to think through what commitment we could ask for, before entering a sales meeting, so we can plan the agenda accordingly. If there is no next step, we are not in control of the sales process.

Theme 6: Paying attention to who makes the buying decision

One of the unique characteristics of B2B buying is the number of decision-makers involved. Corporate Executive Board research in 2015 found that an average of 5.4 people were involved in B2B purchases.[29] If your sale is complex, has a high budget and carries high operational consequences for your customer, it could be even more people. Because of this, we often have to *map the decision-making unit* and understand the *customer buying process*.

Inexperienced salespeople often make the mistake of spending too much time with one friendly contact at a prospect who likes the product/service but has no real influence.

Various schemes have been developed over the years to map decision-makers by categorising their role in the buying process. Typically, these roles include:

- *Budget holder*: The one who ultimately says yes/no to your offer.
- *Technical influencers*: Individuals that set the specifications for your type of product/service.
- *Product/service users*: The ones that will use your offering.
- *Advocate/champion*: An individual who wants your approach to be successful.

Categorising influencers and decision makers in this way can help us adapt our approach to them, for example, when preparing a return-on-investment calculation for a budget holder. For a fuller insight into how to manage and influence decision-making units, 'The qualified sales leader'[30] is an excellent resource.

Some key principles to think about are:

- Try to find a champion/advocate as soon as possible.
- Ask your champion to help you map the decision makers and influencers.
- Establish their level of influence in the buying process.
- Establish their opinion of your produce/service.
- Use your advocates to positively influence doubters.
- Co-create a strong case with your advocate and take it together to budget holders.
- Pay attention to culture, politics and power.

Today, many organisations use their internal experts and key staff to influence customer decision-making processes. For example, you could set up a meeting between your technical expert and theirs to thrash out the specification.

Your sales process can also include checklists to ensure you have identified key decision-makers and met with them during the discovery phase. This approach avoids presenting a proposal that gets rejected because it does not meet the needs of key stakeholders.

Theme 7: Qualification

Perfect time management occurs in sales when we spend all our valuable time with customers and prospects, where the best opportunities for growth exist. If we invest a lot of time in poor quality opportunities, it has costs. For example, losing out to a competitor and coming in second in a long selling process is the most expensive way to fail. The ability to *fail early* in sales, therefore, is often desirable.

Qualification is a structured approach to assessing opportunities at an early stage to help us focus our time on the best ones. A well-known simple qualification tool is BANT: *Budget, authority, need* and *timeline*. The theory is that if we are in touch with someone who ticks all four boxes, then the probability of closing a deal is higher.

This basic approach has been refined by others to be more specific and thorough for the type of sale. John McMahon, mentioned earlier, uses the MEDDPICC approach[31] (*metrics, economic buyer, decision criteria, decision process, identify the pain or initiative, paper process, champion and competition*). This approach has diffused across many tech companies now.

SMEs and start-ups can develop their own qualification criteria, which are super specific to their type of sale.

During the *discovery* and *engagement* phases of our sales process, we can use qualification as follows:

- By asking direct and indirect questions, we better understand who is involved in the decision, what the timeline is and what the measures of success are.
- To test the pain/initiative to see if it is important and shared by several people.
- To guide our approach to meeting the decision-makers, we *cover the bases*.

It should soon be obvious if we are dealing with a real and relatively urgent need or if we are looking at superficial interests only.

Qualification acts like a kind of probability measuring tool: if we can say yes to many of the qualification criteria, then the probability of a sale is high. If we cannot meet the criteria without a significant amount of work, then it may be time to 'reverse out' it or delegate sales work to the customer (e.g. ask them to put together a specification so you can quote accurately).

Theme 8: Sales technology

As we will see in Chapter 12, sales technology has already transformed and will continue to transform the way buying and selling are done. From automating routine tasks to augmenting and improving other customer interactions, anyone involved in B2B sales must pay close attention to these developments.

From general B2B selling themes to your specific sales process and sales methodology

Having taken a whistle-stop tour of the key processes, attitudes and behaviours involved in B2B selling, you hopefully now have a clearer view of how your sales process could work or be enhanced. The next chapter will set out how to derive your sales methodology (way of selling) from your sales process, so it is worth reading the 'into action' section now before proceeding.

Into action

If you don't have a sales process...
Thinking about the type of sales that you are making (transactional or consultative), try to build a first draft sales process using the methodology set out in Chapter 3. The generic B2B sales process phases can serve as a base; now you have a clearer idea of what they look like:

Prospecting
Discovering
Engaging
Proposing
Closing
Securing
Nurturing

In your sales process, note down the key activities that you've just read about that need to take place in each phase, taking care to adapt them to your sector.

If you already have a sales process,
Cross-check what you have with the B2B selling attitudes presented in Chapter 4.

- What are you doing well that needs to be kept?
- What are you missing that should be added in?
- What are you doing that could be improved?

Expert view: Alastair McIvor – Specialist B2B sales trainer

Among all B2B sales trainers, UK-based Alastair McIvor can lay claim to being one of the very best. In a distinguished career lasting 25 years, Alastair has trained sales forces in a staggering variety of sectors and companies.

As well as working with global brands such as PWC, Johnson & Johnson, Bosch, and Google, he has worked with many SMEs and start-ups.

I caught up with him between training projects to get his view on B2B selling in SMEs and start-ups.

Alastair, you have had a huge amount of experience in training B2B salesforces of all sizes. In your opinion, what are key skills that B2B salesforces need to master?

There are quite a range of skills I think, which makes it such an exciting role. Preparation and research before a sales call are essential, as well as having the discipline to ask great questions and listen actively to the answers during sales meetings.

Many salespeople have to work on being comfortable with silence, leaving room for customers to finish. Then there are various functional skills, such as objection handling, proposal writing and negotiation.

I believe patience, resilience and the ability to stay positive are essential life attitudes for sales. For example, if you make a first contact and a potential customer does not come back to you straight away, harassing them continuously hardly ever works.

Similarly, self-belief, inner confidence and being comfortable in your own skin really help.

B2B selling is a busy job, and so time management is a key skill! If you can't manage your time in B2B, it's difficult to be truly successful.

A common issue that start-up founders face is a kind of anathema to being too 'salesy', that is they don't like the idea of selling to others, as they may see it as 'sleezy' or manipulative. What is your advice for founders who don't want to be seen as 'salesy'?

In my training career, I have worked with a significant number of individuals who might be considered 'oddballs' and do not fit the sales mould. They might be creatives who studied art or music. They often have no preconceptions of what sales is.

For example, they might just do something intuitive, like call the CEO of a potential customer without fear, because they don't have the 'sales experience' to limit them.

These individuals are often intelligent, quick-witted and confident. They are very trainable, and once they have something in their brain, they go out and do it. I have seen people like this go from zero sales experience to sales directors quite quickly.

The point is, we don't need to be 'salesy' to be successful. One individual I worked with loved the large corporate sale. He loved connecting and networking with senior managers at potential customers and became very effective at landing large deals.

Also, some people have an allergy to the word sales. This is often the case in pharma and healthcare settings, where clinicians are sometimes recruited into commercial roles. If we reframe sales as 'helping to buy', this changes everything for them because they are used to helping others.

Many SMEs and start-ups won't have access to professional sales training because of budgets or lack of resources. What is your advice to those types of companies to improve their selling skills?

I recently read a book called 'Switch' by Chip and Dan Heath, which has the key message to focus on your strengths and not worry about what you don't have. This is a great message for small businesses. For example, some members of the team might have strength in terms of cold calling, while others are better at building proposals. Playing to your strengths is a good start.

Also, practice different sales scenarios in training and get great at giving each other feedback. Learning together creates energy. Likewise, SMEs can organise a telephone day with a simple competition and prizes. By having fun and taking risks together, a lot of leads can be generated!

Finally, what do you think can be selling superpowers for SMEs and start-ups?

The passion, energy and drive of the founder(s) can really inspire people to follow. Customers and staff buy-in to 'start-up stories'. Also, start-ups that create a culture of working hard and playing hard have fun together and create a perfect storm for success. The team gets to know each other really well and ends up supporting each other when times are tough.

Often, the lack of bureaucracy can foster open-mindedness, thinking without limits and positivity. These attitudes nearly always translate into good outcomes for customers. An agile organisation has more chances to adapt to customer needs.

Notes

1 SPIN is a registered trademark of Huthwaite Inc
2 N. Rackham *Spin selling* McGraw Hill 1988
3 https://www.huthwaiteinternational.com/blog/complete-guide-to-spin-selling
4 M. Dixon & B. Adamson *The challenger sale* Penguin 2012
5 https://www.amazon.co.uk/Challenger-Sale-Control-Customer-Conversation-ebook/dp/B009AG6YLY
6 R. Ward *High performance sales strategies* Pearson 2014
7 J. McMahon *The qualified sales leader* John McMahon 2021
8 The author's consulting firm www.selllinginteractions.com has designed and implemented custom B2B sales methodologies for over 50 clients. The firm also maintains an extensive database of sales research, taking into account other proprietary B2B sales methodologies
9 For a detailed analysis of typical B2B sales cycle times, see J. Atherton *B2B social selling strategy* p30 Kogan page 2023
10 A. Wood Brooks & L. John "The surprising power of questions" *Harvard Business Review* May 2018
11 W. R. Whitten & S. Roy *Precision listening* The international journal of sales transformation Q4 2016
12 Mentioned in A. Wood Brooks & L. John p6
13 Ibid
14 A. Arndt et al "The impact of salesperson credibility building statements on later stages of the sales process" *Journal of Personal Selling and Sales Management* vol. 34 no. 1 (March 2014), 28–29.
15 R. Ward p102 Pearson 2014
16 Ibid., p134
17 B. Hochstein et al "Proactive value creation via structural ambidexterity: Customer success management and the modularisation of front-line roles" *Journal of Service Research* vol. 24, no. 4 (2021), 16–17
18 S. Friend & J. Johnston "Familiarity breeds contempt: perceived sales and service complacency in B2B relationships" *Journal of Personal Selling and Sales Management* vol. 37, no. 1(2017), 47, 55–56.
19 N. Arbel *Data-driven sales* p67 Clearbit 2018
20 https://en.wikipedia.org/wiki/Paul_Watzlawick
21 D. Kahneman *Thinking, fast and slow* Pearson 2011
22 E. Meyer *The culture map* p168 Public Affairs 2014
23 https://www.bbc.co.uk/programmes/m001bdkx is an example of how salespeople are exploited
24 S. Dudley & T. Bryant *Relentless* Behavioural Science Research Press 2020
25 H. Moon & B. Choi "How an organisation's ethical climate contributes to customer satisfaction and financial performance" *European Journal of Innovation Management* vol. 17, no. 1 (2014), 85–106.

26 S. Pryor et al "Salesperson listening in the extended sales relationship" *Journal of Personal Selling and Sales Management* vol. 33, no. 2 (Spring 2013), 193–195
27 N. Rackham *SPIN selling*" p118 McGraw Hill 1988
28 Ibid., p44
29 K. Schmidt et al "Making the consensus sale" *Harvard Business Review* Mar 2015
30 J. McMahon J. McMahon 2021
31 Ibid., p265

Chapter 5

Your unique sales methodology

What are the specific routines, attitudes and processes that define good selling in your context?

What is a sales methodology?

Your *sales methodology* could also be known as *your way of selling*. It's the collection of routines, attitudes, skills and knowledge that brings your sales process to life. It's the set of actions and activities that maximises your chances of success in selling. Mark Roberg calls it the "best practices blueprint".[1] Because every product/service/market combination has its own idiosyncrasies, your sales methodology tries to codify these so that they can be trained, coached and lived every day.

Imagine you have a new starter in sales. Your methodology is what you will train them so that they can be successful as quickly as possible. Even though they may have experience in sales already, your methodology explains the unique aspects of *your* sale that, if followed, will help them adapt quickly. It's also known as your *sales playbook*.

Using the analogy of car maintenance, your *sales process* is the jobs to be done at each mileage, while your *sales methodology* is the detailed 'how to' guide for carrying out each task on the schedule. For example, we might have a task such as *map the decision-making unit* in the discovering phase of a sales process. It serves as a checklist reminder to do the task but does not explain how. Sales methodology goes a level deeper to set out:

- How to do the task?
- Which routines to follow?
- The attitudes and behaviours that support success.
- The skills and knowledge required.

Why do we need a sales methodology?

Without a sales methodology, it's very hard to bring your sales process to life. A sales process is too 'high level'. Too much is left open to interpretation. Quoting Mark Roberg again, "I needed to expose my salespeople to these critical learnings, but also provide them with the flexibility to apply their superpowers".[2] By making your *best way of selling* visible, it is then possible to:

- Train it.
- Coach it in use.
- Recruit individuals that are good at this type of selling/
- Use it as a measure in your performance management process.

DOI: 10.4324/9781003449614-5

- Optimise it over time.
- Automate and augment aspects of it.

A key driver of profitability in any sales organisation is *time to competence*, or in other words, how quickly you can bring in new starters and have them be productive. Your sales methodology is the accelerant to achieve this.

How do we build a sales methodology?

Your sales methodology is derived from your sales process. Recall that we used quite a rigorous process to build it (Chapter 3), so we can reasonably expect that it is a good base to define what good selling looks like.

As with your sales process, it makes sense to have a working group build the methodology, as you will stand a better chance of capturing best practices. The B2B selling principles in Chapter 4 can also serve as a guide to help you.

Firstly, let's deal with some definitions of the building blocks of a typical sales methodology. You may end up using some or all of the components in Table 5.1 at each stage of your sales process.

With these definitions in mind, we can go into detail about how to establish the essential ones for your organisation. There are at least four ways to do this:

1 Derive them from your sales process.
2 Review your existing sales best practices.
3 Look at firms selling similar products to your own.
4 Build on proprietary sales methodologies.

Table 5.1 Potential components of sales methodology

Component	Definition	Example
Routine	An activity or set of activities that increases our chances of success in sales	Preparing questions to ask based on a review of a customer's website
Attitude	A vital attitude that we need to make the sales methodology work	Being genuinely interested when listening to a customer
Skill	A needed ability to enact the sales process	Demonstrating software interactively in front of a customer
Behaviour	A way of acting that positively influences our chances of success	Acknowledging objections without "yes, but..."
Sales tech	Use of technology as part of selling	Completing CRM after a discovery meeting
Checklist	An essential list of checks/tasks to be done to ensure high-quality selling	Completing a full customer site survey before preparing a proposal
Hand-off	Communication with another individual or team to ensure a fluid customer experience/sales process continuation	Joint handover meeting with your technical support team after the deal is closed
Document	Preparation of a key document to record essential information	Preparation of a customised proposal for a customer

Using your sales process to design your sales methodology

This should be your first port of call. For each phase, we can work 'top down', that is, derive logical components that are needed to support the phase. By way of example, recall the school sales process in Chapter 3 (Table 3.3). In the *meet* phase, there is a routine called "dig the pain". This is actually a combination of skill, attitude and routine:

Skill: The ability to ask precise, focused questions that uncover a customer's challenges.

Attitude: To go deeper, to be curious, to listen actively to the stated problems and to explore further.

Routine: (1) Work through the common areas where schools experience physical education challenges. (2) Ask open questions to explore if there is a challenge. (3) When there is a challenge, ask follow-up questions.

Using this example, we might include examples of typical questions to ask in the sales methodology:

"What challenges are you facing in delivering your physical education curriculum?"

"How are these challenges affecting you?"

"Who is responsible for solving the problem?"

"When do you want to fix it by?"

Your sales methodology spells out this kind of detail so that a salesperson can see how to execute it. There are more examples covered later in this chapter.

Using your own sales best practices

One of the stages of building your sales process outlined in Chapter 3 was to inventorise your own sales best practices. If you have anyone in your working group who is good at selling, the chances are they have already figured out some excellent best practices.

This is the equivalent of asking workers on a production line how best to do their job. Because they are doing it every day, you can be sure they have valuable input to give.

Looking at similar businesses

Along the same lines, you can look at what other businesses similar to your own are doing. For SMEs, there is a chance you have someone in the business who has worked for a competitor or in an industry similar to your own. We can always learn from our competitors. Also, searching through your LinkedIn network might reveal someone who can give you some useful insights from working in a related industry.

Building on proprietary sales methodologies

A quick search of any bookstore soon throws up a long list of *how to sell* books. Within these books, you will find some useful building blocks to help you construct a sales methodology, provided that you retain a critical mind, and adapt their recommendations to your own context. Often, they have valuable practitioner knowledge, although sometimes this is subject to either personal or sector bias. Fortunately, there is a growing body of academic research that offers some critique of these texts. The NIU Journal of Selling, for example, compares and critiques sales approaches by Silent Edge and the CEB (Corporate Executive

Board),[3] while the Journal of Personal Selling and Sales Management extensively reviews and critiques the Challenger Sale (Table 5.2).[4]

With insights from these sources, you should be able to form a picture of your 'way of selling'. Building a sales methodology does take time, and if several people are involved, this will extend the timeline, but it does mean you will have an internal group of champions for it.

How should a sales methodology be presented and used?

The core purpose of a sales methodology is to convert strategy into action. We must therefore pay careful attention to how we present and deploy it so that it does not become *shelfware*. Salespeople's home offices are filled with large folders of sales training materials that will never be read. We have to strike a balance between comprehensiveness and brevity. Taking a learning and development perspective is very important here, and if you are lucky enough to have a specialist in this area, then it makes sense to get them involved.

The CIPD (Chartered Institute of Personnel and Development) has an excellent guide to designing learning materials and engaging learners, which can help you.[5] Some ideas for how to deploy your sales methodology include:

- As part of a phased training programme over several weeks.
- Using small 'memo cards' that cover each building block of the methodology.
- Short videos.
- PDF playbooks.
- In your LMS or content management system.

Table 5.2 Some of the more popular sales methodology books and the potential value they can offer

Book	Valuable components for sales methodology
"SPIN selling" Neil Rackham[6]	Questioning methods to demonstrate value
	Keeping control of sales processes
"The Challenger Sale"[7]	Bringing valuable insights to customers
Matthew Dixon and Brent Adamson	Out manoeuvring competitors
"Fanatical prospecting"	Finding new customers
Jeb Blount[8]	Using multiple media to contact prospects
"Social Selling"	Working with social media in sales
Tim Hughes and Matt Reynolds[9]	
"High performance sales strategies"	Managing sales meetings
Russell Ward[10]	
"The qualified sales leader"	Selling high-value complex solutions
John McMahon[11]	Qualification methods
	Managing decision-making units
"The smart sales method"	Finding a good fit between customers' needs and your
Joe Morone, Karen Benjamin	solution
and Marty Smith[12]	
"Whiteboard selling"	Presenting a business case
Corey Sommers and David Jenkins[13]	Interactive sales meetings
"The new strategic selling"	Navigating decision-making units
Robert Millar and Stephen Heiman[14]	Power and politics

- At a point of need, for example, in a workflow management system.
- Enabled by AI to select useful content at the appropriate moment.

Whichever medium you use to capture your sales methodology, it should meet the following criteria:

- Salespeople can refer to it easily in their everyday work.
- It can be used by coaches on the job to explain and train a key point.
- It is motivating and insightful.
- It fits very well with your type of sale.
- It is generally agreed to be useful in helping everyone to sell.
- You can update it without excessive cost and hassle.

Examples of formats for your sales methodology

Your sales methodology should make your sales best practices clear so salespeople can execute them consistently, to increase their chances of success. Let's now look at some examples of how SMEs and start-ups have presented their own sales best practices.

Example 1: A tool manufacturer wanted to train their sales team to be more discerning concerning which retail customers to invest most time with. They developed a pocket-sized memo card that salespeople could use on store visits to remind them of key checks to make. This enabled them to make more informed decisions about where opportunities lay. The key text is shown in Figure 5.1.

Example 2: A tech firm supplying specialist software to car dealerships identified the need to align customer decision-makers and influencers to proceed in their sales process. This phase was called 'align', and they developed an aide-memoire for salespeople as shown in Figure 5.2.

THE STORE WALK

*Learning is not compulsory
...nor is survival*

W.Edwards Deming

A store walk enables us to see
the reality on the ground.

What are we looking for?

o What other woodworking brands are stocked?
o What tools and accessories do they sell?
o What associated products do they sell?
o What kind of tradespeople are in the store?
o How knowledgeable are the counter staff?
o What kind of image does the store present?
o How easy is the store to access / parking?
o How up to date are promotions / stock?
o How good is stock availability?

Based on our store walk:

o How attractive is this retailer to us?
o How much time should we invest?
o What is best way to position us for growth?
o What is the first step?

Figure 5.1 An example of sales methodology for tool retail

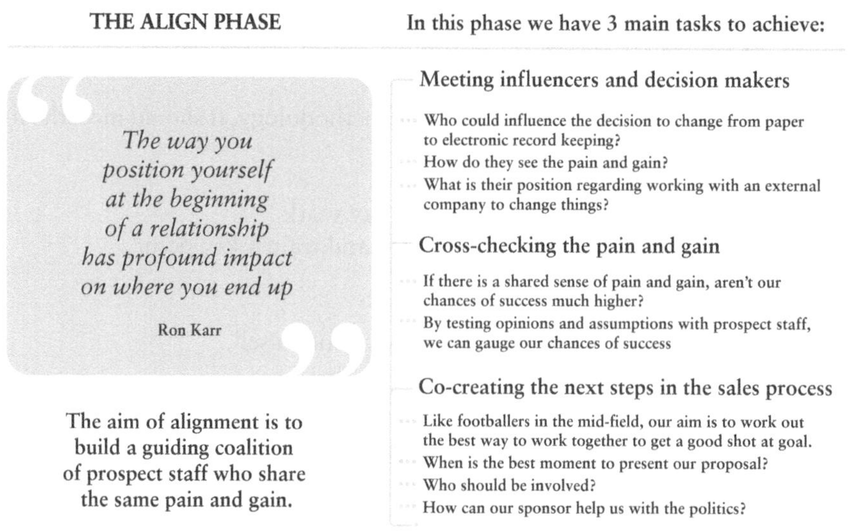

THE ALIGN PHASE

In this phase we have 3 main tasks to achieve:

> *The way you position yourself at the beginning of a relationship has profound impact on where you end up*
>
> Ron Karr

The aim of alignment is to build a guiding coalition of prospect staff who share the same pain and gain.

Meeting influencers and decision makers

Who could influence the decision to change from paper to electronic record keeping?

How do they see the pain and gain?

What is their position regarding working with an external company to change things?

Cross-checking the pain and gain

If there is a shared sense of pain and gain, aren't our chances of success much higher?

By testing opinions and assumptions with prospect staff, we can gauge our chances of success

Co-creating the next steps in the sales process

Like footballers in the mid-field, our aim is to work out the best way to work together to get a good shot at goal.

When is the best moment to present our proposal?

Who should be involved?

How can our sponsor help us with the politics?

Figure 5.2 An example of sales methodology in car dealership software

What are typical building blocks to consider?

Primarily, these are derived from your sales process, as mentioned. Here is a list of potential areas to include in your sales methodology:

- How to prospect (via telephone, LinkedIn, email or other media)
- Example templates for prospecting
- Key messages to attract new customers per sector
- Preparing a reason to call
- Appointment setting
- Questions to ask
- Opening a customer meeting
- Quick pitch for each product/service
- Customer success stories/testimonials
- Typical commitment objectives
- Objections and how to manage them
- Competitive information and how to sell against them
- Checklist for needs analysis
- Influence principles in decision-making units
- Proposal template and guidelines for completion
- Presentation
- Negotiation guidelines
- Ordering process
- Handover guidelines to other internal teams
- Account/customer development plans
- Cross-selling questions
- Up-selling approaches
- Asking for referrals
- Business review meetings

If you are in the very early stages of a start-up or don't have the resources to create this level of content, a 'quick and dirty' version is simply to build a checklist of the main points to remember for the key meetings in your sales process, for example: *First meeting, Proposal meeting, Solution implementation meeting* and *Business Review meeting*.

How can your sales methodology be embedded?

Having done the hard work to codify your way of selling, it still needs to be lived by the sales team every day. This can be done by:

- *As part of onboarding*: Consider sending your methodology in advance of new hires joining your organisation. They are normally excited and motivated to start a new job, and this gives them something to get started on.
- *At induction*: It is essential that new hires realise that your sales methodology is important, and you expect it to be used.
- *In formal training*: Every salesperson on your team should be trained in your sales methodology. Even the experienced ones need to know it.
- *During coaching conversations*: "*What gets inspected gets respected*". If you don't refer to the sales methodology after sales call wash-up meetings, why should anyone think it is important?

Sales training will be covered in Chapter 13 in more detail. Your sales methodology will be a guiding light for this critical activity.

Into action

You will need your unique sales process to get started, so if you don't have this written down, it's best to read Chapters 3 and 4 and finalise it.

1 Bring together a group of four to six sales and marketing specialists, including some of your top salespeople.
2 Work through your sales process from left to right, and for each phase in the process, derive any of the following items that support it:

Routines
Attitudes
Behaviours
Sales technology interactions
Checklists
Hand-offs
Documents

3 Build a master list of the essential components that need to be trained/adhered to make your sales process work. Try to pare this list down to a workable level.

4 For each item on the list, agree on who in the team will work on the detailed content.
5 Set timescales and circulate the developing content among the project team to iterate, improve and ultimately sign it off.
6 When the methodology is complete, apply learning and development best practices to ensure everyone knows about and uses it.

Expert view: Business impact training

Business Impact Training is one of the very best training and consulting businesses in the Netherlands. Founded by a group of highly experienced behavioural change specialists, it helps companies in Europe increase their performance through a variety of training interventions. It has grown spectacularly over the last decade and is recognised for having a very well-thought-out and effective sales methodology.

Jan Bouw, one of the founding partners explains how and why the company uses its sales methodology.

Firstly Jan, what type of customers does Business Impact Training mainly work with?

In a small country like the Netherlands, we tend to focus on small organisations with between 50 and 600 employees. We also work with some mid-sized, international companies with around 500 to 2,000 employees.

We love to work with this size of customer because we typically have direct contact with the board of directors. Companies like this often don't have a supervisory board to ask searching questions about challenges and culture, so we can be a critical counterpart for them. We can be a trusted advisor to the board.

Your organisation is famous for setting a high standard when it comes to sales. You are known for being disciplined and consistent in the way you sell. Why do you think a consistent sales methodology is so important?

Firstly, it gives clients confidence that we are a professional organisation. In our market, we are often the most expensive potential training partner, and so to help customers see why we are 'worth it', we offer them a free training session. This is a key part of our sales methodology, as the 'proof is in the pudding'. During such sessions, we dare to take more risks than competitors by challenging and provoking participants while having fun, so that in just two or three minutes, they are in a unique learning situation. Our competitors may have better slides than us, but our sales methodology lets customers experience how we actually train. Around 85% of customers who participate in a taster session like this go on to buy from us.

Secondly, having an effective sales methodology increases self-confidence in our team because they see it working in action, and this makes them feel good. Self-confidence is vital when we sell at board level.

Thirdly, new sales representatives notice that we have a consistent way of selling when we do joint calls. We always take new staff on sales calls with us. Initially, they just watch, then they progressively take over some sections until they are ready to lead the whole sales call. This approach builds confidence in our new team members, who can go on to be great salespeople themselves.

Once, we recruited a trainer who really did not want to sell. We took her to client meetings to introduce herself as the trainer, and when she saw our sales approach, she was curious and went on to lead client meetings on her own by choice!

A good sales methodology gives routines, and routines give confidence in a selling situation.

What sales routines do you believe are important for your team?

Asking for introductions to new potential clients is very important. We are very proactive in doing this. We use LinkedIn to identify who knows who, and we ask for an introduction as soon as we get our first positive evaluation. Sometimes, of course, clients recommend us to others without being asked, and we very much appreciate that.

Another thing that is important is to define who is good at what. For example, we might have two people make a pitch to a client, a different two to negotiate a contract and maybe others to work on writing a tender. We define roles and use the strengths of people to increase our chances of winning projects. Our sales methodology helps us clarify who should do what according to their strengths. Sometimes this means saying no to team members when they want to get involved in an area which is not a strength for them. This is not without challenges, but overall, they are happy when we win a deal.

Every month we have a sales meeting, and a key routine is for team members to bring a sales situation they faced during the month (good or bad), which we practice with a role-play. The owner of the case takes on the role of the customer, and other team members try different approaches to learn from practical situations. Our sales methodology was built from these sessions so that it reflects real life.

Also, we believe in the power of contacting people regularly. In my earlier days of selling, I was consistently in the top three sellers, and we all had one thing in common: huge telephone bills! They signal effort, hard work and perseverance. And it's vitally important to call customers not just for sales but to be genuinely interested in them. As an example, during the COVID-19 pandemic, I had a number of exchanges with customers that were seriously ill, which is only possible when you have the depth of relationship created by frequent interaction outside of sales meetings.

A good CRM system is very important. We use TeamLeader, a Belgium technology. It is very simple to use, and we have customised it to reflect our sales process, which reinforces our sales methodology.

Opportunities have to be properly qualified at each stage so that a probability of success can be calculated, which improves forecasts. The team can see their results, which motivates them. It is solid and simple, and I think that is very important, as some CRM systems can be very complicated.

Finally, it's important to positively challenge each other. If a deal is sitting in a pipeline forecast for months, we need to challenge each other to remove it. We do this, but we should do it more.

Notes

1 M.Roberg "The sales acceleration formula" p50 Wiley 2015
2 Ibid
3 R. Plank "Comparing the two newest models of sales performance" *NIU Journal of Selling* vol. 14, no. 1, 55–60.
4 A. Rapp et al "Salespeople as knowledge brokers: A review and critique of the challenger sales model" *Journal of Personal Selling and Sales Management* vol. 34, no. 4, 248.
5 K. Beevers et al *Learning and development practice in the workplace* 4th ed Kogan Page 2020
6 N. Rackham *Spin selling* McGraw Hill 1988
7 M.Dixon & B. Adamson *The challenger sale* Portfolio Penguin 2012
8 J. Blount *Fanatical prospecting* Wiley 2015
9 T. Hughes & M. Reynolds *Social selling* Kogan page 2016
10 R. Ward *High performance sales strategies* Pearson Educational Limited 2014
11 J. McMahon *The qualified sales leader* John McMahon 2021
12 J. Morone et al *The smart sales method 2016* Worldleaders inc. 2016
13 C. Sommers & D. Jenkins *Whiteboard selling* Wiley 2013
14 R. Miller & S. Heiman *The new strategic selling* Kogan Page 3rd ed 2011

Chapter 6

Lead generation

What methods could you use to generate new opportunities?

Why is lead generation important?

Customers can go out of business. They can buy less from you. Competitors sometimes take customers away from you. Because of all these reasons, if you don't search out new potential customers, sales will likely decline. Depending on your growth model, finding new customers can be absolutely central to your sales strategy.

Business scaling gurus Aaron Ross and Jason Lemkin believe that "predictable lead generation is *the* lever to hypergrowth" and that "lead generation absolves many sin".[1] If there is a plentiful supply of good fuel to your sales engine, this can only help. If you can make it work, you have gained control of a key growth lever.

Definitions

You've almost certainly come across many lead generation terms: inbound, outbound, above the funnel, in the funnel, marketing-qualified leads (MQLs) and sales-qualified leads (SQLs). Let's define these terms upfront.

Inbound/outbound Mark Roberg of HubSpot fame describes the difference between inbound and outbound marketing very well, and this is summarised in Table 6.1.

Most organisations will use a mix of both methods, according to their context and ambitions.

MQLs: In MQLs, it appears a potential customer is interested in buying/finding out more about your product/service.

SQLs: In SQLs, a salesperson contacts the potential customer and determines that there is an opportunity to be pursued.

Above the funnel: Leads are those that your sales team has not contacted/had contact with yet.

In the funnel: Leads are those that you are in a conversation. They are in a stage of your sales process.

Who is responsible for lead generation?

The definition of these terms is important because it clarifies who is responsible for lead generation activity. Sales and marketing often end up in conflict if lead generation is not joined up. For example, the marketing team might say, "The sales team never follow up the leads we generate properly", while the sales team might say, "The leads we get from marketing are rubbish!".

DOI: 10.4324/9781003449614-6

Table 6.1 Inbound vs. outbound selling

	Method	*Example*
Outbound selling	Contact potential customers with a good fit, and then find out if they have pain.	Buy a contact list of CEOs and contact them.
Inbound selling	Let potential customers with pain find you, then qualify the best opportunities.	Use SEO and well-designed landing pages to generate marketing lists that you follow up with.

Table 6.2 Approaches used for inbound and outbound marketing

Inbound marketing	*Outbound marketing*
Website/landing pages	Referrals
Content (blogs, whitepapers, LinkedIn posts, Videos, Facebook, Instagram, TikTok and podcasts)	Telephone and voicemail
	In-person prospecting
Search engine optimisation (SEO)	Email campaigns/newsletters
Webinars and virtual events	Social media
Product trials	Text/WhatsApp
Targeted adverts	Trade shows
Influencer strategies	Networks/networking events
Relationship marketing	Product-in-use data mining strategies
Sales agents	Marketing lists
	Letter/physical mail

The relationship between sales and marketing really comes under the spotlight when it comes to lead generation. In some organisations, conflict between the two functions is already a problem.[2] Recall that in Chapter 3, part of sales process design involved paying attention to how leads get transferred from marketing to sales. While this may be irrelevant for solopreneurs, if several people are involved, it's important to make sure roles and responsibilities are clearly defined for each stage of lead generation so that there is no lack of accountability or poor handovers.

High-quality discussions in your commercial team about the process of lead generation can be a positive driver for change because you can align on the overall goals and build team spirit to make it work. Technology can enable this, as we shall see in Chapter 12.

What activities can support lead generation?

Table 6.2 shows the typical activities you can use to generate leads, categorised by whether they are inbound or outbound methods.

The good news is that there are many choices! The challenge is figuring out what works in your context and getting the mix right. This takes continual experimentation. Repeated, determined iterative work will get you to a good place.

Fortunately, there is a lot of research and practice to guide you. There is also good research on the best *sequences* of methods to use, which will also be covered in this chapter.

Let's now consider each method in turn and what it can bring to an SME/start-up. Having covered the individual methods, we will then look at how to decide on the mix, what targets to set, and how to measure/manage progress.

Website

While your website may not *need* to generate leads for you, it certainly should not put people off contacting you. In some ways, it is 'table stakes' for doing business. If it's not high-quality and professional, it's unlikely potential customers will go as far as contacting you to discuss their situation.

In his book *Innovative B2B Marketing*, Simon Hall explains that, regarding websites, "There are several characteristics which could be managed to support brand consistency. Creative look and feel should be consistent.... websites and micro-sites should be consistent in look and feel".[3]

Understanding your audience is important here. If you are selling life coaching services, the look and feel will be very different than if you are selling IT services to corporates. The selection of images and colours is very important, and for an excellent in-depth tour of the key principles of website influence, I recommend *Webs of Influence* by Nathalie Nahai.[4]

In summary, the author recommends that when you design your website, it should take care of the following aspects:

- Have a clear purpose that is reflected in its design values.
- Build trust through a good user experience and an appropriate tone of writing.
- Meets your customer's needs by speaking to their experience and context.
- Clear messaging so customers can understand what you do.
- Includes the information customers need.
- Up-to-date content.
- Clear call to action.

As mentioned, your colour palette is important, as it affects our perception. For example, fast food chains often use red and yellow to increase arousal, while financial institutions often use blue to promote calm and stability.[5]

A good website that has been properly set up with well-chosen content is an essential component of lead generation and marketing automation. For example, *landing pages* are typically used in *inbound marketing*. They are essential for marketing automation software (Chapter 12). Digital marketing experts Dave Chaffey and Fiona Ellis-Chadwick believe the number one aim of a landing page is to "Generate response – online lead, sale and offline callback",[6] and so it is important that the *call to action* is very prominent.

If you wanted to attract potential customers to a webinar, for example, you might set up a landing page that enables people to register easily by giving their email and confirming their attendance. You can direct all lead sources to this landing page, perhaps from social media, an email campaign or a QR code.

Content creation

A crucial component of inbound marketing is high-quality content. Every day we come across content on the internet that is interesting to our work and personal lives. If the content is engaging, informative and relevant to us, then we are likely to read on and form a favourable impression of the source.

Content can, of course, span many media types: website, blogs, LinkedIn, YouTube, Instagram, TikTok, Facebook, email campaigns and podcasts. All have the potential to build your brand and presence and incite potential customers to contact you. Paying attention to good content can have several benefits,[7] including improving SEO (as good content gets shared), increasing inbound traffic and helping customers work through their decision-making process (to hopefully buy from you).

So how can we create good content? Many marketing organisations use *personas* to help understand their audiences better. A persona is a written description of your typical customer, designed to help you envisage what they need, and includes things like:

- Their job title
- Areas of responsibility
- Typical challenges
- Education
- Interests

While we must be careful that we don't overgeneralise, personas can be helpful to have in mind when you are creating content.

Marcus Sheridan gives us a pragmatic way to do this in his book *They ask, you listen*.[8] By soliciting questions from potential customers about what they want to know, content can be created that directly answers their needs.

The choice of content you use will depend a lot on your audience and your product. For example, Industrial Cleaning Equipment (featured in Chapter 11) sells highly intelligent cleaning robots, and the company shares short videos of them cleaning iconic locations in the UK, which not only shows how effective they are but also that they are trusted by high-profile organisations.

Search engine optimisation (SEO)

Since the key aim of inbound marketing is to attract potential buyers to you, it's essential that they find you when they search for key terms. SEO is an ever-changing technical discipline, and many start-ups and SMEs will need external support to get it right. Fortunately, it is a well-served market, and by asking around for personal recommendations, you should be able to find a good professional resource.

It is important to be clear-headed about the search terms potential customers might use for your product/service. Ideally, you want to find those where you do not have many competitors. This makes your content more effective because you know buyers will be searching for it and won't find too many of your competitors.

Good SEO and content go hand in hand, then. If you research your key personas, find out what they are looking for and create compelling content that answers their concerns, then you will generate enquiries.

Webinars and virtual events

Inbound marketing relies on selecting customers who have a need and are working through the decision-making process. If your content has been successful in piquing their attention, webinars and virtual events can be great 'next steps' to engage them further.

For customers to buy from you, they must trust you. The *mere exposure effect* tells us that repeated views of 'subliminally presented stimuli' do increase our positive appreciation of a brand or product,[9] so if customers have found your content in several areas, then this can encourage them to take the next step.

Joining a virtual event enables them to go a step further. You can begin a conversation with them because webinars can be made interactive. A well-executed webinar on a very relevant topic will help to increase trust in you as a potential supplier.

It will also provide a bridge to *outbound selling* because you will have an email list of potential customers who have given you permission to contact them (assuming you followed the correct data protection legislation on your landing page).

What makes for a good virtual event, then? Using workshop/training design principles will serve you well here:

- Set clear outcome objectives before building content (what should people do/feel after the session?)
- Use a mix of media/methods to engage (polls, votes and ask questions to individual members of the audience, videos, challenges, breakouts, competitions).
- Bring new insights to the audience that they will talk about afterwards (word-of-mouth marketing).
- Design a logical next step/call to action (to bring leads into your pipeline).

If attendees feel the time they invested was well spent, rather than listening to a poorly executed sales pitch, they are more likely to form a favourable impression of you as a potential supplier.

Targeted adverts

You can substantially increase your reach by using targeted ads in your browser and on social media. This is a specialist area for digital marketers, and you might need external support if you don't have the necessary expertise in your team. Your targeted ads should drive traffic to your landing pages.

Influencer strategies

In any sphere, there will be individuals who are super-connected, respected and listened to. According to Mailchimp, the email marketing specialists, "influencer marketing is a form of marketing that enables businesses to collaborate with individuals who have a following".[10]

They cite the following advantages of using this approach:

- Helps establish credibility and trust
- Cost effective
- Attracts quality leads

Normally, influencer marketing works by agreeing to a commission/percentage of sales for the influencer if they recommend your product/solution. It's important to check that your potential customers do indeed follow the influencer to establish if they can reach your target audience.

Relationship marketing

In some industries, it's possible to identify other players that serve the same market as you but are not competitors. An example would be if you provide accounting services and decide to form a partnership with a legal firm. You can agree to mutually recommend each other's services.

Where reciprocal recommendation is not appropriate, you can still agree to a commission, much like with influencer marketing.

A clear, well-organised process can deliver a steady stream of leads, without too much effort or investment. Chapter 17 goes into more detail about working with partners to optimise this type of relationship.

Sales agents

You might be able to identify *sales agents* that have a good network with your customer base and who would be willing to introduce you to them for a fee. These individuals might be selling another product/service primarily, but they have autonomy to decide what to sell and are good at it.

You can make an agreement about which parts of your sales process they should get involved in. For example, you might pay them a nominal fee for an introduction that results in a first meeting and/or a more substantial fee if the sale goes ahead.

Referrals

Did you have such good service from an organisation that you found yourself spontaneously recommending them to your network? You are now an unpaid advocate for them! They are getting free leads because of you! Not only is this free, but it also has another massive benefit: We tend to trust the recommendations from our network more than we trust messages from potential suppliers.

We should always deliver excellent service so that we build a network of *active references*. Applying the principle that "If we set our standards higher than our clients, then they will never be disappointed" will help!

Rather than waiting for customers to recommend you spontaneously, you can proactively ask them to do so. As soon as you are sure that your customer is happy, ask them for referrals.

You can do this by proactively finding out who is in their network (LinkedIn) or by simply asking them:

> "Is there anyone in your network who might benefit from our product/service? Would be willing to introduce us to them?"

This method is not only free but extremely effective, as you are being introduced to a prospect in the best possible way.

If they are not happy to recommend you, then it is best to know that and deal with the customer satisfaction issue in front of you promptly!

Telephone and voicemail

Nothing divides B2B selling so much as the use of the telephone in outbound selling. You have very likely read the phrase "cold calling is dead" somewhere on the internet. Social media specialist Julie Atherton notes that "Pure cold calling has been on the wane for many years, with 90% of decision makers saying they never respond to cold calls".[11] Jeb Blount, the poster child for the use of the telephone, is less reserved in his comments, saying that the phrase 'cold calling is dead', is normally said by "an inbound marketing, sales 2.0, social-selling-obsessed nitwit".[12]

Meanwhile, a plethora of sales directors are ignoring the debate and blending telephone-based approaches with other media (LinkedIn, texts and WhatsApp) to create *sequences* to reach prospects.

The telephone still has relevance today, for sure. In their fascinating book, *Relentless*, Suzanne Dudley and Trelitha Bryant ran a survey of 4700 sales professionals and found that 31% of them indicated that phone calls are the best method, second only to in-person interactions.[13] Similarly, Trish Bertuzzi, a veteran of setting up successful SDR teams, has done a detailed analysis of what works and does not work. She has discovered that voicemail and email are equally effective and twice as effective as other media.[14]

To understand how best to use the telephone, it is helpful to understand *sequences* and *cadences* for lead generation. Leaders like Bertuzzi have discovered that success rates increase when a variety of media are used to reach potential customers over a defined period. "It's clear that the more depth and rhythm of outreach, the better the sales results".[15]

By analysing the activities of thousands of reps over a long period of time, firms have established optimal sequences of contacts for their services. For example, Bertuzzi discovered that nine touches in 15 days work for her clients.

When potential customers receive approaches through multiple media and in a relatively concentrated period, they receive a clear message:

- This company is serious about getting in contact with me – they must see me as a good candidate for what they are selling (as opposed to the 'one and done' callers).
- Because they are present on LinkedIn, email and have a telephone, it's more likely they are legitimate, not scammers.

The exact sequence and cadence you use may not be so important for SMEs and start-ups, but what is important is consistency and quality. Managing a few opportunities very well is better than emailing 100 prospects in one day and then doing nothing more to follow up.

Your telephone activity, therefore, should form part of a sequence, with the aim that when you make a call, your name is not totally new to your potential customer. Remember the *mere exposure effect*? That's how sequences work.

Here are guidelines for making telephone calls to prospects:

You can hear a smile: Positive attitude and confidence help when you make the call. We can hear a smile through the telephone. Some people are more comfortable using the telephone than others. Confidence comes through preparation for the call and also working on your positive mindset.

The book, *Relentless,* identifies *telephobia* as a specific mindset issue for some salespeople[16] and advises 'sufferers' to tune into the underlying negative self-talk that supports it. For example, you may have experienced rejection when making a call before, and it left a scar. Reframing the situation with positive self-talk, such as "It was just one person who was rude, not everyone is like that", can help.

Personalise your reason to call: If you have researched the person and organisation well (visited their website, read their blogs/news, checked LinkedIn), then you should be able to explain in 30 seconds your 'reason to call' that is 100% relevant to the person you are calling. Written preparation helps a lot here to craft the message. Here is an example:

YOU: "Hi it's X here calling from Y. I imagine I am calling you in the middle of something when would be a good moment to speak?"

THEM: "What are you calling about?"

YOU: "I work for an organisation specialising in social media services, and I noticed that you are running a campaign on Linked-in for your new product Z. The reason to call is that my organisation has deep experience accelerating the sales of new products via social channels, and I can see some potential improvement areas to help you optimise reach. Would you be open for a short meeting so I can understand your campaign objectives and share these ideas with you?"

Be ready for objections: Almost certainly, you will encounter objections when you contact someone for the first time. Make a list of the objections you might reasonably expect and be ready to manage them as discussed in Chapter 4. Typical objections to prepare for include:
"We already have a provider"
"I am too busy right now"
"I don't deal with that".

Request a clear next step: Think about the commitment objective you are looking for and refer to your sales process to figure out what you want to happen next.

Make the next action clear in the calendar: Ensure you send a calendar invite and follow-up email as soon as possible, so everyone knows what will happen next.

If telephone selling is part of your outreach mix, then *Fanatical Prospecting* by Jeb Blount is a very good practical guide[17] to get into the details of what to say and how to manage the conversation.

What to do if we reach voicemail? This can be a very effective part of an outreach sequence. It's helpful to understand what is *not* effective for voicemail: Simply calling again and again and leaving a voice message such as "H it is X from Y company, please can you call me back on 123456789" has a low impact.

Instead, each voicemail should be crafted so that it adds something new. Research done by Essi Pöyry and her colleagues showed that *complimentary messages* drive higher conversion rates than *consistent ones*.[18]

To apply this principle, you might leave a first voicemail such as:

"Hi, it's X calling from Y company. I noticed that you recently acquired a new company to build your presence in the north of the country. I can imagine that will give you some headaches concerning staff integration. We have expertise in this area that could help. I will call again on Monday next week, otherwise feel free to call me on 123456789".

Then, a week later, you could follow up with:

"Hi, its X calling as promised. I am going to send a case history I found today which I think is relevant to your integration situation. We will be discussing it on a webinar in three weeks if you'd like to attend".

Even if your prospect does not respond, each voicemail you leave can increase their knowledge of what you do and build your credibility.

Finally, any telephone strategy only works if you can get through to an influencer/decision-maker. Befriending receptionists and administrators is often a better strategy than treating them as "gatekeepers". Help them become active references for you by acknowledging the positive intention behind what they do.

In-person prospecting

'Dropping in' is alive and kicking today. For some industries, it makes total sense. Jeb Blount quotes the example of a rep selling uniform services on industrial estates. Because he is 'in the area' when he sees preset appointments, it's no trouble to do some research, then drop into a few new prospects whilst out on the road.[19]

Armed with similar research that you would do for a telephone call and with good manners, it's amazing what can be achieved with this method. I know of several reps in the heavy truck sector that use it to good effect. Imagine the impact it makes when a rep turns up in a brand-new truck right outside your premises and asks if you might be interested in finding out more!

Email

According to Simon Hall, in 2016, 83% of B2B marketers were using email as part of their mix.[20] The trend of *permission marketing*[21] has steadily grown, where customers opt in to receive your newsletters, updates and offers. If done well, potential customers value your content and are more likely to purchase from you.

If you have contact consent, then how is it best to encourage them to become a customer? There are two main approaches: *nurturing* and the *direct prospecting* approach.

Nurturing means sending automated emails containing relevant, personalised content so that when the potential customer is ready to buy, they will think of you first. *Marketing automation* software can take care of this, as we shall see in Chapter 12.

Direct prospecting means writing personalised emails to individuals to motivate them to have a conversation with us.

For the nurturing approach, marketing specialists Dave Chaffey and Fiona Ellis-Chadwick use the mnemonic CRITCAL to summarise how to make email campaigns successful:[22]

- Creative design
- Relevant to the audience
- Incentive (it answers the question, what's in it for me?)
- Targeting and timing (pay attention to when and who the email is sent to)
- Integration (is it consistent with your brand?)
- Conversation (your message should encourage a response)
- Attributes (ensure the details are correct, subject line, readability, compatibility)
- Landing page (links lead to your landing page)

For *direct prospecting*, we fully customise what we write. The principles, in some ways, are not different from making a telephone call to a potential customer: good research will serve us well.

Jenifer Dapko and Andrew Artis, writing in the *Northern Illinois Journal of selling*, offer the following advice for writing compelling direct emails[23]:

• Grab and hold attention
• Instil trust
• Communicate a call to action
• Avoid perceptions of spam
• Fine-tune your writing

They suggest that you open your email with a personalised statement that shows you have done your research and that it's not just another generic email. You should then use key ideas from your 'elevator pitch' to explain how your company can help them, followed by an appropriate sign-off. The email subject line should be written last of all as an accurate summary of the contents.

The more personalised and relevant your email is, the greater the chances of receiving a reply. Your email will normally be part of a *sequence*, as outlined earlier, so even if you don't receive a reply, it may still be helping your cause.

Social media

B2B social selling expert Julie Atherton offers several compelling statistics that suggest why social media is an invaluable part of modern lead generation[24]:

• Lead generation costs 75% less using social media compared to other channels.
• 78% of those using social selling outperform their peers.
• 84% of C-level executives consult social media before making a decision.

She goes on to say that "professional networking and relationship building have moved irreversibly online". With these points in mind, social media marketing should nearly always form part of the lead generation mix of SMEs and start-ups.

How can SMEs/start-ups decide which social media channel is best? There are two guiding principles that can help with this decision. Firstly, where are most of your customers interacting? Secondly, how much time and resource can you realistically put into your social media efforts? The most common channels used by B2B SMEs and start-ups in my experience are typically, in order of use:

1 LinkedIn
2 Facebook
3 Twitter
4 TikTok

LinkedIn is often a natural choice because, at least in the USA and Europe, it is the default professional network site, and B2B selling lends itself to professional networks. Also, LinkedIn has a paid version called Navigator, which offers excellent functionality for lead generation. It also integrates with many CRM systems, making it easier to transfer data. For example, uploading your customer list from Salesforce to Navigator is a relatively simple operation. Once your customer list is added to Navigator, it greatly increases its power to find similar businesses and opportunities within your current customer base.

Here are some guidelines to help you generate leads over time using LinkedIn. The principles are similar for other platforms.

Get your profiles in shape: Did you ever notice a potential client check out your linkedIn profile before working with you? What image would you want them to have? The importance of building a high-quality personal profile is underlined by Tim Hughes and Matt Reynolds in *Social Selling*: "When people look at your profile, they have a first impression of who you are. In the past, a first impression would have been made when you were introduced; now because of the internet, anybody can search for you and get a first impression".[25] If you click on your profile on LinkedIn, the site will give you advice on how to enhance your profile.

The first base is to ensure potential customers will see you as a *credible specialist* worth talking to.

To further enhance your profile, you can use *sentiment analysis software* to find out what key words your target audience is using (for example, Hootsuite or Talkwalker). You can then add these key words to your profile description to increase the likelihood of being found.

Julie Atherton makes the point that we should consider the *interdependent brand* when using social media, meaning the interaction between the customer, supplier and individual salesperson.[26] There should be a fit between the *personal brand* of employees and your organisation's brand, so that customers get a joined-up view.

A personal brand is, to some extent, created by how your profile demonstrates your expertise and experience in a particular knowledge area. It is also heavily driven by what you post and how you interact with others.

Measure your social selling index: LinkedIn provides a convenient tool to assess your social selling effectiveness. Using the link www.linkedin,com/sales/ssi, you should be able to locate this free-to-use tool. If you have your sales team do this, you will get an accurate view of their social selling activity. Ideally, you want to score around 60 to 70. If you are below this, then improvements will come from posting, sharing, commenting and connecting with others. LinkedIn gives clear advice on how to improve your score.

Build your community: Metcalf's law states that "the financial value or influence of a telecommunications network is proportional to the square of the number of connected users".[27] The same principle applies to social networks; if you are connected to more potential customers, more opportunities are likely to arise.

Not everyone is comfortable with building a personal network of strangers, and often you don't need to. The chances are you and your team are *not* connected to hundreds of people they already know from these groups:

- People you currently work with
- People you have worked with in the past
- All customer contacts
- College or university cohort
- Suppliers
- Partners
- Friends and family

Simply by 'filling in the gaps', you can greatly extend your network. Mark Granovetter wrote one of the most influential papers ever in sociology, called *The Strength of Weak Ties*.[28] In it, he made the point that new ideas (and leads, in the case of social selling) often come from distant/infrequent contacts in our network.

Share content Simply by making regular, intelligent posts, you and your team will be visible to potential buyers. This is free and only costs a few minutes. Some teams struggle with what to share. Tim Hughes and Matt Reynolds offer the following advice: "Don't be a corporate suit. I know it's tempting to tweet or post on LinkedIn articles your company wants you to post. But come on. If you think they are boring, so will your audience".[29] Because of the interdependent brand already mentioned, it's easy to create the impression that your social media account is just another channel controlled by company marketing.

It's vital, therefore, that you add your personal spin to any reposted content that reinforces your personal brand and furthers your organisation's sales efforts. This is often easy for start-up founders because they have a natural passion for what their company does, and this comes across in their postings.

Some core principles for posting are:

- Be consistent in building your personal brand
- Follow the 80/20 rule – 80% non-sales content/20% promotional content
- Don't confuse your audience by having opinions about lots of different topics.
- Play to strengths: If one of your team members is an expert in X, let them create the content that others can share.
- Think about content that will serve your customers well at all stages of their buying journey, for example, interesting articles that highlight gaps in the way customers go about business or selection tools to help them choose a good provider.

Within these guidelines, there are many styles of content sharing that can work (no doubt you have seen many of them). For example, James Barry and John Gironda identified four successful archetypes: edutainer, motivators, strategists, and mentors.[30]

It is wise to learn the rules of the platform to increase your engagement; for example, hashtags can help, but not if overdone (1 to 3 is a good benchmark).

Support your network: If you give to the universe, the universe gives back to you. More accurately, we can employ the influence *principle of reciprocity* here.[31] If you help your network by, for example, sharing great content, connecting them to others and helping them find a new role if they are unlucky enough to be laid off, you will create many loyal supporters and advocates. Advocates tend to refer you to potential customers and most certainly will support your own social media efforts.

A lot of this work can be done behind the scenes with LinkedIn's message service.

Directly contact potential customers: The same principles we considered for email can be used here, but with a large warning sign. We have all received very clumsy prospecting attempts, where a stranger has mailed us with a comment like "Your profile looks really interesting and I'd love to be part of your network", followed very quickly by a request for a meeting to "discover if you would be in the market for our services".

Either be very direct about the reason to contact a new potential customer or connect first and build a relationship over several months before suggesting that there might be mutual benefit in working together.

LinkedIn Navigator allows users to send 'in-mails', where you have no connection with the individual concerned, so that you can scale up this activity.

Be vigilant Every day, something interesting is likely to happen on LinkedIn. After all, it is your personal update from *your* professional network. Many of the postings you see will be from friends and colleagues. There are several things to check frequently:

- Your LinkedIn messages icon: If a lead does come in, you will want to respond to it as quickly as possible. After all, what impression would a potential customer get if they didn't hear back in a short time frame? In a 2022 blog by Leandata[32] data are presented that shows 78% of companies buy from the first company to reply to their enquiry, and that you are 7x more likely to qualify a lead if you respond within one hour!
- Your update icon: This shows you what interactions there have been with your posts, and it is a good idea to respond to anyone who has interacted with your post. This sends a clear message that you value the interaction and is more likely to result in continued support. Also, people do sometimes post comments like "I'd be interested to find out more what you do…", which is good as a lead.
- Your feed: Spending only five or ten minutes each day reviewing your feed will help you spot opportunities for relationship building and sales.

At the end of the day, LinkedIn is a free, auto-updating address book for your professional network. Even if you do nothing with LinkedIn, it is always worth connecting with everyone in your professional network so you don't lose contact with them.

Text/WhatsApp

Everyone has their own preference for using their mobile device. Being flexible in the channels through which you try to reach potential customers increases the chances that you will reach them. This is also a side benefit of using sequences: You might flush out the preferred contact method for a prospect. According to HubSpot, 95% of text messages are opened within three minutes.[33] I ran a sales training once where a participant conducted the whole end-to-end sales process on WhatsApp.

Trade shows

Many industries have trade shows that bring many customers together, potentially offering a rich source of leads and the chance to meet customers face to face. They are worth considering as lead sources, with the following provisos:

Assess their impact: If you did the trade show previously, what business did you actually secure from it? Was it worth the cash investment?

Use a lead scoring system: Not all trade show visitors are equal. Some visitors will be senior decision-makers for your dream customer. Others are students researching new technology. Just because you have a conversation does not mean you have a lead. Lead scoring will be covered later in the chapter.

Use a trade show sales process: Make sure you have a very clear, succinct and practical trade show visitor engagement approach. How will you manage the three or five minutes they are at your stand? How will you follow-up post-show? What will be the next step you ask them to agree to? If you expect a lot of visitors, it is wise to use the 'gazelle approach' that top restaurants use: that is one individual keeps a sharp eye out for visitors, welcomes them to the stand, and quickly hands them over to your team, who can have a more detailed follow-up discussion.

Note all visitors and follow-up: One of the key rules of building trust is 'doing as we say we will do'. Whenever a promise is made by a salesperson and is not honoured, it *diminishes* your company. It is a form of 'anti-selling'!

Networks and networking events

While networking events sometimes have a bad rap, the right ones can work well. Solopreneurs and inexperienced start-up founders sometimes make the mistake of attending local general business networking events without considering whether there are likely to be any potential customers there. It helps if you have defined an *ideal customer profile* before selecting networks to target; that is a description of what a great customer looks like for your business. Then you can identify groups or events where they hang out.

Many industries have trade organisations that run seminars and events for members. If you are targeting that industry, then clearly attending their network events is likely to be very fruitful.

Not everyone is comfortable going to an event where they don't know anyone. Here are some guidelines to help with network events:

- Don't be a wallflower! Join a group quickly, and with a confident smile, say something like, "Sorry to interrupt your conversation, do you mind if I join your group?" The longer you leave it, the harder it gets to join in.
- Be genuinely interested in others: Ask lots of questions to learn about what they do and why they are here. Who doesn't love that kind of attention?
- If you find yourself with a potentially interesting customer, ask to exchange contacts and follow up immediately after the event with a "nice to meet you" message. Then nurture the relationship until they are ready to discuss any opportunities.
- If you find yourself in the 'wrong' group, don't be afraid to make a swift, polite exit, for example, "I am really sorry I just need to duck out and make a quick call".

If you have a good pipeline of opportunities (Chapter 11), you will not feel pressured to push conversations towards sales. You are simply building your network for the future.

Product in-use strategies

In their Harvard Business Review article, *The Next Great Digital Advantage*, Vijay Govindarajan and Venkat Venkatraman[34] outline how companies are uncovering new sales opportunities by paying close attention to what customers buy and how they use products. In an industrial context, the *internet of things* has created a sea of data that reveals how customers use products and what they might need next.

A great example of this approach is outlined in *Data-driven Sales*, a book put together by the Clearbit organisation.[35] DigitalOcean, a tech company with 500,000 clients, decided to drive growth from its existing customer base rather than find new ones. By carefully analysing spikes in their usage data, they discovered that this was a signal that a customer was getting ready to test a new IT implementation and could be in the market for more services. They trialled different outreach sequences and managed to secure 30% account value growth from these accounts.

If you collect data or have visibility of how your customers use your product/service, it might well be possible to generate leads from it.

Marketing lists

There are numerous lists available from reputable and non-reputable providers out there. Normally, good ones are expensive, and poor ones are cheap, like so many things in life. The message is to do your due diligence before handing over cash!

Letters and physical mail

Because receiving letters is quite rare today, this is a contact method not to be ignored. Handwritten letters and very creative packaging can get your attention. One start-up I work with sends a plastic foot to potential customers with the message "Hoping to get a foot in the door"!

If used as part of a sequence, they can be very effective.

Deciding on the mix of lead generation sources

By now, it is hopefully clear that you have a lot of methods at your disposal. How then should you choose which ones to prioritise? If you have any historical data, you can start with a lead analysis, as shown in Figure 6.1.

By paying attention to the sources of leads and the relative conversion rates for each source, you might be able to make an educated guess for future activities. In this example, the returns from trade shows are questionable (8% conversion rate), while referrals and LinkedIn are much higher (71% and 57%) and should be amplified.

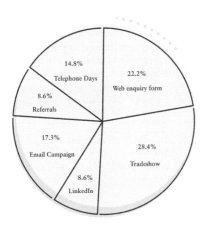

LEAD SOURCE	NUMBER OF LEADS	SPLIT	CLOSED	CONVERSION RATE
Web enquiry form	18	22.2%	9	50.0%
Tradeshow	23	28.4%	2	8.7%
LinkedIn	7	8.6%	4	57.1%
Email Campaign	14	17.3%	4	28.6%
Referrals	7	8.6%	5	71.4%
Telephone Days	12	14.8%	6	50.0%
TOTAL	81	100.0%		

Figure 6.1 Lead generation analysis

If you don't have any historical data, you can make a guestimate and adjust the course en-route based on emerging data. Just about every client I have ever worked with is on a continual journey of refining their lead generation approach. It's near impossible to plan the correct approach upfront.

Measuring and managing your lead generation activities

The process SMEs and start-ups can use to derive lead generation metrics is shown in Table 6.3.

When you have completed this process, you will have the number of leads you need each month to meet your targets. As you figure out which activities are most effective, you will have a set of *activity measures* to manage each week. If you drive these activities every week, you will be in a good position to hit your target.

Sequences, touches and cadences

This was alluded to earlier. Using well-thought-out combinations of lead sources (e.g., social media, telephone and email) can increase your chances of success compared to

Table 6.3 Deriving lead generation metrics

No	Step	Calculation	Notes
1	Calculate the average year-1 revenue from new customers	How much revenue is a new customer likely to deliver in one year?	This helps establish the value of an individual lead
2	Calculate average uplift from cross-sales/up-sell	If you cross-sell a product/ service, how much revenue does it bring in one year?	Ditto, but for cross-selling and up-selling
3	Set growth targets for each activity	According to your growth model, what is the total amount of revenue you are looking for from a) new customers, b) cross-selling and c) up-selling?	You could set the growth target first, then see how many leads you need, or figure out what a realistic workload is for the team and calculate the associated growth
4	Estimate the conversion ratio for each lead source	What percentage of leads are likely to convert for each source?	Ideally, use historical data for this, or you could try 25–50% to begin with and adjust based on incoming data
5	Calculate how many leads are required to meet growth target	Based on the conversion rates, how many leads do you need initially to meet your targets?	A conversion ratio of 50% means you need $10,000 of leads to secure $5,000
6	Adjust for timing effects	Given that your leads will convert sequentially through the year, how many do you need each month to hit your target?	If you win a client that pays $500/month, they will only deliver $3000 if you win them mid-year
7	Publish the targets	Make the targets visible and part of your regular performance management	What gets inspected gets respected

just hammering away on one channel. You might start by contacting a potential lead on LinkedIn, followed by an email a few days later, and then leave a voicemail. In the next week, you could use the same channels again, with slightly different messages (*complimentary messaging*).

Making each contact progressive and bringing new, valuable insights to potential customers is more likely to motivate them to respond to your sequences.

If you are planning to do a lot of activity like this, then it is worth considering a sales engagement platform to support it (see Chapter 13).

Lead scoring

Are all leads created equal? Clearly not! As mentioned in the trade show, example conversations with customers soon reveal that the probability of success varies widely. Some organisations use a *lead scoring matrix* to prioritise which ones to focus on. Sales technology can do this automatically now, and McKinsey found this to be a top use case for AI in sales.[36] The basic principle is like qualification, which is to use a series of questions to establish how attractive the opportunity might be.

Mark Roberg (HubSpot's sales director) introduced a 'buyer journey/buyer persona' matrix to assess leads based on where the customer was in their buying journey and the size of the enterprise in question.[37] This enabled the commercial team to customise (and prioritise) the way they managed each type of lead.

Organisations that field a lot of leads can derive great value from systems like this because it helps them to prioritise where best to focus valuable sales time.

Remember, the fuel you put in the engine defines how well the engine runs! Established sellers can be guilty of the 'eat what walks past' syndrome; in other words, leads come to them, but they are not active in choosing who to work with. Remember, world-class sales organisations choose what to sell to whom and when to do it. For this reason, you might set sector/product targets as well as volume targets.

Lead response time

A few years back, I worked with a sales director who reluctantly confessed to having 200 leads that had not been followed up. This is 'crime number one' in sales: A potential customer contacts you, and you don't follow up straight away. In today's 'always on, I want it now' culture, we have to be super-slick with response times and the quality of response. If you have gone to all that trouble to create good-quality leads, then give them silk glove treatment all the way through the sales cycle.

Into action

If you already have lead generation in place...

Start by analysing the sources of leads and the conversion rates for each source, as shown in Figure 6.1.

Which sources would you move away from?

Which sources should you double down on?

Which new sources of leads could you try?

If you are starting from square one...

Start by writing down your *ideal customer profile* and the typical *personas* that you might need to meet to sell your product/service. What are their concerns/interests?

Work on your website/content/SEO so that if they search for your area of expertise, they find you.

Think about the methods you could use today to reach them (Think email lists, LinkedIn, other networks, tradeshows, telephone and in-person prospecting).

Plan a three-month campaign with defined activity targets each week to make contact with your ideal customers. Review your success after this time and make adjustments based on what the data are telling you.

Expert view: Neil Clarke at Quattro

Quattro is a specialist digital sales and marketing agency and a HubSpot Elite Solutions Partner. Clients across multiple sectors turn to Quattro for help with lead generation, CRM configuration and all aspects of HubSpot implementation.

Their solutions are designed to support businesses of all sizes with the generation and management of leads, from initial contact through marketing nurturing and sales to customer success.

Here, Neil, Digital Director, explains how Quattro helps clients generate leads.

What sort of client work do you specialise in?

Basically, we're an exclusive HubSpot Solutions Partner, so the work that we specialise in is assisting any business that is considering taking on HubSpot or any business that's looking to grow and evolve their marketing, sales and customer service functions.

HubSpot uses the concept of a 'flywheel' to describe the way that potential customers are attracted to a business and then converted into customers and advocates. Our services support each stage of that flywheel.

If someone needs a CRM, we'll configure it for them, bring in their data and then implement the flywheel components around it. These start with attracting potential customers (marketing), pre-qualifying leads and routing them to Business development representatives (BDRs) and then turning prequalified leads into opportunities (sales). We help businesses streamline these processes and automate them using software.

Then, of course, once the deal is done and closed, what happens then? This is where customer service software (service) comes in. We help businesses follow up with customers and manage their whole customer experience with support inboxes, tickets, service level agreements (SLAs) and satisfaction surveys. Those are the core parts of the flywheel (marketing, sales and service) that support a centralised CRM.

In addition to that, customers like their systems integrated, for example, with an internal Enterprise Resource Planing (ERP) system. So, we also do Application Programming Interface (API) integrations.

Website development is also a common request. More and more businesses want their sales and marketing functions in one place, so we build custom lead generation websites on HubSpot that are linked with marketing, sales and CRM.

Going a bit deeper, how do you use technology to support lead generation for your customers?

We think of lead generation in terms of symptoms, problems and solutions. Essentially, your customers are out there. They will be experiencing symptoms of a problem but may not know what the problem is. You need to be found as the resource that helps them diagnose their problem and ultimately find the solution to that problem. Being found online as a resource to solve your customers problems naturally positions you as the solution provider.

If we think about it in a digital world, lead generation begins with search terms or phrases. Prospects will go into a search engine and ask for a solution to the symptom or problem they are experiencing. To be found for that term or phrase, you need to have a lot of well-structured content that is optimised for those keywords and phrases. This content needs to be well organised and can take the form of blogs, website pages, knowledgebase articles, landing pages, guides or wikis. Each piece of content needs to provide the prospect with the information they need but also subtly position you as the solution provider with lots of opportunities to fill out forms or speak to a sales advisor.

Online search has changed massively. It's no longer just about keywords; it's more conversational. Think about how you use Siri, Alexa and Hey Google. You need to be found in a conversational way. We help clients build 'topic clusters' where they can be seen as an authority for a particular topic. The topic cluster contains one very broad key term at its core, surrounded by sub-topic terms that are variants of the central broad term. It takes time to build organic SEO using clusters in this way, but the results are long lasting.

To help businesses manage their digital content and optimise it using topics and clusters, automation software is needed to tackle the heavy lifting. Automation software also plays a critical role in the capture of leads and the management of them, including automated responses and the dynamic routing of enquiries.

Businesses can and often do paid advertising, but if you do paid advertising, you'll always be doing it for fear of not being seen. It's the same as manufacturers who are afraid that if they don't go to a trade exhibition every year, customers will assume they've gone out of business.

Using automation to get your content out there in the right way, to be found by the right people, is going to bring in more qualified leads, and they're going to be better-fit leads because they're leads that found you. That's the crux of HubSpot;

it's inbound marketing. Rather than pushing your message out there, you try to pull prospects in.

If you create content seriously, then you get the rewards. Once done, you will have built a series of digital marketing assets that will continually generate leads for you for many years to come.

Given the potential amount of work involved, what is your advice for start-ups and SMES who are often strapped for resources?

A common problem I've seen when I've worked with small businesses with one or two marketers is that they try to take on too much and try to rank for every product or service they provide. Instead, they need to look at what their business sells the most of and which lines yield the most revenue and start with those first. This will often take them in the direction of real niche products that are easier and faster to rank online. All too often, I've seen marketing teams put time and effort into marketing a product line that performs well but is something that they make very little money on and is problematic to sell. This is where marketing and sales need to work together.

My advice, therefore, is to focus on the products you make the most revenue from. Emphasise the problem it solves, and be laser-focused on it. Start publishing content regularly and make it specific.

Let's say you sell paint. Everyone will be going after the keyword 'paint'; it's too broad. But if you sell a specific type of varnish for certain types of yacht, you're going to be much more specific and, in that specificity, there will be a lot less competition. It's about knowing, really well, what items make the most revenue and the key terms that are specific to them, so you can be found. In starting your lead generation journey, ask yourself the following questions: who are your customer personas? What are they searching for? What are their symptoms? What are their problems? What are your solutions?

Are there any other systems that you think are useful for small businesses to help with lead generation?

There are a lot of systems out there; my advice would be to either build a system from lots of small software vendors and build it best in class for your needs or take on a starter package from one of the bigger vendors in the market and grow with that system.

Email marketing systems like Campaign Monitor, MailChimp or DotMailer integrated with a website on WordPress or Wix are a good starting point. Low-cost CRM systems like Sugar, Zoho or PipeDrive are great for building out sales opportunity management.

I think a lot of businesses are fearful of taking on HubSpot or Salesforce because they think they will cost an absolute fortune. But bigger software vendors like HubSpot offer all-in-one starter packages of marketing, sales and service along with a free CRM, which is a great way to start out. You can add features as you grow or remain on the starter plans. The advantage of this route is that less time is spent linking systems together, and you can get up and running quicker.

Notes

1 A. Ross & J. Lemkin *From impossible to inevitable* p46 Wiley 2016
2 N. Rackham & P. Kotler, *Ending the war between sales and marketing* Harvard Business Review July 2006
3 S. Hall *Innovative B2B marketing* p171 Kogan Page 2017
4 N. Nahai *Webs of influence* Pearson 2012
5 Ibid., p100
6 D. Chaffey & F. Ellis-Chadwick *Digital marketing* 7th ed Pearson 2019
7 S. Hall p141 Kogan Page 2017
8 M. Sheridan *They ask, you listen* Wiley 2019
9 R. Bornstein et al "The generalisability of subliminal mere exposure effects: Influence of stimuli perceived without awareness on social behaviour" *Journal of Personality and Social Psychology* vol. 53 (1987), 1070–1079
10 Mailchimp blog https://mailchimp.com/resources/what-is-influencer-marketing/#:~:text= Influencer%20marketing%20is%20a%20form,promotes%20their%20products%20or%20 services
11 J. Atherton *B2B social selling strategy* p16 Kogan Page 2023
12 J. Blount *Fanatical prospecting* p13 Wiley 2015
13 S. Dudley & T. Bryant *Relentless* p145 Behavioural Science Research Press 2020
14 T. Bertruzzi *The sales development playbook* p160 T. Bertuzzi 2016
15 Ibid., p164
16 S. Dudley & T. Bryant p194 Behavioural Science Research Press 2020
17 J. Blount Wiley 2015
18 E. Poyry et al "Generating leads with sequential persuasion: Should sales influence tactics be consistent or complimentary" *Journal of Personal Selling and Sales Management* vol. 37 (2017), 96–97.
19 J. Blount p201 Wiley 2015
20 S. Hall p131 Kogan Page 2017
21 Permission marketing is the term coined by Seth Godwin in 1999
22 D. Chaffey & F. Ellis-Chadwick 7th ed p443 Pearson 2019
23 J. Dapko & A. Artis "Writing effective prospecting emails: An instructional guide" *Northern Illinois University Journal of Selling* vol. 16, no. 1, 44.
24 J. Atherton p14 Kogan Page 2023
25 T. Hughes & M. Reynolds *Social selling* p29 Kogan Page 2016
26 J. Atherton p78 Kogan Page 2023
27 https://en.wikipedia.org/wiki/Metcalfe%27s_law
28 M. Granovetter "The strength of weak ties" *American Journal of Sociology* vol. 78, No.6 (1973), 1360–1380.
29 T. Hughes & M. Reynolds p55 Kogan Page 2016
30 J. Barry & J. Gironda "Developing social selling influence: An archetypal examination of content strategies" *Northern Illinois University Journal of Selling*   vol. 18, no. 1, 61–63
31 R. Cialdini *Influence – The psychology or persuasion* Collins Business 2007
32 https://www.leandata.com/blog/the-modern-rules-of-lead-response-time/#:~:text=A%20 five%2Dminute%20lead%20response%20time%20is%20the%20benchmark%2C%20 but,mind%20you%2C%20those%20are%20conversions
33 HubSpot *Digital marketing for beginners* 2022
34 V. Govindarajan & V. Venkatraman "The next great digital advantage" *Harvard Business Review* May 2022
35 N. Arbel (editor) *Data-driven sales* p67 Clearbit 2018
36 R. Deveau "AI powered marketing and sales reach new heights with generative AI" McKinsey article May 2023
37 M. Roberg *The sales acceleration formula* p131 Wiley 2015

Chapter 7

Your unique value proposition and pricing

Why should customers buy from you and how much should they pay you?

Why do SMEs and start-ups need to consider their value propositions?

If you have ever seen a rookie salesperson in action, you may have noticed the potential customer grimace as the salesperson listed feature after feature of their product or service. Simply telling a customer all the attributes your solution has rarely leads to much motivation to buy. In this example, the customer perceived little value from the list because the salesperson did not take care to communicate it effectively.

Recall that one of the fundamental questions your sales strategy should address is "What are we selling?" Therefore, your value proposition is part of the jigsaw of sales excellence.

Ideally, you will have a *unique value proposition*. So, what is a unique value proposition, and why do SMEs and start-ups need to develop them?

Let's start with value. What is value? In his book, *Differentiation strategy*,[1] Kevin Holt shows us that this apparently simple concept is poorly understood by managers. He offers the following pragmatic definitions of value:

> "Value is the customer's overall assessment of the utility of a product based on what is received and what is given".

Or,

Value = Benefits − costs

Similarly, Mark Davies, in his book, *Infinite Value*, offers a similar equation-based definition[2]:

Value = Impact − total cost of ownership

A value proposition, therefore, has to offer something that a customer perceives as justifying the cost of actually purchasing it.

Why, then, does it also need to be *unique*? Here we have the leviathan of strategy, Michael Porter, to thank, who introduced the idea of being a *price taker*.[3] Where an organisation does not have a *competitive advantage* (i.e., is differentiated from its competitors), it cannot command a premium price because customers have other identical offers to choose from. He named it *strategic hell*, and that is not a nice place to be in sales.

What does a good value proposition look like?

Kevin Holt cautions us that *benefits* and *costs* are a bit more complicated than they first seem[4] because it is the customer's perception of these that count, and they are not easily measured quantitatively. If you have read anything on sales already, you may well have

DOI: 10.4324/9781003449614-7

come across the idea of *features and benefits* associated with rules like "never sell features, only benefits". A *feature* is typically defined as an attribute or description of a product/service, while a *benefit* is *what value the feature brings to a customer.*

One of the reasons rookie salespeople can look so clumsy is if they forget to fully explore a customer's needs before presenting a recommendation. In this sense, a benefit should always be linked to a need. If we don't understand customer needs, we cannot present benefits. So, it is worth remarking up front that a value proposition must be based on a thorough understanding of customer needs. This is why your sales process should allow for *needs discovery* before *solution presentation*, so that you can present a true value proposition to them.

So, what are the types of value we can provide to customers? Mark Davies offers the following key areas[5]:

- Improve customers' revenues
- Reduce customers' costs
- Improve customers' reputation
- Improve their overall business strategy

How does your own product or service help your customers in these four areas? Being clear on that is very useful in asking the right questions to build a customised value proposition.

In addition to these four fundamental areas, research carried out by Eric Almquist and his colleagues identified an incredible 30 distinct areas that B2B buyers value.[6] Their research offers a fascinating insight into the great number of emotional and psychological benefits that buyers value. These areas are summarised in Table 7.1. Keeping these in mind can help you be much more expansive and creative in the ways you build your value propositions.

A key objective in B2B selling is to identify which sources of value are most important to customers through skilled questioning, active listening, and emotional intelligence. This requires a mix of operational questions to discover the *functional* benefits on Almquist's list and more indirect, personal questions to uncover *emotional, life-changing* and *social impact* sources of value.

Table 7.1 Sources of B2B value

Functional	Emotional	Life changing	Social impact
Saves time	Reduces anxiety	Provides hope	Self-transcendence
Simplifies	Rewards me	Self-actualisation	
Make money	Nostalgia	Motivation	
Reduces risk	Design aesthetics	Heirloom	
Organises	Badge value	Affiliation	
Integrates	Wellness	Belonging	
Connects	Therapeutic value		
Reduces effort	Fun		
Avoids hassle	Attractiveness		
Reduces cost	Provides access		
Quality			
Variety			
Sensory appeal			
Informs			

What aspects of our offer can we play with to differentiate our value propositions? Francis Buttle and Stan Maklan offer seven areas where value propositions can be differentiated in their book, *Customer Relationship Management*[7]:

Product: How can this be customised?

Price: How can it be differentiated for customer segments?

Promotion: How best to customise communications and offers?

Process: How could you create a unique process for your customers that they value?

People: How can you put talented, well-trained people in front of your customers?

Physical evidence: What tangible items can you offer to reinforce your services?

Bringing the elements of a value proposition together

How then can we begin to bring these elements together? *Value-ology*, written by Simon Kelly and his colleagues, offers the mnemonic 'MUSICAL' to help you structure your value proposition[8]:

Monetary calculation (What are the financial benefits minus costs?)

Unique (What is it that differentiates you from competitors?)

Spend (How much a customer is prepared to spend?)

Impact (How does your value proposition benefit your customer?)

Capability (Why are you uniquely qualified to deliver value?)

ALigned (How aligned is your value proposition to the key needs of your customer?)

Again, the need to be unique is emphasised. You are probably aware of *unique selling points*, which are another way of articulating your competitive advantage, so that you don't end up in strategic hell.

Methods like MUSICAL help us identify our value proposition by finding answers to these six key questions:

1 Who are we selling to? (sector and role)
2 What are their challenges and ambitions (business and personal)?
3 How does our product/service address these points?
4 What value does it bring to them (business and personal)?
5 Why are we unique?
6 What is the evidence that we can deliver on the promise?

Many larger corporates capture this information in *battlecards*, which are typically 1-pagers that cover these six points, so that salespeople can use them in the field, along with key questions to being conversations with. Technology can also enable this, with tools like tablets running content management software that ensure salespeople have the latest information at their fingertips. The exercise of creating a battlecard is useful in that it forces us to clearly articulate our value by writing it down. If it is clear in our heads, it stands a chance of being clear in customers' heads!

An example of a value proposition

Imagine you are a salesperson for an organisation selling industrial cleaning equipment. You have a new robot that can be deployed to automatically clean large open areas. It has the following features:

Table 7.2 A sample value proposition for industrial cleaning equipment

Key question	Value proposition
1 Who are we selling to?	Managers of outsourced cleaning firms who have the contract to keep the shopping centre/mall clean
2 What are their challenges and ambitions?	1 Maintaining acceptable hygiene standards in a post-COVID era 2 Keeping costs under control to stay profitable 3 Finding and recruiting suitable staff 4 Getting all the work done in time for opening hours
3 How does our product/ service address these points?	1 By removing human error, our machine ensures a consistent, high-quality clean across all floor space 2 Less staff are needed to clean the same area, meaning labour costs are reduced 3 Less staff are required, and their work is more rewarding and high-level, meaning retention is easier 4 Several robots can be deployed at the same time to shorten the total cleaning time
4 What value does it bring to them?	Reduced staffing costs Increased customer satisfaction through consistent high cleaning Less anxiety related to staffing issues Fulfilment and pride in using the newest technology
5 Why are we unique?	The sole manufacturer of this cleaning robot, with its customer-friendly route-programming function
6 What is the evidence that we can deliver on the promise?	Customer testimonials at three major shopping centres are featured on the company website

- The robot can run for eight hours on one charge.
- It can be programmed to clean floors with a surface area of 10,000 square metres.
- Uses 10% less chemicals than a human operator.
- Reduces bacterial residuals on floors by 20%, compared to humans.

What could your value proposition be? Using the six questions above, it might look as shown in Table 7.2, based on selling the solution to a large shopping centre/mall.

Note that there is very little mention of *features* in the value proposition. It tries to take a customer-centric perspective. Some organisations try to encourage customer-centric thinking through the use of *personas*, that is, researched descriptions of typical customers and their challenges/ambitions. In this example, the persona is a typical manager of an outsourced cleaning firm, and the value proposition addresses the typical KPIs and concerns they experience.

Also, value propositions tend to be more effective when focused on specific sectors and roles because every individual's needs are unique.

Who should be involved in the creation of value propositions?

In their seminal paper *Ending the War Between Sales and Marketing*, Philip Kotler, Neil Rackham and Suj Krisnashwamy[9] warn of the need to fully align the two functions to be effective. Indeed, a core message of *Value-ology*, mentioned earlier, is to use value propositions to align sales and marketing. Both functions need to be involved in the generation and formulation

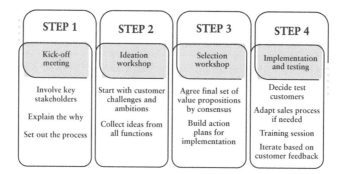

Figure 7.1 Value proposition design process

of value propositions. However, these are not the only two functions that can create value propositions. Technical and production staff are equally likely to think of new use-cases for your product/solution. For this reason, it's a smart idea to set up a working group to align with your organisation's value proposition. Much like sales process design, cross-functional teams tend to lead to more diverse thinking, creativity, and ownership in implementation.

A typical process for value proposition design is shown in Figure 7.1.

Good change management principles always have to be taken into account when managing sales teams, because in many cases, it is a lonely job with high levels of autonomy where it's difficult to see what is actually happening in front of customers (although this is changing with technology). Therefore, the process is designed to create buy-in and champions as part of the design, so you have the best chance of implementation on the ground.

Testing the quality of value propositions

A good way to test your emerging value proposition is using the four questions developed by the Boston Consulting Group start-up team for testing new business concepts[10]:

Desirability: Does the customer's problem/benefit really matter?

Feasibility: Can our solution really fix it?

Viability: Can our idea beat our competitors?

Scalability: Will the idea scale up?

The sales learning curve

Whenever new go-to-market approaches are introduced, such as a new value proposition, it's useful to think about *sales learning curve* effects.[11] This is effectively the amount of time it takes your salesforce to discover how best to sell a new product/value proposition and is discussed in Chapter 9. The sales learning curve can be accelerated by effective, rapid effective knowledge sharing.

It's worth remembering that not all salespeople will take new value propositions to market with the same level of gusto. Coaching on the job is often, therefore, an essential component of introducing new value propositions. This will be covered in Chapters 9 and 12.

Demonstrating value before presenting price

Having looked at the case for value propositions and how to construct them, it is important to deal with a common question that often comes up from those new to sales, "What do I do when a customer asks for the price early on in a meeting?". It's a common aphorism amongst salespeople to *sell value before price*. The basic principle is that if a customer does not fully grasp the value of your solution before they see the price, they might experience *sticker shock*, i.e., the feeling that your solution is overpriced.

This logic underpins most sales process design, where we try to discover the needs and ambitions that a customer has before showing how our solution addresses them and finally presenting the fees/price/investment.

It is generally sensible to acknowledge requests for prices with a response such as:

"You are very wise to ask about our fees upfront. If it's ok with you, could I ask a few more questions to establish what solution would work best for you, so I can give an accurate answer?"

That is why value propositions are covered before pricing in this chapter. On the other hand, if a customer appears to really want to know pricing upfront, trying to deflect the question is likely to appear evasive and untrustworthy. In these circumstances, it's just best to give a ballpark figure, using a *proud of price* attitude (more of that later).

With this in mind, let's now turn to the often-neglected area of pricing.

Why do we need to pay careful attention to pricing?

Recall that increasing prices is one of the six fundamental levers we can use to grow. Peter Hill's excellent book *Pricing for Profit*,[12] makes the point very clearly, "The quickest and greatest impact on profits comes from simply charging a little more on the price". To see the impact of discounting or *'selling yourself cheap'*, we can look at the effect on your gross profit. A number of tables exist in the sales communities that show this. Table 7.3 is an example.

If you don't have tight control of pricing, a seemingly reasonable 10% discount to *get a deal over the line* means you would need to double your volume of sales based on 20% gross profit! If you have a sales team with quite a lot of pricing autonomy, this can be a disaster.

This chapter will explore strategies for setting your prices and most importantly, how to present and discuss them in a B2B sales context.

Table 7.3 The effect of discounting

Current gross profit	20%	40%	60%
Discount offered:	The sales volume has to increase by the percentage below to make the same overall gross profit:		
5%	33%	14%	9%
10%	100%	33%	20%
15%	400%	60%	33%

The proud of price attitude

Are you proud of the prices you charge? Or do you feel uncomfortable discussing prices and squirm when the topic comes up? "Hesitation to communicate cost and payment" is one of the "16 faces of call reluctance", also known as "close reluctance/arranging payment reluctance", identified by George Dudley and Shannon Goodson.[13] The authors found it is surprisingly common, even among seasoned salespeople, with 49% of sales reps with greater than five years of tenure experiencing it.

If we are nervous, uncomfortable or apologetic when we present our prices, what message does that send to customers about our belief in our value? Therefore, whatever pricing we end up with, it is vital at the outset to develop conviction about why we are excellent value and worth the fees we charge. This is sometimes referred to as the *proud of price attitude*. If we are confident in our value, then it shows.

As outlined above, it is common for salespeople *not* to be proud of price and to ask their managers to sanction discounts. Peter Hill suggests this is because "Most of the people that businesses employ to sell are simply not appropriately trained to do that role".[14] It can also have to do with the fact that management has not explained *why* maintaining prices is essential. It is hard to justify a price if you don't understand why it is needed. Managers and founders can help the situation by communicating the money your organisation invests in quality, training, product development and customer service to help salespeople understand the rationale for price levels.

How then should we communicate a price to demonstrate '*proud of price attitude*'? Simply, without justification or apology, this is the best way:

"Our fee for this service is X" ...silence.

The proud-of-price attitude also plays out if/when we get into a negotiation. In B2B selling, it is sometimes a reality that we have to negotiate, and having a strong belief in our value prevents too much profit from being given away.

Setting prices

How do organisations set prices? Dr. Christian Homburg offers three 'formal' methods that are typically used[15]:

- Cost-based pricing
- Competitor-based pricing
- Value to customer pricing

And in addition, two other common, more 'ad-hoc' approaches are used[16]:

- Best guess pricing
- Last year's price plus an arbitrary increase

Of all these methods, Peter Hill argues that *value to customer pricing* is the only viable, long-term approach.[17] Dr Christian Homburg is a bit more nuanced in his point of view, stating that "The price will always stem from a mixture of the results of the three approaches",

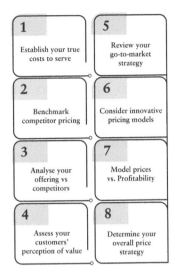

Figure 7.2 Different perspectives on pricing

going on to add, "However, we have frequently observed that value-based pricing is given insufficient weight".[18]

So, with these perspectives in mind, how can SMEs and start-ups set prices effectively? Figure 7.2 shows eight typical perspectives that can be used to help you reach a solid pricing approach. Here follows a description of each:

Establish your true cost to serve

Clearly, understanding the actual profit that your sales generate is essential information so that you can set prices that deliver the profit you want to achieve. If insufficient profit is generated for each transaction, it can severely impact the possibility of growth, unless you have external funding. Admittedly, getting accurate cost-profit data can be challenging for any business. Your financial specialist may well be able to help.

Benchmark your competitors' pricing

If you have competitors, checking out their pricing gives you a sense of the market's pricing range. Ideally, this should be done with either *mystery shopping* or by *asking through a friend* to get actual figures. The aim of this research is not so that we can copy or undercut competitors, but to get a general sense of the market and help with your positioning decisions.

Analyse your competitor's offering

Unless you are very lucky, it is highly likely that you will face the "We already use your competitor" objection at some time in a customer meeting. Without a thorough understanding of how you are different, it will be very difficult to justify a higher price. By creating your unique value proposition and understanding what your main competitors offer, it will be easier to position yourself to charge higher prices.

Assess your customers' perception of value

As already stated, *value-based pricing* is likely to be the best route to growth and profitability. How then can we establish the value we offer and the prices we should charge for it? There are several options:

Discover it during your sales process: The discovery stage of a sales process enables us to fully understand our customers' *pain and gain* before presenting our solution and price proposal. Often, this can be quantified to directly measure the value of our solution. For example, if your solution saves your customer labour hours, this time and cost savings can be estimated.

Test the limits: Sales folklore says if you don't lose a small percentage of customers each year because you are "too expensive", then you are definitely too cheap. Peter Hill is at pains to point out that we should not base our pricing on the cheapest buyers in the market.[19] It is very common for salespeople to tell you that more could be sold if prices were lower. If no one has complained that your prices seem high, then this is almost certainly a signal that you are not charging enough!

Analytical methods: The *Van Westendorp Price Sensitivity Meter* is an analytical way to use customer feedback to ascertain a range of acceptable prices,[20] avoiding the typical risk of bias in the answers. Figure 7.3 explains the method in more detail.

Review your business strategy and context

Years of selling on the internet and e-commerce have spawned many different approaches to pricing and competing. *Digital Marketing*, by Dave Chaffey and Fiona Ellis-Chadwick, gives a good overview of some of these.[21] At a basic level, organisations can choose *premium pricing* (skimming the market for the highest payers and thus reaping high gross margins)

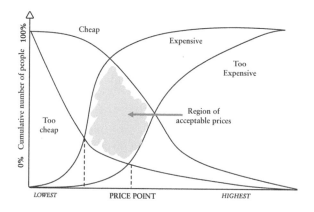

Data is collected by asking customers at what price point your offering is:

    1. Too cheap to have faith in
    2. A bargain worth paying for
    3. Expensive enough to seem reliable
    4. Too expensive to purchase

The cumulative number of customers giving the figure is plotted on the vertical axis. The range between the dotted lines shows the acceptable pricing range.

Figure 7.3 The Van Westendorp price estimation method

or *penetration pricing* to rapidly gain market share.[22] Organisations that have a *winner takes all strategy*, i.e., to become the dominant player in an industry as quickly as possible, often use penetration pricing so competitors cannot catch up. This approach is common for internet businesses that go for scale before profits. But, of course, it requires deep pockets to enable. For cash-strapped start-ups, a premium pricing model might make more sense.

Two other important factors to consider are *pricing transparency* and *dynamic pricing*.[23] In some sectors, competitor prices are very visible on the internet, especially where price comparison websites exist. Similarly, some industries (airline travel, hotel booking) change prices according to demand, and these factors have to feed into pricing strategies. For a more detailed view of strategies in these environments, again, 'Digital marketing' is a good source.[24]

Consider innovative pricing methods

There are so many ways you can price. Pricing specialist Rafi Mohammed urges us to "look at other industries for inspiration".[25] His excellent Harvard Business Review article offers a menu of pricing approaches to consider,[26] which SMEs and start-ups can draw great inspiration from. Some examples are:

- Unlimited or all-inclusive plans
- Metered pricing (i.e., pay for usage only)
- Split usage, leasing or renting (e.g., time share)
- Prepaid plans
- Progressive pricing
- Auctions
- Royalties
- Off-peak pricing

As well as these options, at least four pricing approaches have been shown to help increase sales growth and margins. These are:

- Good-better-best pricing (G-B-B)
- Directional pricing
- Decoy pricing
- Segmented pricing or price discrimination

G-B-B has become very common in many sectors, especially subscription services. It involves having three or more product/services levels for your offering, from basic to premium. The basic idea is to appeal to different customer segments by varying the amount/quality of benefits at each level. Rafi Mohammed again gives the example of US insurance provider Allstate, which introduced G-B-B in 2005. By 2008, they had sold 3.9 million policies using this model, with 100,000 new ones per month.[27] The author gives several reasons why organisations might want to employ this pricing model:

1 The premium level generates high margins.
2 The basic level attracts price-sensitive customers.
3 The premium version can boost the perception of your whole brand.

4   The lower priced option can serve as an entry point for your organisation, boosting sales of other products/services that you offer.
5   Some consumers will focus more on *which option to buy* rather than *Should I buy?*

To help decide on feature sets, the author offers a list of parameters that can be adjusted to build the tiers, for example: *volume, service level, waiting period, warranty,* and *flexibility.*[28]

In setting the prices for each tier/level, be aware of the psychological effect of *anchoring.* Much research has been done on this, especially by Daniel Kahneman and Amos Tversky in their well-read book *Thinking, Fast and Slow.*[29] For example, they discovered that if two groups of people were asked, "How tall is the tallest redwood tree?" preceded by the question, "Is it taller than 1200 feet?" or "Is it taller than 180 feet?" then the average answer of each group was 844 feet and 282 feet, respectively. In other words, being given an irrelevant value upfront significantly affected the guesses generated. Nathalie Nahai, an expert in online influence, gives a practical example of this in action on internet auction sites that allow a reserve price to be set. Vendors that set a higher reserve price were shown to receive higher overall bids than vendors using a low reserve price.[30]

Thus, when setting your tier pricing, it's important to consider whether you want to set the anchor high or low. If your *premium option* comes up first, then customers may well be happy to pay slightly more for the *standard offer.* Alternatively, you may want to *anchor low* to give impression of being a low-cost provider and simulate up-sell and cross-sell later (as airlines routinely do by showing the seat-only price as the headline).

Although we commonly visualise websites when we think of how prices are presented, in B2B selling, it's highly likely we will personally present prices, giving us a lot of control over how they are presented and in which order.

If you have ever eaten in a fast-food restaurant, you will almost certainly have come across *meal deals* that effectively nudge you to spend more. This is known as *directional pricing.* To quote Peter Hill again, the idea of directional pricing is "to encourage customers to buy the products that you want them to buy".[31] Of course, G-B-B pricing can be a way of implementing directional pricing by making the option you want to sell look more attractive.

If you are not in a subscription business, directional pricing can be enabled by selling *bundles* of goods and services. The clever design of bundles means you can create offers that are of *high value to customers and low cost to you,* thereby increasing profit margins. Peter Hill gives the example of adding a *petrol mower kit* to a basic lawnmower sale, which includes items like engine oil, free first-year service and a cleaning kit.[32] While cheap to provide, it can easily be added to the sale when a customer is in *buying mode* and generate significant additional profits.

Firms also use directional pricing in a very transparent way, by offering volume discounts. This can be effective where covering high fixed costs is attractive to your business model.

Another technique explored by Nathalie Nahai to influence customer spending decisions, is *decoy pricing.*[33] Here, a redundant, unattractive pricing option is presented to nudge buyers to go for the premium option. While seemingly irrational, because humans are essentially irrational in their decision-making, it can work.

Finally, we can look at *segmented pricing,* or *price discrimination,* as Dr Christian Homberg calls it.[34] This involves charging different prices to different groups of customers, for example, by *customer characteristics, geography, channel, volume,* and *time of purchase.*

This has been shown to increase profitability overall, but it is not without risk. If customer groups talk to each other, it could cause much anger. Many start-ups and SMEs often have price discrimination by default, as new customers are taken on at different times with different discounts/costing assumptions.

Price discrimination works best when differing value propositions are constructed for each segment. For example, you might target your largest most important customers with a faster service response time, for which they pay a premium.

Model prices vs. profitability

Armed with all the insights from the preceding sections, it is valuable to look at how different pricing approaches might affect your overall profitability. For start-ups and SMEs with limited data analytics capabilities, this might involve using a spreadsheet and building a cash flow model for the year ahead. You'll need to make some assumptions about what you could sell and when the sales will come in.

Forecasting and target setting are covered in more detail in Chapter 10. For now, the idea is to play around with different scenarios and their impact on your profit. Don't forget to add in any costs that providing new service/product offerings incurs.

Determine your overall pricing strategy

Once you have decided on the way forward with pricing, it's time to implement it. Dr Christian Homburg warns us of the need for good pricing control: "In many companies, price discipline can only be described as poor".[35] He gives the main reasons for this:

* It's not clear who sets the price and who is allowed to discount.
* Process and procedures do not exist for checking what price is actually achieved.
* Salesperson's incentives are often based on volume, not profit.

Because of these factors, implementing a new price policy is essentially a change management challenge, especially if you want to substantially increase your prices. This implies:

* Good and frequent communication reasons your policy and the reasons behind it
* Definition of clear roles, responsibilities and limits of authority concerning discounts
* Training to help salespeople practice the *difficult conversations*
* Metrics and monitoring to assess progress and actual prices achieved
* Review and iteration of the approach based on learning with customers

Death before discount

Hopefully, by now, the importance of setting profitable prices, presenting them confidently and checking that you actually achieve them is clear. Does that mean we should never discount? The answer is, of course, "it depends".

The attitude of *death before discount* is useful, in part, because it is closely linked to the idea that *what is given free has no value*. If we give concessions too easily, they are not valued by our negotiating partner. This is because of the psychological phenomenon of *effort justification*; that is, the harder we work to achieve something, the more we value it.[36] Perhaps more importantly, knowing the impact that even small discounts can have on profit, resisting the urge to give 5% or 10% to close a deal has a significant impact on our profits.

That said, there are situations in B2B selling where negotiating and discounting do help to get deals over the line.

Do we need to discount?

Most professional buyers work on the assumption that there is no harm in asking for a discount. Thus, it's normal to be told you are "too expensive" or "If you can shave off 10%, we can give you the deal". How then do we objectively assess the need for a discount?

Useful insight can be given by analysing the *power and dependency* relationship we have with our customers. Key account gurus Diana Woodburn and Malcom McDonald offer this insight[37]: "Power is obviously linked to the perceived degree of dependency on the partner... dependency increases as the size of the business with the trading partner increases".

Andrew Cox, an expert on power mapping and supply chains, identifies four types of buyer–supplier relationships.[38] Understanding the relationship you have with your customer is very helpful in establishing what is likely to be possible in a negotiation. Table 7.4 shows the characteristics of each type of relationship, and the consequences for negotiation.

To understand our power position, it helps to understand the sources of power we can have and, of course, over time, try to build them, so the need for discounting is less. Woodburn and McDonald offer these, among other, sources of power for sellers[39]:

- Your criticality to your customer
- Your share of their purchases
- Your patents and monopolies
- Your key differentiators
- Your access to information

Table 7.4 The different types of power and dependency relationships

Relationship	Characteristics	Consequences for negotiation
Buyer dominance	Many suppliers like you in the market with similar offers.	Expect frequent requests for discount.
	This customer represents a significant percentage of your turnover.	Business can easily be lost if you don't differentiate.
Supplier dominance	Little competition for your services.	Little need to give discount.
	Your customer really values/relies on your offer.	Easier to retain customers, provided you don't get complacent.
Interdependence	You are deeply embedded in your customers operations and important to them strategically. They are a 'key customer' for you.	Frequent meetings and negotiations. Little real need to discount other than to 'save face'.
Independence	Neither you nor your customer really relies on or needs the trading relationship.	Finding time with buyers may be hard. Provided your service is good, then relatively safe business.

- Your recognised relevant experience
- The switching cost for your customer
- The competence of your account managers

So, to return to the question, "should we discount?", understanding your power position is the first step. If you are in a position of power where your customer is dependent on you, the answer is no, and a *proud of price attitude* prevails. If you face a dominant buyer, then maybe you have to negotiate today and work on your power position for tomorrow.

How best to prepare for a negotiation?

If you expect to have to negotiate, it pays to prepare well. A tool used by many negotiators is *a matrix*. A sample is shown in Figure 7.4. How does this help us? If we prepare in advance:

- We do not need to do calculations in our heads while simultaneously trying to negotiate with a skilled negotiator.
- Figuring out the elements that are possible to negotiate gives us the creativity to find a solution, rather than getting stuck on only one issue.
- Preparing for each element avoids being blindsided by our negotiating partner, bringing in 'new' options.

As you negotiate using this preparation, the following guidelines can help secure the best outcome:

1 *Take time to reach a good agreement*: Explore possibilities, and don't jump on the first solution offered. Haste on the part of a salesperson often smacks of desperation, which a good negotiator will spot immediately.
2 *Start high*: If we start with our lowest offer, we have nowhere to go; it's the equivalent of 'negotiating with your back against the wall'.
3 *If you give a concession, ask for a compensation in return*: For example, *"If we agreed to waive the delivery charge, could you commit to a bulk order of x units?"*.
4 *If you decide to concede, do so in micro-steps*: Recall the potentially severe effect on profit of discounting and the psychological effect of *effort justification* from the buyer's side.

ITEM TO NEGOTIATE	DISCOUNT LEVEL	DELIVERY FEE	PAYMENT TERMS	SERVICE OPTION
Outcome:				
Ideal outcome	Full price - 0%	$25 per delivery	15 days	Service $200/month
Realistic outcome	-2.5%	$10 per delivery	30 days	Service $150/month
Min acceptable outcome	-5%	$free delivery	45 days	Service $125/month
Walk-away point	Below 5%		Longer than 45 days	

Figure 7.4 A negotiation matrix

5 *Check progress towards a deal regularly*: This can head off *figureheading* and *nibling* negotiation strategies (where buyers are testing the waters, ready to come back with more demands later). One way of doing this is with *trial closes*, e.g., "With this offer, would you be ok to go ahead this week?"

6 *Alternate between negotiation substance, process, and relationships* If you are getting stuck on the details of % discounts or payment terms (substance), you can also focus on the process (the way the negotiation is conducted) and the relationships (the importance of working together). For example, "It looks like this area is a bit challenging for us. Why don't we reschedule and meet next week with the latest market demand information? We do really value the partnership with you and want to make it work."

Negotiation is a very useful skill for sales managers and start-up founders, and if you find yourself in frequent commercial negotiations, it is worth following a negotiation training programme to work on this.

Prices increases

One last important pricing area in B2B selling is the importance of securing prices rises regularly. Many organisations do this annually, but it can be done more frequently if market conditions demand it. Without discipline in pushing price increases through, profits will gradually erode, especially in times of high inflation.

It is another example where the *proud of price attitude* is important. Research done by Professor Nick Lee at Warwick Business School and Tim Riesterer at Corporate Visions[40] has shown the most effective way to frame price increases in this regard is what they call the *Why Pay Framework*:

1 Document the results achieved to date to achieve a *positive priming effect*.
2 Reinforce the reasons your customer took the decision to work with you in the first place to leverage the *status quo bias*.
3 Introduce your newest capabilities, which will help you shine versus your competitors.
4 Anchor high and offer a loyalty discount. "Normally the increase is 10%, but if you can sign up for two years, we can reduce that to only 5%".

Coupled with strong price discipline, your price rises are a strong contributor to your overall growth strategy.

Into action

To make progress with value propositions and pricing, it's a good idea to do a short audit of your current situation.

Value propositions

If you have a sales team (or at least some people selling), ask them to *write down* what they believe the company value proposition is, then compare notes.
Is it consistent? Do people have wildly different ideas?
Use the process outlined in Figure 10.1 in this chapter to sharpen up your value proposition.

Pricing

There are several ways you can audit pricing. It could be done by a product, a sales-person or a customer. Depending on your business, select a sample of 5–10 of these, and review the actual prices charged over the last 12 months. Then try to establish the costs associated with each sale and, thus, the true profitability.

Which items are profitable?

Which items need to be improved?

What controls can you put in place to ensure price erosion does not occur in the future?

What training does your team need to help them implement a new pricing approach?

Expert view: Speciality food ingredients

For reasons of conflict of interest, organisations do not usually like to 'lift up the hood' on their pricing and negotiation practices. This case example is based on a real organisation selling food additives (FoodCo) and their approach to price defence.

The food sector has some notoriously tough negotiators in it, especially those in retail who deal with many suppliers and where margins are critical. Therefore, pressure on prices in the food supply chain is ever-present.

Foodco has a number of specialist products with unique value propositions, where it should be possible to defend margins against discount demands from buyers. However, the sales team did not feel confident in these tough negotiations to defend their prices.

The company instigated a phased training programme for its sales force that covered the following critical areas in B2B selling:

- Understanding customer needs and pain points
- Selling the value of Foodco's solutions
- Mapping the power relationships
- Understanding the procurement mindset
- Preparing for negotiations with a matrix
- Practicing the 'proud of price' attitude
- Practicing negotiation

The training was scheduled to be just ahead of the annual price rise discussion. The response of the sales team was very positive. Armed with a real understanding of the true power they had, they felt much more comfortable saying no to requests for discounts, substantially improving margins and profits as a result.

They reported that doing the research and preparation well before the negotiation helped them have conviction and clarity in the heat of negotiations, thus demonstrating that "*The most common way people give up their power is by thinking they don't have any*" (Alice Walker).

Notes

1 K. Holt *Differentiation strategy* Routledge 2022
2 M. Davies *Infinite value* Bloomsbury 2017
3 M. Porter "The five competitive forces that shape strategy" *Harvard Business Review* 2008
4 K. Holt p16 Routledge 2022
5 M. Davies p91 Bloomsbury 2017
6 E. Almquist et al "The elements of value" *Harvard Business Review* 2018
7 F. Buttle & S. Maklan *Customer relationship management* p160 Routledge 2015
8 S. Kelly et al *Value-ology* p30 Palgrave Macmillan 2017
9 P. Kotler et al "Ending the war between sales and marketing" *Harvard Business Review* July 2008
10 N. Furr & K. O'Keefe "The hybrid start-up" *Harvard Business Review* March 2023
11 M. Leslie & C. Holloway "The sales learning curve" *Harvard Business Review* July 2006
12 P. Hill *Pricing for profit* p19 Kogan Page 2013
13 S. Dudley & T. Bryant *Relentless* p164 Behavioural Science Research Press 2020
14 P. Hill p157 Kogan Page 2013
15 C. Homburg et al *Sales excellence* p63 Springer 2012
16 P. Hill p48 Kogan Page 2013
17 Ibid
18 C. Homburg et al p65 Springer 2012
19 P. Hill p93 Kogan Page 2013
20 N. Arbel *Data-driven sales* p10 Clearbit 2018
21 D. Chaffey & F. Ellis-Chadwick *Digital marketing* p203 Pearson 2019
22 Ibid
23 Ibid
24 Ibid
25 R. Mohammed "Expand your pricing paradigm" *Harvard Business Review* Jan 2023
26 Ibid
27 R. Mohammed "The good-better-best approach to pricing" *Harvard Business Review* Sep 2018
28 Ibid., p111
29 D. Kahneman *Thinking, fast and slow* p119 Penguin 2011
30 N. Nahai *Webs of influence* p166 Pearson 2017
31 P. Hill p182 Kogan Page 2013
32 Ibid., p79
33 N. Nahai p168 Pearson 2017
34 C. Homburg et al p65 Springer 2012
35 Ibid., p68
36 A. Waytz *Beware a culture of busyness* p58 March 2023
37 D. Woodburn & M. McDonald *Key account management* p140 Wiley 2013
38 A. Cox *Supply chains, markets and power: Mapping buyer and supplier power regimes* Routledge 2001
39 D. Woodburn & M. McDonald p141 Wiley 2013
40 N. Lee & T. Riesterer "When challenging the customer backfires" *The International Journal of Sales Transformation* (May 17), 36–39

Chapter 8

Sales organisation structures

What structure is most appropriate for your sales approach and stage of growth?

A tricky challenge

Settling on which sales structure to implement is a notoriously difficult decision for any business. For start-ups and Small and medium enterprises (SMEs), this challenge is often magnified because:

- The first hire may be a significant financial stretch for self-funded start-ups.
- The HR issues involved (hiring, role changes, restructuring).
- Unclear advice on what the sales roles should be.
- The difficulties in actually transitioning from one structure to another.
- Founders have no sales background/experience.

Getting beyond the 'solopreneur' stage can be tough, and a common question asked by start-up founders is "*What type of salesperson should be our first hire?*". Personally, I have seen that founders often believe that if they hire a *cold caller*, it will solve all their sales problems, as if there is a cadre of sales magicians out there that can compensate for all the sales inadequacies in a start-up.

How then to move forward? Growth will clearly be severely limited if start-ups and SMEs cannot break through the hiring challenge. To answer this question, let's first look at the signals that tell us it's time for a change.

Growing pains

Many organisations experience *growing pains*. Larry Greiner established that they typically go through similar challenges on their growth journey. In his seminal work *Evolution and Revolution as Organisations Grow*,[1] he identified five 'crises' on the journey as an organisation gets bigger:

1 A crisis of leadership (who will lead us out of the start-up challenges?)
2 A crisis of autonomy (how do the leaders delegate key tasks effectively?)
3 A crisis of control (how does a growing organisation coordinate all the departments?)
4 A crisis of red tape (how to deal with the frustration created by control?)
5 A crisis of the unknown (what will be the next challenge?)

Greiner believed that revolutions were needed at each stage for organisations to move forward. These crisis points often involve restructuring to address them.

DOI: 10.4324/9781003449614-8

Grenier's initial concept has been built on over time and applied to the start-up and SME contexts. As mentioned in chapter 3, Jeffery Rayport and his colleagues identified "3 stages of venture growth"[2]:

- Exploration (finding a product-market fit)
- Extrapolation (finding a profit-market fit)
- Exploitation (fine-tuning its business model and competitive advantage)

Their experience in working with new ventures is that finding a *profit-market fit* is one of the distinguishing features of successful start-ups.[3]

What these models tell us is that if you are going to grow, you will almost certainly have to review your structure and processes so that your organisation is fit for purpose. You might end up introducing new roles or even new specialist teams to optimise your growth trajectory.

Is it your time to make a change?

Here are some signs that you might need to address your sales organisation's structure:

- You are a solopreneur, and your growth has flatlined.
- You want to rapidly scale your organisation.
- Your go-to-market approach has changed.
- You have capacity issues in meeting sales/customer demands.
- Profitability is not where you want it to be.
- Customer dissatisfaction because of lack of access to your team.
- High attrition rates in certain sales roles
- Salespeople spend too much time on non-value-added activities.
- Coaching and training are not getting done.
- Recurrent conflict between team roles.

If some of the points on this list resonate with you, then it's probably time to review your structure. This chapter will introduce a decision-making process to help you do that and include some examples of typical structures start-ups use to get off the ground. Firstly, let's consider some of the key issues concerning sales structures.

Structure follows strategy

Alfred Chandler's famous quote has already been mentioned in the context of building a scalable organisation. If we have a sales strategy as outlined in Chapter 2, then we can figure out what structure will best enable its execution.

The sales strategy effectively tells us the *work to be done*. If we know that, we can decide who is best placed to do the work and what skills they will need. Sales management expert, Javier Marcos Cuevas, expresses this as "Organisations should be designed according to processes and activities rather than people. The raison d'etre of organisations is to perform tasks, not to accommodate people."[4]

A common objection to this approach that does need to be addressed right away is, "What do I do about my existing team?". Very few people are in the luxury position that they can sack all their current team and start again (neither would most people want to).

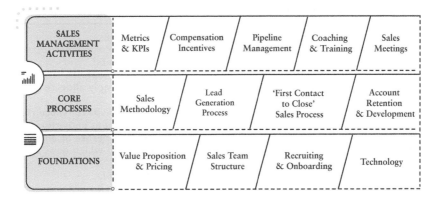

Figure 8.1 The elements of a scalable sales organisation

Of course, some or all of your current team will feature in the new structure. If we start with the *ideal scenario* first, then we can take pragmatic decisions about the current team with that vision in mind.

Figure 8.1 serves to remind us of the foundations, core processes and activities that you might consider in deciding the *work to be done*.

In some ways, organisational design in sales is analogous to figuring out what the best roles and responsibilities would be to assemble a car on a production line. We need to decide who does what, where the handovers should be, and ultimately how many people we need to meet our throughput target.

The key structural decisions to be made

Table 8.1 shows some of the key questions you could work through to design your sales organisation.

To manage these choices, sales organisations have developed a wide range of specialised roles over time. Understanding these can help start-ups and SMEs evolve on their growth journeys. Table 8.2 shows some typical roles found in sales organisations today.

So, with all these choices and options, how can we decide on the best structure to adopt?

A decision-making process for organisational structures

Figure 8.2 shows the process we can use.

Let's use an example to see how it works. Table 8.3 shows a completed table using this method. In this example, an SME is considering three options for its new structure. Option 1, the TSM model, means each salesperson is responsible for finding new customers and retaining existing ones in a defined territory. Option 2 separates out these tasks, with some of the team responsible for finding new customers and the rest for account management. Option 3 is a variant of option 2, but includes a new role, *sales operations manager*, who effectively takes a lot of routine tasks and non-sales activities away from the team. The organisation has chosen four decision criteria to help make a decision. Of course, this can vary, and other decision criteria will be looked at.

Table 8.1 Key organisational design questions

Dimension	Key questions and guidance for start-ups and SMEs
Size of salesforce	How many people do we need to hit our targets? *Salesforce sizing methods are covered in this chapter.*
Temporary vs. permanent roles	Should we employ new permanent roles or simply allocate projects to the existing team? *Temporary roles are an excellent choice for start-ups to reduce costs.*
Outsourced vs. permanent staff	Should we outsource some business development activities? *Outsourcing is a great way to buy in essential expertise at an early stage.*
Personal selling vs. automation	Which activities are best done by humans, and which ones can be automated? *Chapter 12 addresses this question in more detail.*
General sales role vs. specialised roles	Should we have one role covering the whole sales process or specialise in various sections, e.g., new business representatives and account managers? *Highly standardised sales processes often benefit from role specialisation.*
Sales and delivery vs. split roles	For service organisations, should salespeople deliver what they sell, or sell for others to deliver? *Combined roles tend to increase customer satisfaction but reduce growth.*
Technical sales rep vs. split roles	Should we employ people who have deep technical knowledge and train them to sell, or employ salespeople and back them up with a technical support team? *Difficult to recruit technical expertise is typically best separated from sales roles*
Inside sales vs. field sales	What should be the balance between field-based and office-based roles in the team? *Customer preferences can guide your choice here, as modern buyers often prefer short virtual meetings or calls.*[5]
New business vs. customer retention and development	What should be the balance of business development and customer success roles (those responsible for helping customers get the most from your offering)? *Your growth model (Chapter 2) should provide a clear answer to this.*

Table 8.2 Typical sales roles

Role	Description
Sales development representative (SDR)	Responsible for 'opening the door' to new prospects and qualifying needs before passing onto an account manager.
Account manager (AE)	Takes leads from an SDR, closes the deal, and typically hands over to a CSM (see below).
Territory sales manager (TSM)	A TSM has a growth target for a region and autonomy about how to achieve it. The role includes winning new customers and retaining existing ones.
Key account manager (KAM)	Coordinates internal roles to manage a small number of critical large accounts.
Technical sales representative (TSR)	A TSM with specialist technical knowledge. Can be responsible for delivering billable service too.
Customer success manager (CSM)	Responsible for ensuring customers get the most from products and services, so they renew contracts, and become advocates for your organisation.
Technical support or 'pre-sales'	A customer-facing role who works with prospects and customers under the guidance of a sales representative. It is useful where very specialist technical knowledge is required.

(Continued)

Table 8.2 (Continued)

Role	Description
Customer service	A role focusing on dealing with customer enquiries, orders, invoices, and other matters to ensure customer satisfaction.
Inside sales representative or 'Telesales'	Similar to an SDR, it may include the management of smaller accounts by telephone to save field visits.
Channel/distribution manager	Responsible for managing distributors or channel partners by providing training, resources and targets.
Merchandiser	Where sales are done through a distributor/partner, this role helps with point-of-sale materials or on-site training.
Sales manager	This role manages a team of representatives and is responsible for the implementation of the sales strategy.
Sales trainer	This role provides training in product knowledge and selling skills.
Sales operations manager	This role/function removes 'non-sales' activities from salespeople to increase their focus on selling. It may include the production of quotes, proposals and booking appointments. Often looks after CRM and the sales tech stack.
Sales enablement manager	This specialist role coordinates marketing and sales dictates to the sales team so they receive the right content, coaching and training at the right time. Avoids information/initiative overload.
Sales academy manager	This is a learning and development specialist, typically in place where an organisation has a lot of standardised training to deliver. A variant of the sales enablement role.
Sales director or VP sales	All sales roles ultimately report to the sales director, where there is a separate marketing director/VP of marketing.
Chief revenue officer	All sales and marketing roles report to the 'CRO'.

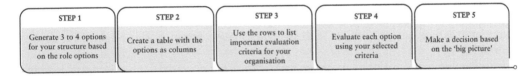

STEP 1	STEP 2	STEP 3	STEP 4	STEP 5
Generate 3 to 4 options for your structure based on the role options	Create a table with the options as columns	Use the rows to list important evaluation criteria for your organisation	Evaluate each option using your selected criteria	Make a decision based on the 'big picture'

Figure 8.2 A decision-making process

Table 8.3 Example structure evaluation table

Criteria	Option 1 TSM only	Option 2 Hunters and farmers	Option 3 Hunters, farmers and sales operations
Cost	Comparable to existing costs	+£100k per annum for new hunter role	+£150k for new roles
Hand-offs	Best option as no hand off	Need to agree process and change targets/commissions	As option 2, but sales ops can assist with the process of making it smoother
Recruitment	As today	Could be difficult to find credible industry hunters	Existing team member for sales ops role. Need to recruit 2 x hunters
Transition	Minor, easily managed	Will need HR support + new role descriptions and territory changes, salary evaluation, etc.	As option 2 Sales ops expected to be relatively easy to set up

Note that the table does not generate 'one right answer' necessarily, but what it does do is:

- Make the options clear.
- Provide an objective evaluation of each option using pre-selected, logical criteria.

By restricting the number of choices and using clear decision-making criteria, typically taking a decision is easier.

What decision criteria can be used to decide on structure?

In the example above, *cost, hand-offs, ability to recruit* and *transition practicalities* are used to evaluate the choices. A fuller list of areas to consider follows:

Cost and potential revenues: Clearly, one of the biggest barriers you are likely to face is the cost of your new structure. This should be offset against the potential revenues you expect to achieve.

Conflicts and silos: Your new design should try to avoid inadvertently creating conflicts by building silos, cliques or other dysfunctional arrangements.

Recruitment The ability to find the roles you would like in your new organisation might be an important point, especially if you require highly technical roles. Recruitment is covered in Chapter 16.

Hand-offs If you decide to specialise by role, for example, having new business acquisition roles that handover to account executives, then this means managing handovers. Is this feasible for your product and service?

Fit with your sales process It goes without saying that your chosen structure should enable your sales process effectively. Highly standardised sales processes lend themselves to specialised, discrete roles, a trend strongly evident in technology sales that typically have SDRs, AEs and CSMs to cover the end-to-end sales process.

Job design The range of activities that are specified in a role will affect the level of motivation people experience in fulfilling it. If the role is very repetitive, this might drive up staff attrition.

Training implications Often, a change in structure will necessitate training and education. How feasible is this?

Practicalities of transition It's one thing to design the perfect structure and another thing to actually make it happen. While it is more or less inevitable that some short-term pain will be experienced in transitioning, the realities of doing it are important to think through, for example, the effect on customers.

HR and legal Restructuring often involves careful attention to employment legislation, whether we change job roles and responsibilities or go for a full restructure.

Development track Start-ups often get sales work done with interns, new graduates and relatively junior roles to save cost. Organisational structures can be designed with progression in mind, e.g., a TSM can become a KAM if they flourish in the basic sales role.

The sizing decision

A vital issue that just about all sales organisations must deal with is: how many people are needed? Good salespeople do not come cheap, so this is an important question to ask, especially for start-ups that might not have deep pockets for recruitment.

There are potentially three commonly used methods[6] to estimate the size of the salesforce you will need. They are:

- The breakdown method
- The build-up method
- The incremental method

The breakdown method

The underlying assumption in the *breakdown method* is that each salesperson can deliver a certain amount of revenue. If you have a salesperson today who is managing $500k of sales, then if you want to deliver $2.5 million in your budget, you will need five salespeople.

This is a quick, simple method, but it has limitations. Firstly, there might not be the same sales potential in the customer base that each salesperson is allocated. Secondly, humans are not robots, and so each salesperson is likely to actually deliver different results according to their skills and motivations.

The build-up method

This works by estimating the actual workload required to achieve your sales strategy. For example, if you set targets for each salesperson to retain 20 accounts and find ten new ones, you can make a best guess at the amount of time it takes to do this, e.g.,

Time taken to manage and retain 20 accounts

An analysis of your call history shows that typically one visit per month is needed for each account, which involves:
2 hours' meetings
2 hours' travel
1 hour' admin
Therefore, total time invested = 100 hours/month or 1,200 hours per year (150 days per year, based on an 8-hour day).

Time taken to find and win ten new accounts

Your CRM history shows it typically takes five sales calls to win a new account, involving:
5 hours' meetings
10 hours' preparation, calls and emails per new account
2 hours' travel per account
Total = 17 hours per account, or 170 hours/year (21 days per year)

Servicing the ten new accounts

Based on closing them sequentially through the year, this will add:
30 hours/month
Total = 360 hours per year (45 days per year)

Other activities, such as internal meetings, training and holidays, are added to at the total workload. In this worked example, the sales representative would be expected to spend 216 days on selling activities per year. Allowing 46 working weeks per year (230 days – after weekends and holidays are taken out), this sales representative would have 14 days spare for internal meetings and training each year.

Calculations like this are notoriously controversial, as they are built on 'average, typical' customer management scenarios, which rarely materialise. Nonetheless, they can be a useful input into your decision-making.

The incremental method

If we had a fountain of cash, would employing more and more salespeople generate more sales and profit? The incremental method says NO! There is typically a finite number of customers in a market, and therefore your overall potential is limited by other factors than the size of your sales team.

The point at which the cost of the extra salespeople equals the expected profit that is generated by them is the optimum number. For a more detailed worked example of this method, I recommend *Sales Force Management* by Mark Johnston and Greg Marshall.

There is also a fourth strategy for salesforce sizing, which is sometimes justified. Where an organisation wants to quickly capture market share to become the dominant player in a sector, it might decide to invest in capacity ahead of demand to lock in long-term profits. Where you have a fantastic new product and growth funding in place, this strategy has been shown to be more successful than start-ups that tried to *earn their way* to market share.[7]

Start-up sales force structure examples

In practice, every start-up and SME must find their own unique route to growth, through a variety of innovative structures. Great entrepreneurs are masters at bringing disparate expertise together in service of their cause.

Figures 8.3–8.5 show some common models used by start-ups to 'get off the ground'.

You can, of course, imagine many variants and adaptations of these models that would better suit your own unique context.

Your growth model is your *north star* here, because it should spell out very clearly the *work to be done*. As an example, in the SaaS business, customer retention is absolutely key to growth. Aaron Ross and Jason Lemkin recommend that a customer success role is a "single-digit hire", in other words, one of the first ten hires.[8]

Similarly, if your growth model means the acquisition of many new customers, then your structure would likely be a balance of marketing expertise (focusing on inbound leads) and sales development representatives (focusing on outbound leads). Trish Bertuzzi's research showed that organisations below $10m typically get 41% of leads from marketing, while organisations of $250m+ only get 29% via this route,[9] so the balance can shift on the growth journey.

Managing the transition

Having arrived at a decision on the 'ideal structure' to execute your sales strategy, you then have the practical reality of transitioning to it with your existing team. This process may

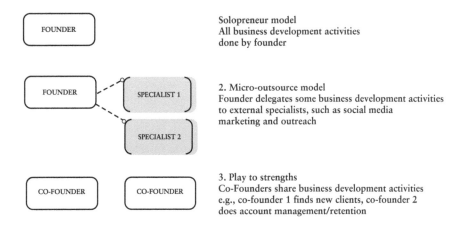

Solopreneur model
All business development activities
done by founder

2. Micro-outsource model
Founder delegates some business development activities
to external specialists, such as social media
marketing and outreach

3. Play to strengths
Co-Founders share business development activities
e.g., co-founder 1 finds new clients, co-founder 2
does account management/retention

Figure 8.3 Alternative structures

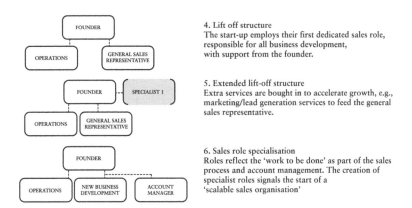

4. Lift off structure
The start-up employs their first dedicated sales role,
responsible for all business development,
with support from the founder.

5. Extended lift-off structure
Extra services are bought in to accelerate growth, e.g.,
marketing/lead generation services to feed the general
sales representative.

6. Sales role specialisation
Roles reflect the 'work to be done' as part of the sales
process and account management. The creation of
specialist roles signals the start of a
'scalable sales organisation'

Figure 8.4 Alternative structures

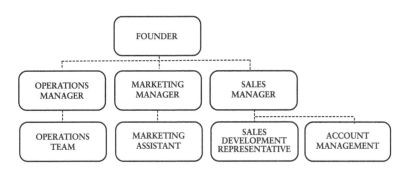

8. SME Foundation structure
Most services are in-house, delivered by dedicated roles, with line management
in place to co-ordinate activities, and provide coaching/support for front-line staff

Figure 8.5 Alternative structures

involve compromising on the ideal of working with the staff you actually have available/can likely recruit. Carrying out a restructure is a book in itself, but at the highest level, here are some guidelines for managing the transition:

Ensure you follow the correct legal process for your territory: For example, by putting the team on notice that there will be a restructure, they will be required to apply for roles in the new structure or suggest an alternative, acceptable arrangement. Start-ups and SMEs are advised to seek specialist HR help from an external consultant agency to avoid problematic legal missteps.

Take great care with change communication: Sell the problem of the current structure and set out the 'why' behind the new structure. Explain and plan how the transition will be managed with minimal disruption. Excite people with the aspirational view of the new structure and the opportunities it brings. Plan for quick wins and share success.

Prepare detailed job descriptions: The discipline of preparing job descriptions for each role in your new structure ensures no tasks get missed and that everyone is clear on their responsibilities.

Make the change swiftly. Long-drawn-out changes sap motivation and create rumours of other restructuring/negative changes.

Treat the team with dignity: If your restructure means losing some team members, make sure they are treated well and get career counselling/support if possible.

Summary

Renowned management guru Peter Drucker said, "Good organisation structure does not by itself produce good performance, but a poor organisation structure makes good performance impossible".[10] Like a butterfly emerging from a caterpillar, if SMEs and start-ups do not regularly review their structures, then growth is likely to be restrained. At the same time, senseless restructures rarely fuel growth!

Into action

Take a moment to reflect. Are you experiencing any of the challenges listed that signal it's time for a change?

- You are a solopreneur, and your growth has flatlined.
- You want to rapidly scale your organisation.
- Your go-to-market approach has changed.
- You have capacity issues in meeting sales/customer demands.
- Profitability is not where you want it to be.
- Customer dissatisfaction because of a lack of access to your team.
- High attrition rates in certain sales roles.
- Salespeople spend too much time on non-value-added activities.
- Coaching and training are not getting done.
- Recurrent conflict between team roles.

If you are, then use the decision-making process outlined in this chapter:

1 Generate three to four options for how your structure could look (Don't forget part-time roles, outsourcing, and the variety of sales roles that now exist).
2 Make a list of three to six decision-making criteria (e.g., cost, fit with the sales process, growth potential, possibility of recruiting).
3 Evaluate each option against the criteria, adding the text to a table.
4 Discuss the options with someone who knows your company well to help you make a decision.
5 When you've decided on the best option, figure out how you could move towards it based on your current situation. Don't forget to take care of the HR and change factors.

Expert view: Transformational growth at OEE

OEE Consulting, now part of Concentrix/Webhelp and rebranded as Gobeyond Partners, enjoys an excellent reputation as a high-quality operational excellence/customer journey transformation consulting firm. It built its reputation by focusing on improving service delivery and customer satisfaction at major UK blue-chip companies, including RBS, Willis, Lloyds Bank and P&O Ferries.

The organisation went through a period of rapid growth, overseen by its MD, Mark Palmer. When he took over the helm in 2008, the business turned over £4.9 million. By 2023, under his tenure, it had grown to £33 million. To achieve growth on that scale, it involved major changes to the way the team was structured. Mark explains his philosophy for growing the business.

How would you describe the structure when you arrived?

The structure was haphazard. We had probably 25 clients. And one of them dominated 50% of the revenues (British Nuclear Fuel). Many people were involved in the largest client and at least three of the main directors.

We also had a few financial services clients, with probably just as many directors involved in each account. So, there was no real clarity in terms of what we were doing with each client and how we were going to grow them. We didn't understand what the client's problems were or how, therefore, our capabilities could be positioned to solve their business problems.

There was a lot of positivity when a lead came in, and we'd all burn the midnight oil and work as a team in a very open way. Very often, we would win work because we were innovative and because we could turn things around very quickly and competitively. But there were no repeatable processes or content that we could reuse. We were starting from scratch every time, coming back to answer the same questions in terms of who we were, what we did, and our standard price. All those questions needed to be asked every time we were responding to an RFP.

So how did you change the structure to make it more effective?

I was fortunate because I'd worked for a large French corporate where the disciplines of key account management were inculcated in me. The first initiative that I introduced was to agree on a single point of accountability for each account. This guarantees you're going to give the same price to a client because the price is agreed by the same person each time.

I also wrote down simple things, for example, what the responsibilities of the key account director were. We introduced a strategic account management planning process that takes you through the critical areas: Key people in our orbit performed a basic SWOT analysis of what the challenges were that a client was going through, which forced us to define our capabilities in terms of client needs, which led to a much better framing of our products, services, and capabilities back to the client.

The key account is also about ownership. It's all about having clear accountability. So, one person did all the contracting, the payment terms, the solutioning, the project oversight with project managers functionally working for them, the cash collection and revenue generation going forward. This end-to-end accountability meant there was no internal blaming. As an account director, you were responsible for all of it.

What other principles would you say were important in helping you really grow as a business once you've got the key account structure right?

I would say don't get bogged down with "bogs and drains" stuff like car parking, ERP systems and kitchen designs. It's much better to keep a laser focus on markets, cash and developing people's skills. I'd been encouraged by people to have a finance, HR, IT, and sales function, but I wasn't convinced that it would work at OEE. I really wanted the markets, sectors, and clients to be front of mind, so I made sure the top table roles were those people who were looking after the key accounts and when we were large enough, the sector MDs.

It was essential that we were all customer-focused and essentially got up every morning worrying about the financial markets, the broader economy and what columnists were saying about our clients, so we could see what was happening and react rapidly. The client had to be the hero of our narrative. We had to be thinking about their problems rather than worrying about whether we had the best business card or financial accounting system.

It meant we had eight or nine people who were all really thinking in the same way and worrying about the same things, but also learning. For example, if we were doing a project with Lloyds Bank, would there be valuable learnings for RBS or Deutsche Bank?

Clearly, growth on the levels you achieved meant a lot of structural changes for the team. How did you help them personally transition?

Firstly, I think it's true to say that not all the people we started off with made it through the major growth phase. Around 50% made it, and 50% didn't.

Secondly, we took a lot of trouble to write things down in a collaborative way, to explain what we were looking for. The business had a numerical engineering legacy, which meant very bright people had been hired who were good at modelling and capacity planning.

They saw themselves as specialist consultants who were good at solving complex problems. But it didn't mean that we should give up on them, because some of them could adapt and develop into leaders.

For example, I'm pleased to say that one of our original specialists, Simon, is now a sector MD. His sector turns over £6 million in revenues on its own. He is a great example of somebody who went through that journey.

We spent long evenings setting out the vision and explaining the 'why'. We explained why it was important to adopt new working practices and new ways of thinking, writing down and sharing what we needed.

We understood very quickly that attitude was more important than deep technical ability. We had enough deep technical ability. And 90% of the problems that we faced didn't require deep technical ability only 10% did. So over time, our recruitment processes reinforced the behavioural sets, which made it progressively easier to coach the next generation.

If there's anything I would come back to, it's recording, sharing and documenting how you want to work and where you want to be. It enables you to manage the changes, coach around them, and stay on course over the long term. Values and vision always beat targets and processes.

Notes

1 L. Greiner "Evolution and revolution as organisations grow" *Harvard Business Review* May 1998

2 J. Rayport et al. "The overlooked key to a successful scale-up" *Harvard Business Review* Jan 2023

3 Ibid., p59

4 J. Marcos Cuevas et al *Sales management* 4th ed p49 Palgrave 2016

5 P. Thaichon et al "Hybrid sales structures in the age of e-commerce" *Journal of Personal Selling and Sales Management* p297, vol. 38 (2018)

6 M. Johnston & G. Marshall *Sales force management* 13th ed p157 Routledge 2021

7 A. Zoltners et al "Match your sales force structure to your business life cycle" p3 *Harvard Business Review* July 2006

8 A. Ross & J. Lemkin *From impossible to inevitable* p53 Wiley 2016

9 T. Bertuzzi *The sales development playbook* p35 T. Bertuzzi 2016

10 Quoted in J. Marcos Cuevas et al 4th ed p48 Palgrave 2016

Chapter 9

The work of sales managers in start-ups and SMEs

How do effective sales managers spend their time?

What do good sales managers do?

So far, we have looked at building:

- A sales strategy
- A growth model
- A sales methodology
- A team structure to 'get the work done'

These building blocks set a clear plan for growth and make your specific way of selling visible. This work is essential to building a scalable sales organisation. Not much will happen, though, unless we actively manage sales. So, what does good sales management look like?

This will, of course, depend on how much time you can give it. Start-up founders often juggle many balls at once and cannot realistically dedicate 100% of their time to this activity. Nonetheless, an understanding of the core principles will help founders make an informed choice about what to prioritise and what routines they can drop without too much detriment.

For full-time sales managers of Small and medium enterprises (SMEs) this chapter will help you reflect on your own routines to see if they can be enhanced.

Research published in the Journal of Personal Selling and Sales Management identified 14 key skills needed for sales managers[1]:

1 Understands general trends in the industry
2 Understands the overall strategy of the organisation
3 Make decisions consistent with the company's strategy
4 Provides effective verbal feedback
5 Role model for the sales force
6 Designs and builds effective teams
7 Creates a supportive team environment
8 Manages team dynamics
9 Understand the importance of new tech
10 Implements sales force automation
11 Implements customer relationship management (CRM)
12 Sensitivity to cultural issues
13 Understands global selling programmes
14 Understands salesperson evaluation metrics

DOI: 10.4324/9781003449614-9

The study shows the broad range of activities sales managers can get involved with and therefore, why it is understandable that start-ups and SMEs can get baffled by what good sales management looks like!

To help narrow our focus, a study in 2019 found that the most important activities carried out by sales managers that were perceived to enable sales performance fell into four key categories[2]:

- Coaching (helping salespeople perform)
- Collaborating (bringing the sales team together to solve problems)
- Championing (influencing internally to help salespeople sell)
- Customer-engaging (building relationships and helping the sales team progress deals)

These four categories serve as a good classification system to practically demonstrate routines that you can implement in your business to help drive growth.

Coaching

Why is coaching one of the four essential activities for a sales manager? As a manager/founder, you are responsible not just for your own 8–10 hours per working day but for the combined hourly input of all your team. Sales is a lonely profession, where much of the work done by your team is not visible to you. For this reason, having motivated, competent, consistent sellers doing great work every day in your team will very clearly influence their overall output. And there is no output more visible than a sales target!

As far back as 1998, sales coaching was already well-established. "Sales coaching has long been cited by sales professionals as a critically important means used by sales managers to enhance the performance of their salespeople".[3] Research by the Bain organisation has found that "top performing reps have more frequent and higher quality interactions with their managers, such as one-on-one sessions and weekly pipeline reviews".[4]

Coaching is not just for large organisations. Research carried out by Michael Sweeney[5] found that those SMEs who carry out sales coaching have cited the following benefits:

- More engagement
- Higher motivation
- More self-awareness
- Better staff retention
- Less sick time
- Higher morale
- More productivity

So, what does good coaching look like? Without getting into the debate of what exactly is or isn't coaching, under this broad umbrella, there are several types of coaching that effective sales managers regularly use:

- Pipeline coaching
- Deal coaching
- Coaching skills and behaviours
- Data-driven/AI coaching
- Peer coaching

Each of these will be examined in turn.

Pipeline coaching Often done weekly, the objective of this conversation is to help your team stay on top of the opportunities they have today and the ones they should develop for tomorrow. It will be covered in greater depth in Chapter 11.

Deal coaching is done on individual opportunities to help salespeople overcome obstacles and advance opportunities through the pipeline. Combined with pipeline coaching, this activity is a very important driver of results.[6] Sales enablement gurus Bryon Matthews and Tamara Schenk believe this activity has the most impact on early-stage deals because if sales managers wait until opportunities are advanced, then most of the focus is on pricing/discounts.[7] Increasingly, technology and AI solutions are becoming available for this, and they will be covered in more detail in Chapter 12.[8]

Coaching skills and behaviours is where the focus is on your sales teams' habits, routines, attitudes and behaviours to help them be more effective overall. This is often done when a sales manager attends a joint sales call with a customer (face to face or virtual) led by the sales representative. The objective is to observe the salesperson in action, help them understand their strengths and areas for development, and ultimately increase performance.

Many larger organisations mandate this activity, and if done well, it can be highly effective on a number of levels. Firstly, "We are the experts of our intentions, while others are the experts of our behaviour". In other words, we are often blind to our behaviour, and an observer can hold a useful mirror up to us.

Secondly, focusing on development is known to build engagement. Research done by Marcus Buckingham and Ashley Goodall, presented in the Harvard Business Review, identified "In my work, I am always challenged to grow" as one of eight critical dimensions that drives engagement.[9]

So, what types of coaching behaviours drive results? Carlin Nguyen and his colleagues at California State University[10] have created an effective coaching scale that identifies three specific areas of sales coaching that drive performance. These are shown in Table 9.1, with some examples of each.

In practical terms, there are three key touch points during joint sales calls where you can have a high impact using these approaches, as shown in Table 9.2.

How often do we need to do coaching like this? A good rule of thumb used by many larger organisations is a *minimum of one joint sales call coaching meeting per month per team member*. If you are a full-time manager of a sales team, then you are probably used to

Table 9.1 Key areas of sales coaching

Adaptability	Involvement	Rapport
My manager adapts his coaching style to my needs and preferences. My manager understands that each salesperson is different, having varying strengths and weaknesses.	My manager observes me as I sell to clients. My manager brings to my attention how I can perform better as a salesperson.	My manager understands me on a personal level. I can tell my manager anything.

Table 9.2 Key touchpoints for sales coaching

Touchpoint	Typical activities	Outcome
Before a joint sales call	Customer Research. Setting a *commitment objective* (see Chapter 4). Prepare how to lead the sales call. Anticipate and prepare for objections. Organise any demos and documents. Agree roles during the meeting.	Your sales team gets the message that 'preparation = 90% success'. You both understand the commitment you are looking for and the plan to achieve it. You can show commitment and credibility to the customer.
During the call	Let the salesperson lead while you observe. Take your turn when it adds value. *Show how*, if appropriate, to help your salesperson learn.	You have concrete, observed feedback to give to your salesperson.
After the sales call	Do an 'after action review': *"What do you think you did well?"* *"What could you improve?"* Give your feedback: *"I think you did X really well."* *"I think you can improve Y, by doing Z."* Complete follow-up actions from the customer meeting. Enter key information into your CRM/other sales technology.	The sales team builds confidence upon hearing their strong points and is motivated to improve based on their areas for development. The importance of *doing what you say you will do* is reinforced. You are a role model for CRM usage.

ride-along days, where you spend a whole day with each member of your sales team during the month, doing several sales calls. Although this can be hard to fit in, alongside the many other responsibilities sales managers have, it really is a strong driver of performance.

Where you have new salespeople joining your organisation, bring them along to sales meetings with your best salespeople so they can see good sales in action as quickly as possible. The craft of selling needs to be learned on the job, and by progressively handing over more of the sales call to manage, your new team members will grow in confidence and competence.

Data-driven/AI coaching: Increasingly, the technology exists to give objective feedback to salespeople based on multiple data sources. These could be your team's use of CRM, response time to leads, conversion rates, use of content and so on. SAP has been using this approach for a while to guide its sales team[11] by sending them a monthly report of these key metrics that forms the basis for a coaching discussion.

A fascinating study by Irene Nahm and her colleagues showed how AI can be used to identify 'hot streaks', that is, runs of high performance in individual sales reps. The team also experimented with ways to improve the efficiency of the call centre by prompting breaks when sales reps experienced 'cold streaks'.[12] The use of technology to support sales organisations will be covered in more depth in Chapter 12.

Peer coaching: Salespeople can learn a lot from each other. If you are a busy sales managers or founder, putting experienced salespeople together with new hires for joint sales calls is an excellent way to upskill them in a time-efficient way.

In summary, good sales managers use a variety of coaching mechanisms to ensure that everyone in the team is continually stretched and helped to improve.

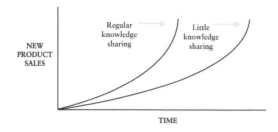

Figure 9.1 The sales learning curve

Collaborating

When many salespeople essentially operate individually, why is collaboration an essential sales enabler? Firstly, in their article *The Hidden Power of Teams*, Marcus Buckingham and Ashley Goodall found that doing work as part of a team was the biggest single predictor of employee engagement.[13] Even if salespeople don't *need* to work together, working together helps motivation considerably.

Secondly, sales teams face a number of challenges, and these are often easier to overcome with a group. For example, aggressive competitor moves, objections, price pressure and difficulty finding new leads. Collaboration increases learning, and faster learning translates into better sales. A good example of this is during a B2B product launch. Despite the very best research and planning, until sales conversations actually take place, no one really knows how best to sell a product. The sales learning curve shown in Figure 9.1[14] shows how increased knowledge sharing can increase the growth in sales of new products.

Since many start-ups are essentially testing a new approach to the market, accelerating the sales learning curve can be very important. You can do this by regularly bringing the sales team together (virtually or in-person) to:

- Share successful sales moments.
- Share challenges and obstacles to overcome.
- Ideate ways to overcome challenges.
- Involve technical and marketing specialists to help solve front-line issues.

A third benefit of bringing people together, sometimes more difficult to quantify, is that with social activities, sales meetings can be good fun, and teams often value this.

Many organisations have routines based on regular sales team meetings. How often should you bring the team together, and with what agenda? Table 9.3 shows some typical formats that are used. Pipeline review meetings will be covered in more detail in Chapter 11.

Championing

Numerous studies have shown that salespeople very easily get taken away from their core job of selling. Oracle's 2015 whitepaper quotes Accenture's research, finding that as much as 2/3 of salespeople's time is spent on *non-sales* activity.[15] Good sales managers identify time-wasting activities and lobby internally to change them. Karen Peesker and her colleagues found that good sales managers act to protect their team from internal requests that steer them away from their core work.[16]

Table 9.3 Types of sales meeting

Meeting type	Frequency and format	Notes
Pipeline review	Weekly Virtual or stand-up	Focus on key activities in the next week to progress opportunities. Experts are present if needed. Coaching approach is short and efficient.
All-hands meeting	Quarterly In-person or face to face	To update the sales team on organisational changes and connect to a wider organisation.
Knowledge sharing	Event-driven (e.g., product launch, target-setting, external shocks) In-person or face to face	To set up and progress projects outside of core sales work.
Team building	Bi-annual or part of quarterlies Ideally in-person	To help the sales team feel connected and part of a supportive team.

There may be many areas where you want change, including the commission scheme, the structure, training, technology, and so on. Your ability to sell the need for change, put forward a good case, and manage internal influence and politics is a very useful set of skills to enable your team to sell.

A *gold standard* objective for a sales leader is to build an organisation that can deliver sustainable, predictable revenue and profit growth without them having to be 'in the action' at all times. Championing plays a role in creating this by thinking like an architect, where the mission is to build a high-performing sales organisation.

Customer engaging

One of the biggest traps that new sales managers fall into is that of becoming a *super-rep*. Many sales managers are recruited from a sales background because they over-achieved on their targets, not because they were excellent managers. This can result in them investing too much time in front-line selling (frequently bringing big deals over the line) and not enough time in managing people. On the other hand, good sales leaders can really help their team with intelligent customer engagement. You can do this as a founder/leader in several ways:

- Using your network to 'open doors' for your sales team
- Top-to-top meetings with your customers to understand their needs in more depth
- Being assertive with customers regarding pricing and service scope
- Making things happen inside your own organisation to support salespeople's customer-centric work

Beware of the trap that senior managers can fall into for joint sales calls: being a *loose cannon*. This term was coined[17] for CEOs who turn up to visit customers, make false promises, and fail to deliver revenue growth or improvement in relationships. It is important that if you engage with customers, you also empower your sales team. A common example of this problem is when a customer requests a discount from your team, doesn't get it and then call you. If you negotiate with the customer, then guess who they will call next time. It's vital, therefore, that you make it clear that day-to-day contact is with your team, not you.

When used wisely, your contact with customers can create new opportunities and accelerate those already in the pipeline. You can *show-how* during joint sales calls and provide excellent role-model training for your team.

Of course, for start-ups and smaller SMEs, it may be that you have to look after some customers simply because of a lack of staff. That is okay, but do everything you can to delegate as much as possible so that you can free up time and, crucially, develop customer management skills in those around you. One of the biggest growth opportunities you can give anyone in sales is to hand over one of your best accounts to them and coach them to success. Poor managers sometimes hang on to the best accounts for themselves, take the glory for good sales, and berate their team for not finding any new opportunities. Maybe if they had the chance to develop the best accounts, they would stand a better chance of winning new ones!

Building your week

Having read all these options for good sales management routines, you might be forgiven for wondering how best to actually allocate your time. Table 9.4 shows a typical week for a full-time sales manager at an SME, while Table 9.5 shows a typical week for a founder, dedicated approximately one day out of five to sales management.

Table 9.4 Week in the life of a full-time sales manager

	Monday	Tuesday	Wednesday	Thursday	Friday
AM	30 min pipeline call with team Update forecast for the board Sales admin	Field coaching with rep 1	Product management meeting Marketing meeting	Field coaching with rep 3	General admin Chasing up deals and updates
PM	Travel Customer meetings	Field coaching rep 2	Work on RFPs, proposals and pricing requests Ad-hoc calls with the team	Field coaching rep 4	Internal meetings Planning/admin for the coming week

Table 9.5 Week in the life of a founder doing sales management part-time

	Monday	Tuesday	Wednesday	Thursday	Friday
AM	Pipeline call with the team Internal management team meeting	Internal meetings and development work	1:1 coaching calls with the sales team (remote) Marketing meeting	Internal work	Strategy work to develop the sales team (hiring, tech, etc.)
PM	Meeting with the CFO and CTO Internal 1:1s	External networking event Customer engaging	Attend customer meetings remotely Internal work	Internal work	Internal work

Every founder and sales leader has to find their own rhythm for the week, based on their unique circumstances. Remember, "what gets inspected gets respected", and "what you pay attention to grows". Regardless of your situation, those around you will very quickly pick up on your priorities and what is really important to you. For this reason, having regular contact moments built into your calendar where you focus on coaching, collaborating, championing and customer engagement, sends a very clear message that growth is important and also that you are willing to invest in the human dimension of sales. We must remember that a scalable sales organisation depends on engaged, competent people with clear goals and the motivation to succeed. Primarily, that will come from you and the sales management routines you put in place.

Management, leadership and culture

Let's not forget that aside from all the sales-specific activities sales managers can engage in, they also need to be good 'general' managers, meaning they can bring out the best in their teams. Personally, I have had the privilege to work alongside many very talented sales managers who are excellent at adapting the way they work with different individuals.

Many sales teams have a very broad range of people on the job for very different reasons. Some are independent sales rock stars who crush their target others are perhaps anxious and underconfident, but have a potential to be solid core performers.

Covering the principles of good management is beyond the scope of this book. There are so many inspiring and useful management books to guide us, and I am sure readers of this book have already digested quite a few. For a deeper view into leadership styles and behaviours specific to sales managers, you could start with:

Sales Excellence Dr Christian Homburg et al. (Chapter 9)

Rethinking sales management Beth Rogers (Chapter 11)

Sales management Javier Marcos Cuevas et al. (Chapter 5)

At the end of the day, you, as the sales leader, are the role model. You set the standards and the culture of the team, intentionally or by default. An excellent sales culture goes a long way towards motivating and retaining high performers, so good management skills are worth investing in. This is especially important when top sales performers get promoted. Just because they can sell well does not mean they can manage well!

Other sales management routines

There are other activities that sales leaders may get involved in, and many of these are covered in future chapters:

- Target setting and forecasting (Chapter 10)
- Hiring and onboarding (Chapter 16)
- Credit control (if not done by finance)
- Business plan and strategy (Chapter 2)
- Marketing

Given all the tasks sales managers have to complete, a core foundation skill is clearly excellent time management!

Into action

Which sales management routines do you have in place today at your SME?
  Go through the quick diagnostic below and try to address the gaps you have found.

	We don't do this	We do this sometimes	We do this consistently
Pipeline coaching			
Deal coaching			
Joint sales calls			
Training			
Development projects			
Peer coaching			
Knowledge sharing			
All-hands meeting			
Team building			
Championing improvements			
Senior management customer meetings			
Target setting			
Forecasting			

Expert view: Gareth Motley, national/regional sales manager

Gareth has built up an impressive track record of recruiting and managing high-performing sales teams for some of the biggest global brands in pharma and healthcare. SMEs and start-ups can learn a lot from this sector, as it has a history of investing heavily in good management practices.

Q1. What do you think are the really essential routines that a sales manager should instil in a sales team?

I think it's key to get started with good routines from the off, setting clear expectations and guidance for the team. That then enables people to have a good structure. Weekly and daily planning is a great start. I like them to do that on a Friday, so they've got a good working plan for Monday morning and are productive right from the start of the week.

I like to agree on regular coaching points in advance so that people know what's coming. This means there's no surprise for them, and they can plan accordingly. As a coach, it's good to see people when they feel they are at their best. That's a really, really important thing. Also, if there are challenges, you can deal with them as they arise rather than being reactive.

A mix of coaching methods makes sense. During COVID, there was quite a lot of virtual coaching, so people got used to it. Face-to-face coaching is also vital, as is freeing yourself up for short periods of time on the telephone, so you can coach people through smaller challenges as they arise.

Another routine that's practical and quick is to focus people on their in-call objectives. So, going into a sales call and asking what a good outcome looks like helps. Then post-call, asking the individual to grade the call: Did we achieve a good outcome? I use a traffic light system, red, amber or green, with red being, no, I didn't get close, amber meaning I was partway there, or green, I definitely achieved the goal. You can then begin your coaching session with both parties aligned from the start. Why do you feel that happened? What else could you have done? etc.

It makes for a quite punchy, future-focused post-call analysis, allowing you to transition quickly to key coaching points and the next call objective. It's quite a simple process, and I've found teams have responded well to this approach.

I'm currently managing a big team over a large geography, so it's challenging to be there for them all the time. I am seeking to build in self-coaching as a mindset, using the voice record function on a smartphone. Good tele-sales teams listen to their own calls all the time, and I've experienced very polished technique using this method, so I've got my sales team to trial that. They ask customers if they don't mind recording a meeting for personal training purposes, and then review the call afterwards. It can be difficult to hear yourself for the first time, but they pick up so much subtlety. Things like tone of voice, clarity of delivery as well as the use of silence within a call. I've seen marked improvement in individuals who do this.

Q2. In a lot of jobs, reps are out on the road on their own, so how do you keep people engaged with the business and not feeling too lonely?

Over the last three or four years, the engagement piece has been really key, partly because virtual working has become more routine. I think the time when you're together with individuals or teams is precious, and therefore, you've got to make the most of it.

What I've found with individuals is that it is vital to seek to understand them on a personal level. One way I like to do this is by walking and talking rather than having a traditional face to face over coffee, because some people find it easier to open up this way. I'm also seeing some nice places as a result!

I think team time is really important. It's vital that geographically distributed teams spend quality time together. Bigger companies often arrange team activities, although I am not always a fan of 'forced fun'. Time together over a nice meal in a pub, restaurant or social environment is enough because it gives people time to talk with their colleagues, something that is not always possible in big, structured corporate meetings, where people can be herded around from session to session.

Time together is also important for best practice sharing and problem solving. It's also important for reward and recognition. This can instil a spirit of competition within the team, where people strive to achieve.

The other area that boosts engagement is involvement in the strategic and operational planning side of things. This helps people's buy-in and feel some level of ownership for the direction that the organisation is going in. This is key to your connection with an organisation.

Doing personality profiles like 'Insights' or 'Myers Briggs' is useful because the team better understands themselves and how they interact with others. This is also good for working with customers. You can co-create a team charter following an exercise like this. It is useful for agreeing on how individuals in the team engage and want to be engaged and the values and behaviours they can hold each other accountable to.

On top of these activities, a lot of little things make a difference. Gestures like recognising birthdays and religious festivals, e.g., sending an Advent calendar, while not huge investments, do create engagement. People recognise that they are part of something bigger, part of a diverse team and that people are caring for and thinking of them. A very simple example in my team is that we have a 'Friday song'. We take it in turns to put a YouTube song in our WhatsApp group. Everybody hears it, and it creates a buzz. I've picked up lots of ideas from members of teams over the years that contribute to good harmony and engagement within teams.

Recognising the individuality and strengths of the people in your team and the experiences that they bring is another vital element of an engaged team. There are lots of different ways to get a good result, so don't try to fit people into a box of a certain way of selling.

The more you can spread the appreciation of each other's added value and create a culture of interdependence where they will seek each other's advice, the better the results. I've seen sales teams in the past tear each other apart because of too many similar personalities or character traits and a lack of diversity, resulting in a culture of too much internal competition. It's a careful balance.

Development plans are an important part of the sales management mix too. Some individuals may be less keen than others. For some people, it's an awkward process, while others really value the focus on their future aspirations, and it keeps them motivated. It's just about recognising the different needs within the team here.

The final thing to talk about is the darker side of sales management, where you pick up on an interpersonal or performance issue. My advice is to get on these quickly. Don't allow them to grow and become unmanageable monsters. Understand them, the individuals involved and tackle them asap. It's all about being honest and open with each other. It's critical that you're not seen to have favourites too. I've seen and experienced this first hand, and it doesn't make for a great environment.

So, in summary, have a few simple, easy-to-follow structures and processes, and don't neglect the soft skills of sales management. Reward the good and nip issues in the bud. You can have all the processes in the world in place, but you still have a team that's not engaged if you don't lead the team and the individuals within it.

Notes

1 T. Powers et al "An assessment of needed sales managers skills"' *Journal of Personal Selling and Sales Management* vol. 34 (2014), 207
2 These are terms used by K. Peesker et al in "A qualitative study of leader behavior perceived to enable salesperson performance" *Journal of Personal Selling and Sales Management* vol. 39 (2019), 323
3 G. Rich "The constructs of sales coaching: Supervisory feedback, role modelling and trust" *Journal of Personal Selling and Sales Management* vol. 8 (1998)
4 J. Lee et al "Three strategies to boost sales and marketing productivity" *HBR Digital Article* (June 2023), 3
5 M. Sweeney "Can a coaching culture improve the levels of performance of salespeople in SMEs?" *The International Journal of Sales Transformation* no. 4.2 (June 2018), 35–38
6 T. Baumgartner et al *Sales growth* p213 Wiley 2016
7 B. Matthews & T. Schenk *Sales enablement* p112 Wiley 2018
8 Ibid., p123
9 M. Buckingham & A. Goodall "The hidden power of teams" *Harvard Business Review* May 2019
10 C. Nguyen et al "Dimensions of effective sales coaching: Scale development and validation" *Journal of Personal Selling and Sales Management* vol. 39 (2019)
11 Included in the "our view" section of the journal "Using data to drive effective coaching" *The International Journal of Sales Transformation* no. 4.2 (2018), 7
12 I. Nahm, M. Ahearne, N. Lee & S. Tirunillai "Managing positive and negative trends in sales call outcomes: The role of momentum" *Journal of Marketing Research* vol. 59, no. 6 (2022), 19
13 M. Buckingham & A. Goodall *Harvard Business Review* May 2019
14 M. Leslie & C. Holloway "The sales learning curve" *Harvard Business Review* July 2006
15 J. Fuster "*5 tips to improve sales performance* Oracle whitepaper 2015
16 K. Peesker et al vol. 39 (2019)
17 N. Capon & C. Senn "When CEOs make sales calls" *Harvard Business Review* March 2021

Chapter 10

Targets, forecasts, budgets and KPIs

What are the essential measures to manage sales organisations and how can we derive them?

Which numbers matter?

Global CRM giant Salesforce produced a handy guide to sales metrics,[1] which includes the quote "You have to keep your eye on the ball, but which one?". In this chapter, targets and sales metrics, or KPIs, will be unpacked to help you choose the right ones for your business.

What is the value of a good set of metrics? At least some of the benefits include:

- To focus everyone on achieving sufficient sales to meet your profitability/growth targets.
- To measure progress towards your goal.
- To ensure the right work gets done today that leads to results tomorrow.
- To focus everyone on implementing your specific sales strategy.
- To provide an objective basis for compensation, rewards and incentives.
- To coach individuals and teams to success using meaningful data.

With so much at stake, it's time to dig into the key classes of sales numbers, starting with target setting and then moving on to the other sales metrics that help you manage progress towards those targets.

Definitions

Firstly, some definitions will be used in this chapter.

Sales target: Also known as quota in the US, this is the desired revenue to be achieved for an individual, team or organisation in a specific period.

Sales forecast: This is your best guess concerning the level of sales you will achieve in the next period, based on the information you have at this point in time.

Sales budget: The amount of money that is expected to be invested to achieve your target, including fixed and variable costs.

Sales metrics: Any quantitative measure that is used to establish progress towards your target.

Target setting

The process of setting targets will vary greatly from a solopreneur/small start-up to an established SME where target setting is already well established. Intimately linked with target setting is sales forecasting. To set a target is to make a forecast, and forecasts are an

DOI: 10.4324/9781003449614-10

essential part of business budgeting as they help other departments make investment and activity decisions.

Many start-ups have to 'take a leap of faith' when it comes to forecasting, because there may be no historical data to build a forecast from. Nonetheless, a 'best guess' is very helpful to establish profitability and viability for a start-up and enables you to sense-check the sales *work to be done* to see if it is practical.

With this in mind, Javier Marcos and his colleagues outline three main methods that organisations use to build forecasts[2]:

- Market research and customer knowledge
- The consensus approach
- Objective techniques

Market research techniques involve trying to establish the requirements of customers by asking a sample of them. Although in principle a good idea, the practicalities of actually doing it are challenging and often prone to errors. This tends to be used more in larger organisations that have the resources to carry out such estimates.

The *consensus approach* is commonly used in organisations where the sales team and their managers have sufficient knowledge of the customer base to estimate the sales that could be achieved at each. The forecast is built up by adding together all the potential sales for each customer. This approach often makes sense for start-ups that have enough knowledge of a few customers to make a reasonable estimate of what can be sold.

The *objective method* involves using various statistical techniques for estimating demand. For example, analyses are available for estimating *when* customers will buy (Sir David Cox pioneered the method for this, called *survival analysis*, in 1972, for biostatistics purposes[3]). If you have access to a data scientist or specialist in time-series forecasting, this can be a powerful way to build your forecast.

Top-down and bottom-up forecasts

A common problem in sales organisations is a lack of ownership of the target by individual salespeople. This typically occurs when sales targets are 'imposed' by senior management, resulting in little buy-in from them. Imposed sales targets can be demotivating because:

- They are based on last year's customer performance, which might not be relevant any more.
- The same growth potentials are often assumed across regions, which might not be accurate.
- The target is perceived to be unrealistic.
- The process used to arrive at the growth target lacks credibility.

One way to avoid this is to use a process of bottom-up predictions from your sales team and top-down ambition from your senior team. For an SME, the calendar might look like the one in Table 10.1.

By using a top-down (owners/managers set the company growth target) and bottom-up (reps say what they believe is possible), it should be possible to get better buy-in to a more realistic target.

Table 10.1 Sales target planning calendar

Month	Activity
August	Ask each salesperson to review their customer base and forecast what growth is possible, considering the products and services that could realistically be sold to them. Ask them to estimate how many new customers they expect to win.
September	Aggregate the individual forecasts to arrive at the overall sales number. If it does not meet your company's expectations, go back to the sales team and ask them to find an extra x%. Discuss and negotiate with each team member to arrive at an ambitious but achievable target.
November	Build your sales budget (i.e., the cost of delivering the sales target). Submit the budget forecast for board/senior management sign-off. Make any last-minute adjustments if needed.
December	Brief the team on the targets for the new year, so they hit the ground running on January 1st with a clear target.

Table 10.2 The time-based nature of revenue development

Product	Jan	Feb	Mar	Apr	May	Jun	Totals
Diagnostic survey			$3,000 1 survey	$6,000 2 surveys	$6,000 2 surveys	$9,000 3 surveys	$24,000
Social media support					$2,000 1 client	$4,000 2 clients	$6,000
Marketing content support					$2,500 1 client	$5,000 2 clients	$7,500
Totals			$3,000	$6,000	$10,500	$18,000	$37,500

Taking care of the time-based nature of sales revenues

Managing cash flow is often one of the most critical issues for start-ups to ensure viability. Often, there will be a considerable lag between the formation of a start-up, and the first revenues hitting the bank. In accounting, there is a useful expression to guide us: "Profit is vanity, cash is sanity". Given the potentially long sales cycles that can exist in B2B sales, it is important to recognise this time factor in your forecast. One way to do this is to build your forecast in a similar way to a cash flow projection. Table 10.2 shows an example of a start-up selling digital marketing services.

In the example in Table 10.2, the start-up proposes to use a diagnostic survey to help clients see where their marketing needs are. This will result in a lag between the sale of the diagnostic and fee-earning from marketing support. Also, not all diagnostics will result in the sale of support services, and this is also reflected in the forecast.

Understanding when sales will convert to cash significantly helps growing organisations make the right cost commitments at the right time. Thinking through the steps and timing of your typical sale will add all-important pragmatism to your target.

Point-based quotas instead of revenue targets

Where you are interested in selling specific products to specific customer segments, it can make sense to use a points-based quota system.[4] This means reps might get more points for every dollar they sell of one product (the one you want to push) than if they sell another product (which you want to de-emphasise).

The sales budget

Chapter 2 sets out the fundamental questions that need to be answered for your sales strategy, including, "What resources will be needed to enable the strategy?". The information you have pulled together to answer this question should be used to estimate the costs required to deliver your desired revenue. You may need to adjust either the cost line or the top line to arrive at an acceptable level of profitability. This is an important 'reality check' to ensure you have thought through the practicalities of achieving your desired growth.

Besides targets and budgets, what other metrics are useful?

Once we have set the targets and budgets, what other metrics should we have? While there is debate over whether management guru Peter Drucker actually said it, the quote "What gets measured gets managed" is often attributed to him. Similarly, "Vision without action is a daydream, and action without vision is a nightmare" is another management quote of uncertain origin that speaks to the same sentiment. Without useful metrics, it's going to be difficult to know if you are on track, and even harder to manage present-day activities to make sure you stay on track.

Your metrics should flow directly from your sales strategy and could include some or all of the following:

- Lead generation metrics (to ensure you generate enough opportunities).
- Opportunity management metrics (linked to your *core sales process*).
- Account management metrics (for example, customer retention and cross-sell targets).
- Product mix targets (to ensure you sell the right things to the right customers).
- Cost performance targets (to ensure you meet profitability targets).
- Organisational fitness targets (employee recruitment/retention/engagement)
- Customer satisfaction and advocacy (Net Promotor Score for example)

For start-ups chasing high levels of growth, lead generation and opportunity management metrics will be very important, so these will be covered first.

Lead generation metrics

Aaron Ross and Jason Lemkin state that "predictable lead generation is *the* lever to hyper-growth".[5] There are several commonly used metrics to track lead generation:

New leads in the pipeline (Total the number of news leads each month.)[6]

Average age of leads in the pipeline[7] (Total the age of all leads in the pipeline/number of leads in the pipeline.)

Pipeline creation rate[8] (By what percentage does the value of all the opportunities in your pipeline grow each month?)

The number of new leads you generate is an example of a 'lead measure'. This means it gives you a good indication of what's to come. By contrast, the amount of sales in a month is a 'lag measure', that is, a 'rear view mirror' metric. Keeping a close eye on and driving the number of leads you generate will be a very good step to generating sales growth.

Opportunity management metrics

The importance of defining your *core sales process* was outlined in Chapter 3. If you generate a reasonable flow of leads, you want to be sure as many as possible get converted to sales and, eventually, happy customers. So, what metrics support your core sales process?

The absolute masters of sale metrics have to be Jason Jordan and Michelle Vazzana, whose book *Cracking the sales management code*, is an invaluable guide to designing sales metrics.[9]

They identify three essential metric types that founders and SME managers should know about, as shown in Table 10.3. These are invaluable for managing your core sales process:

The key point about these different types of metrics is that you can't change an *outcome measure*. As an example, if you managed to complete a marathon in four hours, you cannot now change the time or the *outcome*. However, during your pre-race training, you can pay attention to the mileage and quality of your efforts. These are *activity measures*, which can and do influence the end result of your next race.

Sales objectives are a kind of intermediate measure that predicts whether you are on track to hit the result. Returning to the running analogy, your VO2 max will improve with training and can be a good predictor of your race potential. Doing the activities (mileage, speed sessions) will improve your VO2 max, which, in turn, will increase the chances that you will beat four hours next time.

Smart sales organisations figure out, with reasonable certainty, which steps they need to take to close a sale. As an example, the automotive sector has long realised that if potential customers can be talked into taking a test drive, then the chances of an actual purchase greatly increase. Once a potential customer experiences that 'new car smell', and takes the wheel of the car, their emotional commitment to buy often increases. Because of this, the sales manager of your local dealership can target their sales team to arrange *x number of test drives each week*, knowing that if 'x' is achieved, 'y' sales can be expected. Jordan and Vazanna term this the *causal chain*.[10] If you understand the activities that lead to results, you can manage your sales effectively.

How can you establish the causal chain for your organisation? It should be your *core sales process*, of course. If you did a good job of optimising that, then you can be reasonably confident that measuring activities in the early part will lead to sales in the latter part. Indeed, there should be a very strong relationship between your sales process and your sales metrics.

As an example, one sustainability consulting organisation I worked with established pre-sale client workshops to explore their environmental policy, which often resulted in

Table 10.3 Three essential classes of sales metrics

	Description	Typical example
Activity measures	Track day-by-day activities that lead to sales (a 'lead measure')	Number of product demonstrations made/week No. of calls to potential customers
Sales objectives	Measure progress made as a result of sales activities	Number of potential customers signing up to join your marketing webinar Retention rate of existing customers
Outcome measures	Measure the end result (a 'lag measure')	$ sales per quarter/year % market share

follow-on sales. The *number of pre-sales workshops* then became a key activity metric to track and manage every week. If no workshops were arranged for the coming week, then the sales team knew they had to get busy finding willing prospects to participate.

Other metrics to tune the core sales process

As will be outlined in Chapter 10, *pipeline management* and sales process metrics should help us see:

- How many opportunities do we have at play?
- How many make it through the pipeline?
- How fast do they move through the pipeline?

Accordingly, three other metrics we can use are *opportunity value per sales process step*, *conversion rates* and *deal velocity*.

Starting with the *opportunity value per sales process step*, Table 10.4 shows a typical pipeline view for an SME selling PR and marketing services. We can see that the company has closed $5k this period and has $61k of potential work in the funnel ($15k+£$33k+$16k). With estimates about when the work might close, the company could quite easily forecast its revenues and decide if there are enough opportunities in the pipeline.

Some companies take this a step further by estimating *the probability to close* and the *expected close date*. This enables the forecasting of revenue by time period. Sales technology can do this automatically, meaning if salespeople keep CRM up to date, a probability-adjusted forecast can be made at any time.

This method is not without pitfalls. It depends on the disciplined use of qualification criteria at each phase of the sales process. I have seen more than a few organisations use a fixed probability percentage of, say, 25% if a deal is in a needs-discovery phase and 50% if a proposal has been sent, for example. Without strong qualification definitions, each salesperson can allocate opportunities quite differently, resulting in a prediction with poor validity. Similarly, every customer is different, so making broad assumptions about probability like this only works if you have a large data set (where errors can average out). For start-ups and SMEs, this is unlikely to be true.

Tracking the *opportunity value per phase* then enables us to monitor and manage progress towards our target.

Conversion rates are another very useful measure to assess the effectiveness of your sales approach. Figure 10.1 shows a lead flow analysis for a company selling software. Their sales process involves exploration calls to see if there is a potential need, followed by product demonstrations, and then a proposal. The analysis shows the progress of 60 calls to reach prospects, with conversion rates in each subsequent step.

Table 10.4 Opportunity values per phase of a sales process

Phase	Discovery	Agreement of scope	Proposals	Closed
Prospect:	Prospect A $10k Prospect B $5k	Prospect C $10k Prospect D $15k Prospect E $8k	Prospect F $16k	Prospect G $5k
Total	$15k	$33k	$16k	$5k

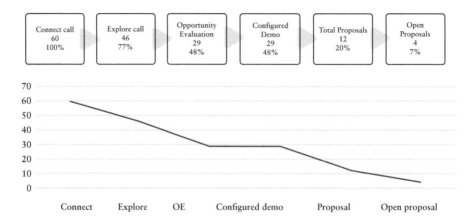

Figure 10.1 Lead flow analysis

For example, of 60 initial leads, 46 'explore calls' were set up (conversion rate = 77%). This is actually quite good and showed that the sales team were persistent in following up on the leads to arrange an initial meeting. From these 46 explore calls, 29 product demonstrations were arranged (conversion rate = 48%), which is also a good success rate. But the number of proposals made (12) following the 29 demonstrations (conversion rate = 41%) shows that only just over a third of customers receiving a demonstration were interested in a proposal. This is not a good success rate. For B2B sales organisations making proposals in a multistage sales process, a good start point for discussion is a two-thirds conversation rate (66%). This is because a proposal should only be created when:

- Your customer needs are understood very well.
- You know the decision-makers.
- The opportunity is 'qualified' according to your criteria.

Under these circumstances, we have good reason to believe our proposal will hit the mark. If not, then a lot of time is being wasted creating proposals that are not relevant to your customer – hardly a win-win situation!

In the case of the software organisation, this suggested that either the customers were not qualified effectively (that is, they were unlikely to be really in the market for the product) or that the demonstrations were a 'turn-off'. The company worked on both areas (better questioning and qualification early in the sales process, resulting in a much-improved personalised product demonstration). In this case, conversion rate metrics played a critical role in improving the sales process.

To measure how fast opportunities move through your pipeline, you can use a *deal velocity* measure. This is essentially the amount of time it takes to go from a lead being registered to your customer signing up. It's very similar to the average age of a lead in the pipeline but measures the '*enquiry to close*' time.

Leads that sit around for a long time raise questions, unless you have a long sales process by nature. Often, it's a sign of poor-quality leads, poor qualification or a lack of attention from your sales team.

Hyper-growth start-ups and SMEs

Start-ups and SMEs that really want to grow fast should pay close attention to:

- Pipeline creation rate
- Conversion rate
- Deal velocity
- Account retention rate
- Referral rate

In simple terms, this means:

- Generating more opportunities.
- Winning more of them.
- Winning them faster.
- Keeping more opportunities that you win.
- Treating them so well brings in even more business.

Savvy start-ups and SMEs continually experience different sales processes and technology, to arrive at the most effective approach to optimise these metrics.

Having considered the core sales process metrics, let's now look at retention and referral metrics.

Account management metrics

Defining account management metrics is one of the trickier areas of sales management and depends so much on the specifics of your business. Your growth model (Chapter 2) will help guide you in selecting the best metrics.

Typical metrics used by sales organisations are:

Raw retention rate: What percentage of accounts have stayed with us since last year?

Number of interactions: How many meetings/exchanges took place in a given time period?

Number of business reviews: What percentage of our accounts did we complete a formal business review meeting?

Profitability: What is the actual cost to serve the account vs. revenues gained?

Account growth: What percentage growth did we achieve year over year?

Cross-sell index What is the number of product lines/services we sell per customer?

Account plans in place: What % of our accounts have a formal account plan in place?[11]

Referral rates:[12] How many referrals did we receive from existing customers?

The activities that support these metrics are covered in Chapter 14.

The supporting cast of metrics

As outlined earlier in this chapter, there are many potential metrics we could use. Product metrics are valuable when, for strategic reasons, it's important to sell certain products. For example, you might have a core software to sell that opens the door to all kinds of other add-on services. Ensuring that this is sold as a priority fuels further growth. You might have performance vs. budget metrics to ensure profitability/viability.

Customer satisfaction is always important, because growth is going to be very hard if your customers are not happy. There are a number of ways to measure it:

- The *net promotor score* is a very common, freely available measure used by organisations[13] to measure satisfaction and advocacy. For more information, see www. netpromoter.com.
- The *customer effort score* is a 'new kid on the block' and is based on the premise that the easier it is to do business with you, the more likely you will be recommended.[14]
- *Retention rate* Customers don't stay if they are unhappy.

Beyond these measures, you might need to derive some more specific measures based on your sales strategy. Table 10.5 has examples of other sales-specific metrics that organisations use to guide them:

Table 10.5 Potential metrics for your sales organisation

Metric	Description
General categories	
Customer lifetime value	The average revenue you receive from a customer during their time with you.
Customer acquisition cost	Your best estimate of how much it costs to win one customer.
Average order value	To assess the productivity of your sales efforts.
Forecast sales vs actual sales	To measure and improve your sales team's ability to accurately predict who will buy and when, so you can plan expenditure/investment effectively.
Sales to new vs existing customers	To estimate how much time salespeople are 'hunting' versus 'farming'.
Percentage of sales by segment	To figure out which segments are most active for you and therefore where to allocate investment.
Salesforce metrics	
Sales team retention	The number of salespeople that stay with you year-on-year. High attrition rates are expensive and damaging to customer relationships.
Time to competence	The average time it takes you to train a salesperson to be productive. Reducing this aids growth and profitability.
Hours of sales training completed	To help you assess how well supported your sales team is.
Percentage of selling time vs. admin and non-sales activities	To reduce non-value-added time in the sales team's diary.
Lead generation metrics	
% of leads by source	To identify which sales/marketing campaigns are most effective
Inbound lead response time	To measure how quickly you respond to incoming leads/enquiries. Customers expect swift response times.
Demo show/no-show rate	Useful measure if you book online demos with potential customers. More than 20% of no-shows typically mean customers have not been properly qualified for the demonstration[15]

Selecting the key metrics

Clearly, there are a lot of metrics that you could use. The principle of 'Don't be a DRIP' is useful here, that is, 'Data rich, information poor'. Often, a 'less is more' approach with metrics is wise, so that you and your team can work with them regularly and with conviction.

Well-designed metrics can become excellent coaching tools. Thinking about the running analogy, who wouldn't want to pay attention to this week's training mileage if they can see it will genuinely help them achieve the faster marathon time they desire? Introducing sales metrics as a way of coaching the team to be excellent salespeople is often an easier change to manage than introducing them as a way of micro-managing their activities.

In the next chapter, the pipeline management meetings will be covered. For them to work, you will need a set of relevant, useful sales metrics to coach your team. For example, you might say, "we need to make more contacts to new prospects, because today, it's clear we don't have enough pipeline to make the target".

Although this message may not be easy to deliver or hear, it is important to face reality as soon as possible; otherwise, the sales strategy is simply a wish, not an actual plan for success.

Knowing that you need to get more miles run this week to meet your target marathon time may not be easy, but if you really want to achieve it, it's better to find out now while you still have time to change things. Exactly the same is true in sales: if we leave it too late, then achieving the result is impossible because many sales processes simply do not happen in one day! Metrics should help us manage sales in this way.

Into action

Depending on where you are on your metrics journey, try one of the three activities below.

For absolute sales management beginners/new start-ups

If you have built your sales process, as outlined in Chapter 3, are you reporting the volume of opportunities in each phase yet? If not, that is step 1, as illustrated in Table 3.2.

If you have not built a specific sales process yet, you can start with a proxy version with headings such as *first meeting, proposal,* and *sales closed.* Reviewing this every week will help you pay close attention to your opportunities (or lack of) and manage them through to the close.

For developing start-ups/SMEs

If you have opportunity tracking metrics in place, it's time to pay attention to the 'accelerators'. What are your conversion rates at each phase? What is the average residence time in the pipeline? What can you do to shorten each phase of the sales process and increase the conversion rates?

For well set-up SMEs

If the core sales process is well monitored and managed with sales metrics, then it's time to review your whole growth model (as outlined in Chapter 2). Do you have metrics in place that enable you to manage all aspects of it? For example, cross-sell, account retention, referrals, customer satisfaction and retention metrics. And do you have good measures for supporting activities like recruitment, staff retention, training and cost control?

Expert view: Trend Tool Technology

When it comes to Wood Working, Trend Tool Technology is the go-to organisation. Trading since 1955, the company has a vast range of specialist woodworking tools and routers, loved by professional tradespeople as well as hobbyists around the world. To support its comprehensive distributor network, Trend employs a specialist sales team who acts like business partners.

In 2019, Trend installed Phocus, a retail metrics and insights tool for their sales team. Phocus replaced a previous system where data had to be extracted to spreadsheets, which was not up to date and difficult for salespeople to work with. With Phocus, data are updated twice per day, and the sales team now has confidence in it.

Mike Tideswell, Sales Director, tells us more about how Phocus supports sales, and the metrics Trend uses.

Q1. Why do you think it is important to use metrics and KPIs in a sales organisation?

Accurate metrics enable us to track promotions, review sales of new products and assess retailer performance. Over time, we have put different emphasis on different metrics, which has enabled us to drive what was important at the time, for example, profit, new products, new SKUs, reducing stocks in the warehouse or de-emphasising certain product lines.

Metrics help us to improve sales. For example, we can look at trends, go back to retailers and ask questions to uncover opportunities.

Q2. Which specific metrics help you run your sales organisation?

We only use a limited number of metrics. Previously, we looked at maybe too many metrics. For our business, we typically pay attention to new products, top sellers, promotions, margins, 'while stocks last', obsoletes and our Premium Tool Centres range.

Around 90% of our retailers stock our 'top 70' range because these are core consumables. We look at the performance of all these areas so that our sales team can put together promotions to help both the retailer and Trend drive increased sales. We can present data from other similar businesses and explain to customers that they are quite like them; then the data say what should be possible for sales.

Q3. How do you encourage the sales team to use the metrics?

Most importantly, make them easy to use. That's essential. Because Phocas is mobile-friendly, they can access data on their phone, laptop or iPad and also have daily, weekly or monthly reports sent to them. They are in control, which is exceptionally useful. They can go back to data from 2008 and look at patterns in our retailer's sales. They can look at changes over time and work with retailers to close gaps.

Each person has their own dashboard with a set of key reports, which makes it easy for them to see where they are. If some metrics are tracking lower, they can ask their colleagues for ideas. We don't use metrics as a stick; they are more of a carrot.

The metrics we have are super-relevant to the sales team, and they are all targeted and incentivised on them.

Q4. What advice would you have for other SMEs who are not sure which metrics and systems to use to manage their salesforces?

Start with the customer. I ask myself, if I were in front of a customer, what exactly would they want to know? How much time do you have with them? If a customer's attention span is limited, the data we share needs to be valuable, so we constantly check if our dashboard is set up well. We don't want to faff around moving from one screen to another. Our system allows us to do this, so we can get the information a bit faster.

Also, make sure the metrics used make salespeople's roles enjoyable. If they can do what they need to do – share and pass on relevant data to customers – then this will help them own the metrics.

Notes

1 Salesforce inc *The sales metrics that matter: Six experts, six themes, one invaluable guide*
2 J. Marcos et al *Sales management* 4th ed p248 Palgrave 2016
3 M. Grigsby *Marketing analytics* p85 Kogan Page 2018
4 M. Johnson & G. Marshall *Sales force management* 13th ed Routledge 2021
5 A. Ross & J. Lemkin *From impossible to inevitable* p46 Wiley 2016
6 Salesforce blog *What are the most important sales KPIs?* 2022
7 Ibid
8 A. Ross & J. Lemkin p96 Wiley 2016
9 J. Jordan & M. Vazzana *Cracking the sales management code* McGraw Hill 2012
10 Ibid., p32
11 Ibid., p121
12 Salesforce blog 2022
13 For more information visit https://www.netpromoter.com/know/
14 https://blog.hubspot.com/service/customer-effort-score
15 T. Bertruzzi *The sales development playbook* p229 T. Bertruzzi 2016

Chapter 11

Pipeline and opportunity management

How can we best manage this most essential of sales tasks?

Pipeline management: The beating heart of sales management

Charles Dickens' novel *A Tale of Two Cities*, begins with the quote, "It was the best of times and the worst of times". *Pipeline management* meetings can be like this. I have sat in on numerous sales meetings, where each sales representative anxiously explains what they expect to sell, moving slowly around the table from person to person, like a kind of creeping death. Predictions are often nothing more than wish lists, fuelled by the pressure of the sales manager to 'lay out a good stall'. These meetings can be pointless, stressful, dull and quite demotivating.

On the other hand, good pipeline management meetings are a very important driver of sales performance. McKinsey describes regular reporting as a key tool to "set the tempo of performance".[1] Citing a client in Denmark (TDC), they showed an increase of 75% in orders closed using daily objective setting with pilot sales teams. The CEO of TDC was quoted as saying, "It raised the clock speed of our sales team". Javier Marcos Cuevas offers other benefits,[2] including "More clarity in terms of where each opportunity stands" and "Better communication as it provides a common way to view opportunities".

Pipeline management is a form of *performance management*. If done well, it can materially affect your sales results. It is also known as *funnel management*, *opportunity management*, *sales review* and just straight-up '*sales meetings*' in some organisations. It is done weekly, monthly, quarterly or ad hoc, according to an organisation's habits.

So, what does good pipeline management look like? Let's begin by understanding at the individual level what is involved and why, therefore, it is a 'core sales attitude'.

The rules of effective pipeline management

Anyone who has spent any time at all selling will know that before very long, someone (maybe yourself if you are a solopreneur) will ask, "What are we likely to close this month/quarter?". It's pretty much impossible to run a business without some idea of what revenues can be expected and when. And if you want to grow a business, then you will very likely have defined growth targets to achieve.

Rather than waiting for that difficult conversation with your boss and/or another stakeholder, it's far better to take personal control of your pipeline of opportunities. Without a pipeline of high-quality opportunities, any sales achieved are most likely due to luck, not agency.

DOI: 10.4324/9781003449614-11

Seasoned salespeople will instinctively know how *not to* manage their pipeline. There are a few 'golden rules' that serve us well:

1 If you don't fill your pipeline with enough new opportunities, it will dry up eventually.
2 If your pipeline has too few opportunities in it, you will appear desperate in front of the few opportunities you do have, thereby further reducing your chances of success (Experienced buyers detect desperation very easily).
3 If your pipeline management is sporadic, you will have feast and famine in your workload.
4 If you don't pay attention to the quality of opportunities in your pipeline, then you will have high dropout rates, and many embarrassing conversations with management.
5 If you have too many opportunities in high-intensity phases (creating proposals, for example), you will have highly stressful periods of overwork and potentially frustrated customers who are left waiting for products/services.
6 If you don't manage each opportunity in a high-quality way, conversion rates will be poor, and customer satisfaction/advocacy will be low.

One way to think about pipeline management is to imagine yourself as the operations manager for a vintage car repair shop. You only have a certain amount of capacity, and if you don't pay attention to the quality and quantity of jobs you take on, it's going to get messy. Perfection means having a steady, manageable flow of high-value repairs. It is the same with pipeline management; you want to be working in a sustainable way with high-quality prospects and clients.

Visualising your pipeline

Many start-ups and SMEs will use their CRM systems to visualise their pipeline. Indeed, this is often a key selling point for CRM systems. Pipelines are often shown from left to right, while funnels are typically shown from top to bottom. The beauty of using visualisation for pipelines is that you will get an instant view of your ability to meet your sales target and the sales work to be done going forward.

Figures 11.1 and 11.2 show some hypothetical visual pipeline distributions for four start-up founders who are responsible for the end-to-end sales process.

Scenario 1 Not enough in the pipeline: If there are only one or two opportunities at each phase, this can be risky. We can never be sure that a customer will buy. If one or two of these opportunities drop out, then it's going to be difficult to hit a growth target.

Scenario 2 Prospecting has stopped: There are no opportunities for first contact, but a lot of product demonstrations are going on. Because the demos take time, the start-up has stopped filling the pipeline with new opportunities. There may be a flood of sales in the short term, but there will be a long period with nothing.

Scenario 3 Feast and famine: This pipeline has lots of discovery calls, which is good news for now, but as they move through to demos and proposals, the organisation is likely to be under severe time pressure. Deft planning will be required to manage the workload and avoid feasts and famines.

Scenario 4 Poor qualification This start-up apparently has a lot of opportunities in each phase, but on closer inspection, very few in the proposal phase. This could indicate that the 'opportunities' in the earlier phase are not very high quality. This organisation might benefit

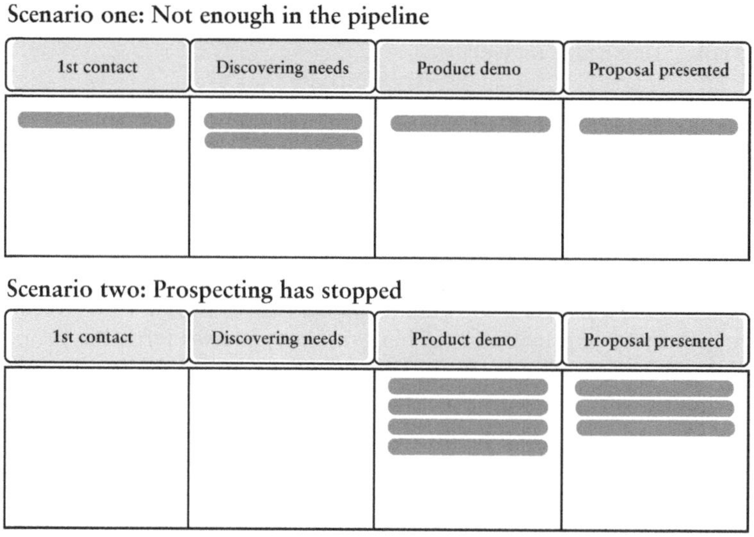

Scenario one: Not enough in the pipeline

1st contact	Discovering needs	Product demo	Proposal presented

Scenario two: Prospecting has stopped

1st contact	Discovering needs	Product demo	Proposal presented

Figure 11.1 Pipeline image

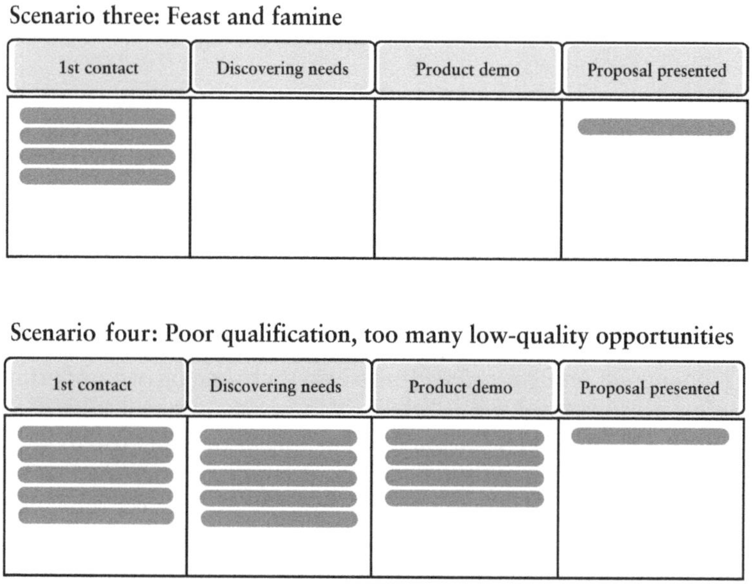

Scenario three: Feast and famine

1st contact	Discovering needs	Product demo	Proposal presented

Scenario four: Poor qualification, too many low-quality opportunities

1st contact	Discovering needs	Product demo	Proposal presented

Figure 11.2 Pipeline image

from being more selective and managing a few high-quality opportunities well, thereby achieving a substantially higher close rate.

When I work with entrepreneurs new to sales, I strongly recommend them to have a 'meeting with yourself', once per week to review their pipeline. As mentioned, taking ownership of your opportunity management is one of the most important attitudes in sales, and it needs to be done regularly to have a good effect.

The *'meeting with yourself'* format means taking a step back from daily action (e-mails, telephone calls and other interruptions) to take the 'helicopter view':

• What are the pipeline priorities this week to move the opportunities forward?
• What do I need to plan over the next 1–6 weeks to maximise my chances of success?
• How best to organise my diary to focus on the right opportunities?

Essentially, it's a combination of time and opportunity management, answering the question, "Where best to invest my valuable time?".

As mentioned in the previous chapter, this often means facing the hard truth that we don't have enough activity today to hit our target tomorrow. By taking personal responsibility for this, we can avoid nasty disappointments that are impossible to recover from in the last quarter.

Qualification

This theme was introduced in Chapter 4 as an essential B2B routine. In pipeline management and forecasting, it really comes into its own. Why? Because opportunities that are not qualified properly are often 'lottery tickets' or 'wish-list sales'. One of the very strong messages in the Qualified Sales Leader,[3] is the importance of having clearly defined language in pipeline management discussions, as well as a strong qualification model (MEDDPICC in that case).

By way of example, one sales rep might visit a prospect and think to themselves, "hmmm, that customer could use our services" and then add it to their pipeline report as a 'lead'. Another salesperson might wait until they have a conversation with a senior manager working at the prospect who confirmed a genuine interest in buying before adding the opportunity to their pipeline. Clearly, both 'opportunities' have very different probabilities of success.

When looking at our pipeline of opportunities, we must have a good reason for placing them at a certain stage of the sales process. We also have to be brutally honest about our chances of success. Qualification helps with this by using an objective frame for checking each opportunity.

Using the simple qualification approach of 'BANT' as an example, if you don't yet know if there is a budget for your solution, then this should raise a red flag for that opportunity. Similarly, if there is no timescale for the implementation of your solution, then possibly it won't happen until next year.

Once there is rigour and objectivity about the definition of each opportunity at each phase of your sales process, then forecasting can become more accurate. With better qualifications comes an improved ability to define what sales work needs to be done this week/month.

For this reason, it makes sense to define your own qualification criteria for opportunities so that you can gauge the probability of success and guide what needs to be done next to increase the chances of success. BANT is a good starting point for building your qualification tool. Also, try to figure out what other essential preconditions are needed. Table 11.1 shows some examples:

Table 11.1 Examples of specific qualification criteria in different sectors

Sector	Essential preconditions
Speciality chemicals	Hazard/safety approval
	Achieves pilot testing criteria
Software	Engagement with IT to sign-off compatibility
	Scope agreed
Consulting	Business case established
	Stakeholder map completed
Food additives	Labelling requirements met
	Production trial completed

Table 11.2 Qualification criteria per phase of sales process

Phase	Selecting	Relating	Discovering	Framing	Proposing	Closing	Cross-selling
Stage-gate criteria	The prospect meets our sector criteria	We have identified a guide who supports us	We have a next meeting We have risk committee approval	Pain and gain defined Decision making process known	Proposal presented	Deal closed Delivery team in place	We have contact with at least three key personnel

Your sales process should support effective qualification at each stage. It is better to 'fail early' in sales (i.e., pull out of a sales process) than to fail at the last stage, when lots of work has been done. Therefore, if you build checks in at each stage of your sales process, it will help you ensure only high-quality opportunities proceed through it.

Checklist/stage gates

Some organisations use checklist criteria at each stage of their sales process to act as aide-memoires for the work to be done. If all the activities have not been done for each phase, then the opportunity stays in the phase it is.

Table 11.2 shows an example of sales process for a B2B financial services solution, with the associated checklists at each stage. In the financial services sector, companies often need to perform certain checks to ensure compliance (e.g., proof of source of funds to prevent money laundering). Also, an opportunity might need 'internal risk committee sign-off' before progressing to the proposal stage. Building these into the sales process aids qualification by ensuring they are 'top of mind' in all sales interactions with your customer/prospect.

From individual pipeline management to team opportunity management

Having set out the core principles of individual pipeline management, how does this translate into a team context? From a history of day-long 'creeping death' sales territory reviews, the zeitgeist is shifting to more regular, shorter, action-driven meetings. As outlined earlier, partly this is due to mounting evidence that the "tempo of performance" can be quickened by shorter review-act time cycles. It also echoes the stand-up huddles used in agile software development.

For SMEs and start-ups, I believe weekly pipeline calls are a good starting point, although each organisation will have to find their own workable rhythm. Weekly calls keep the pace up, but also allow plenty of sales time each week. They can be done face to face, on a conference call or a virtual meeting, according to the location of your team.

What, then, are the essential parameters for a good weekly pipeline meeting?

Guidelines for effective pipeline management meetings

The group coaching principle Psychological safety is an important element of healthy organisations.[4] Some readers may have participated in sales meetings that were little more than a diatribe from a stressed sales manager, 'holding court' with their sales team. Each person does their very best to dress up their inadequate sales pipeline, only to receive no praise, just invective to "sell more and sell it faster". It's hardly surprising that this leads to gaming, inaccurate reporting and a growing intention to leave the job.

An alternative approach is to focus very heavily on 'bringing the best out of people' during the meeting. Coaching has already been covered as a key lever for performance, and if your sales team feels you have their interests at heart, it will go a long way towards facilitating honest, open discussions. It will also lead to more accurate forecasts, as it breaks down the perceived need to 'show a good pipeline'. Aaron Ross and Jason Lemkin say it like this: "Look at your sales funnel and understand conversions through every stage…If most reps are struggling in the same area, then don't blame them, it might be something outside their control".[5]

You should coach your team to adopt the key pipeline management rules already covered in this chapter, encouraging them to take personal responsibility for this.

Chapter 10 explores the potential metrics you can use to measure and manage progress. For the pipeline management meeting, the core sales process metrics will form an essential foundation of your coaching approach. Let's recall some of the metrics you might use:

- Value of opportunities at each phase.
- Expected close date.
- Probability of closing the deal.
- Conversion rates at each stage of the pipeline.
- Deal velocity (average age of leads).

If you have created a group coaching culture, then it is natural to discuss these metrics to help everyone on the team. For example, you might discover that one of your team members is really good at closing proposals based on their conversion rate. You could then pair them up with someone who is struggling with a lower conversion rate. If someone is struggling with 'feast and famine', then you could have a team ideation session to help them manage their pipeline more effectively.

Having effective metrics to discuss in your pipeline meetings introduces an 'elite athlete performance centre' mindset to your culture, i.e., using data to help the team win.

Focus on problem solving: One of the key roles you can play as a sales manager is helping advance opportunities.[6] Salespeople face all kinds of challenges as they sell. Some are created by customers (e.g., the need for proof, senior management involvement, guarantees), and some are created by internal staff (e.g., "we can supply that product in that timescale"). This is a time to roll your sleeves up and find ways to solve these challenges. It can involve using your seniority to convince clients or your internal influence to get things done. For some organisations, it's a good idea to have marketing and technical people in the meeting

Table 11.3 Example action plan from a pipeline review meeting

What	Who	When
Agree project scope with client X	Sales rep A	By the end of this week
Arrange for our technical support manager to call client Y to check for compatibility with our software	Tech support manager	Today
Make contact with two new prospects	Sales rep B	By Thursday this week
Present proposal to client Z	Sales rep C	This week

if they are part of the solution. In this way, the meeting develops a culture of everyone pulling together to win deals.

Plan-do-review: The old adage of "what gets inspected, gets respected" is our friend again here. Each pipeline review meeting should end with a short summary of actions, as shown in Table 11.3:

Note that these actions are '*short term*' and focused on accelerating the progress of opportunities through the pipeline. Each meeting should start with a review of last week's action plan. This cycle of plan-do-review builds a *culture of action* in service of winning deals. The discipline of agreeing on concrete actions and following up on them also increases individual accountability.

To support psychological safety, it makes sense to praise actions achieved and encourage salespeople to share how they were successful for others to learn. For actions not completed, ask, "What do you propose to get them complete?". If individuals regularly miss their actions, then it's time for a 1:1 to explore what is happening and what needs to change so that they can complete their actions.

Prioritise the most important opportunities: Because you want a quick 'huddle' type meeting that leaves people energised and ready to act, you won't be able to go through all the opportunities. That would be creeping death again! Therefore, you will need to choose which ones to discuss. Typically, this will be either:

- Each rep's top 3–5 priority opportunities for the week
- The top ten opportunities for the team

Use CRM where possible for pipeline review: Any extra admin you ask salespeople to do takes them away from front-line selling. Ideally, regular data entry means that each rep's pipeline is always available on your CRM system. Sales technology is covered in the next chapter. The visualisation and management of pipelines is a key function your software should facilitate, as this activity is so central to sales management. As the world of sales technology advances, software is available to automatically update pipelines according to changes in your prospects' propensity to purchase.[7]

Pipeline management and forecasting

If you have a clearly defined sales process appropriate to your type of sale, and *if* you have clear qualification criteria in place, *if* your team's pipelines are up to date, then high-quality forecasts will follow. There are a lot of *ifs* in that sentence!

Accurate forecasting is a hallmark of a high-quality sales organisation, as it is only possible with these high levels of discipline. The benefits, of course, are clear to see, especially if you are looking for/have external funding in place. Your investors will not appreciate wildly inaccurate forecasts or nasty surprises!

If forecasting is critical to your business plan, then you could consider including the accuracy of the forecast as an incentivised performance measure. A *Percentage deviation* from the forecast is sometimes used to support this.

Into action

As mentioned in this chapter, to set up effective pipeline management, you will need:

- Your sales process clearly defined.
- A system to track it (CRM or spreadsheet).
- Clear qualification criteria for your opportunities.
- A regular cadence with the team, ideally weekly.

This is such a critical activity for managing growth that if you don't have it in place today, it's worth getting started as soon as possible, even with a manual approach that can be improved over time.

- Aim for a 30–60-minute meeting once per week.
- Invite those people who can influence the success of deals in the pipeline.
- Select the key opportunities to discuss.
- Figure out the next concrete action for the opportunities.
- Use group intelligence to overcome obstacles and accelerate deals.
- Distribute a short written action plan.
- Praise good work and coach your team to success.
- Finish on time.

If you already have this in place, consider using the key opportunity metrics to coach your team:

- Value of opportunities at each phase.
- Expected close date.
- Probability of closing the deal.
- Conversion rates at each stage of the pipeline.
- Deal velocity (average age of leads).

Expert view: Caitlyn Lewis at Supplier Day

Caitlyn Lewis is the founder and CEO of Supplier Day, an innovative organisation specialising in virtual supplier engagement events. Working with some of the most well-known global brands, such as Siemens, Pfizer, Johnson & Johnson and BP, Caitlyn has built up an enviable business from scratch. Clients work with Supplier Day to run strategic events for suppliers to harness innovation and collaborative thinking across their supply chains.

Caitlyn came from a sales background and, from the very start, introduced high-quality pipeline management routines.

What do you think has contributed to the stellar growth of Supplier Day?

I think, first and foremost, we were able to respond really quickly to market conditions during COVID. We understood that there was a massive opportunity for virtual events at a time when people couldn't do anything else.

The ability to very quickly do something has helped us massively. It's also meant that we really don't have any competitors yet. Beyond that, having some extremely well-known big brands as clients helped us win more clients. I think this is quite an important point. Siemens was our very first client, and when I brought them on board, we were very clear about the fact that they were client number one. And because of that, we discounted our services by 40% with the understanding that they would allow us to write a case study about the project and that they would act as a client reference too.

We also iterated our service frequently, something we still do today.

As the founder of the company, I like to get really involved in our client work to help me understand exactly what their pain points are and how we can then adjust our services to help them.

We're now three years old, and I think this is the first year that we're going into with more of a predetermined service and product set because we feel like now we know what our clients want. We have also delivered these services for long enough to know how to do them and how to do them well with a sustainable margin.

How did you manage your pipeline to ensure you brought in more clients?

Since I've started to build the sales team, I have focused on getting rid of the noise and getting rid of the crap. Salespeople are often opportunistic that's what makes them successful, but this can come with the risk of hanging on to deals that aren't really going anywhere.

So, very early on, I was really clear, even with myself as the sole salesperson, what a buying client looked like. Things like, am I speaking to the decision-maker? Has a contract value been determined? Is there a deadline for the project? There were other things very specific to our industry that I identified very early on that indicated to me whether it was a good opportunity or not.

In terms of pipeline management, being very clear on our target customer and qualifying them in or out is very important.

How did you start to operationalize the pipeline management with the sales team?

We have always had a CRM in place. I think it was the very, very first thing that I implemented because I come from a sales background. We would then have weekly sales meetings, and if I'm honest, I don't know if they were ever excellent sales meetings because, in a start-up, what you need to discuss changes all the time.

I don't think I really focused on the nuts and bolts of selling, like are you making the right number of calls, conversion rates. The sales meetings were more about evaluating opportunities, for example, asking salespeople who they were talking to, why they believed there was an opportunity and how we could find a solution. The meetings were also an opportunity to talk about where they are getting stuck and how we could progress opportunities or just get rid of them. The weekly meetings kept the urgency up, which is one of the most important things when you are trying to manage cash flow as part of start-up growth.

We have experimented with different stages of the pipeline, going from very simple standard stages to more complicated, specific ones. We have settled on simple stages now. I am not sure it matters which business you're in: the main thing is, are the opportunities qualified for each or not? Are you kind of pitching to them? Or are you developing and negotiating a proposal? Are we closing the contract? I don't think we need an overly complicated deal-stage pipeline.

Would be your opportunity management advice to founders who might not have a sales background?

You might consider it a 'cop out', but my advice would be to start a business in an industry that you know, or in an industry where you have a network and connections. I didn't, but I was extremely lucky to have investors that were very well established, and it was their network that enabled me to bring on our first three clients. They introduced me, and then I closed the projects. This great start helped us build an ongoing, strong pipeline.

In the B2B world, it's hard to start something when you don't have a network of potential customers. But at the same time, the whole point of entrepreneurship is to do something new, and I would never want to stifle anybody's motivation to do it!

Notes

1 Baumgartner et al *Sales growth – 5 proven strategies from the world's sales leaders*" 2nd ed p216 Wiley 2016

2 J. Marcos Cuevas et al *Sales management* 4th ed p60 Palgrave 2016

3 J. McMahon *The qualified sales leader* John McMahon 2021

4 I. Nembhard & A. Edmondson *Psychological safety: A foundation for speaking up, collaboration and experimentation in organisations* The Oxford Handbook of positive organisational scholarship August 2011

5 A. Ross & J. Lemkin *From impossible to inevitable* p155 Wiley 2016

6 K. Peesker et al "A qualitative study of leaders behaviours perceived to enable salesperson performance" *Journal of Personal Selling and Sales Management* vol. 39 (2019), 323. The authors describe one of the four key roles of a sales manager as "Customer engaging…. interacting with customer to help progress sales deals.

7 "How top performers outpace peers in sales productivity" *McKinsey Article* July 2023 online article https://www.mckinsey.com/capabilities/growth-marketing-and-sales/our-insights/how-top-performers-outpace-peers-in-sales-productivity

Chapter 12

Sales technology

Why is successful selection and deployment of sales technology so important for growth?

Why is the deployment of sales technology vital?

As David Bowie once said, "Tomorrow belongs to those who can hear it coming".[1] We live in very exciting times for sales leaders as technology transforms the way we sell rapidly.

As far back as 2016, an article in the *Harvard Business Review* predicted that "by 2020 customers will manage 85% of their relationship with an enterprise without interacting with a human".[2] Similarly, the authors found that "40% of sales activities could be automated using current technology".

Since that article was written, the ecosystem of sales technologies available has grown exponentially, along with the potential use-cases. So, there are myriad ways that sales technology could potentially help your business. Making the right choice can therefore be challenging, and clear thinking is required to avoid some of the pitfalls associated with all these options.

On the other hand, avoiding sales technology altogether with a 'head in the sand' ostrich strategy is likely to prove disastrous. If your competitors successfully implement technology, they can quickly overtake you, especially if it improves the customer experience and makes the buying process better.

Sales technologies have the potential to improve service, reduce cost to serve, increase win rates, increase the number of leads and remove non-value-added activities from salespeople, thereby allowing them to focus on where they can best add value.

So, let's begin our journey by looking at the very wide range of applications that already exist to see what they could do for your business.

The salestech landscape

Vendor Neutral is a US-based organisation whose mission is to help clients make smart choices about the use of sales technology, from the definition of where it can add most value through to the implementation and delivery of results.

Vendor Neutral works with the *Salestech Landscape*,[3] which is updated and maintained by Nicolas De Kouchkovsky, who has made a mission out of charting sales technology providers.[4] This helps them deploy the best technology for their clients.

In 2023, Vendor Neutral recognised over 1,000 sales technology providers and 350 CRM providers.[5]

So, where on earth do you start? By looking at the big picture first, it can open our eyes to what's possible, so that we can later narrow down the right choices for our context.

We can use the analogy of visiting a supermarket to explain this.

DOI: 10.4324/9781003449614-12

Imagine if you did meal planning by only ever considering the recipes you already knew. Yes, you would eat food you were happy with, but you would miss out on all the wonderful possibilities that exist if we browsed just a few aisles in the supermarket. We would find ways to save time with the ever-growing range of ready meals. We would find all kinds of new exotic flavours and healthy ingredients that are available now.

When we shop at the supermarket, we don't get paralysed because there are so many choices. This is because we go with purpose, knowing what we need and how much budget we have.

So it is with sales technology. We will first browse the universe of solutions before introducing a rigorous process to select what could be the right solution for you. We will also see that there are some 'tried and tested' recipes that start-ups use, which can simplify this process.

Sales technology and marketing technology

You might be wondering how sales technology fits with marketing technology (*martech*). There is, of course, a lot of crossover. Darrell Alfonso, a veteran of martech implementation, sees the role of martech "to attract and retain customers",[6] so in practice, most organisations will have a 'tech stack' which spans both sales and marketing. Martech includes tech that does marketing-specific jobs (for example, content management for brand image control), while sales technology does sales-specific jobs (for example, pipeline management).

To navigate this complexity, I will leave out the *marketing-specific* technologies and focus on the possible technologies that could support growth for Small and medium enterprises (SMEs) and start-ups.

What are the main categories within the sales tech landscape?

Table 12.1 gives the 52 main categories described in the Salestech Landscape under six main category headings. Within each category, there are multiple vendors, with new ones emerging every week. New categories will no doubt be created that are not in the existing landscape, such as the nature of business innovation. Dan Cilley of Vendor Neutral explained to me that he experiences 15–20 new technologies emerging every month and that existing vendors are increasing their functionality to capture more market share.[7]

Without going into great depth about what each category can deliver, there is clearly a very broad range of sales technology that can enhance your sales and marketing efforts.

The technologies cover all parts of a sales process, from finding potential customers to retaining and developing existing customers. They also cover a very wide range of other tasks that sales organisations get involved in, for example, onboarding and training.

How can SMEs and start-ups decide which technologies to use?

Just like when we go to the supermarket, it's helpful to be clear-headed in choosing what technology is right for your organisation. Darrell Alfonso sees four common mistakes that organisations make[8]:

- Buying too many tools
- Shiny-object syndrome
- Underutilising tech – 'Shelfware syndrome'
- Being feature-driven rather than strategy-driven

Table 12.1 The main categories of sales technology in 2024

Key area	Engagement	Productivity and enablement	Sales intelligence	Pipeline management	Pipeline instrumentation	Sales management
1	Interactive demos	Sales engagement	Prospecting database	Pipeline management CRM	Account planning	Sales incentives and commissions
2	Email tools	Sales assistant	Account data	Customer success management	Deal/revenue intelligence	Sales planning and territory quota management
3	Email deliverability	Guidance and recommendation	Financial intelligence	Account based platform	Conversation intelligence	Partner relationship management
4	Video tools	Mutual action plans	Technographic data	Lead to account matching and routing	Sales activity capture	Sales content and collaboration
5	Dialer	Content sharing and digital sales rooms	Intent data	Eco-system and co-selling management	Product-led sales	Onboarding and training
6	Call management and distribution	Extended reality	Contact data	Workflow automation	Sales data visualisation	Sales coaching and team performance management
7	Chat	Appointment scheduling	Relationship intelligence		Price optimisation	Sales gamification
8	Conversational commerce	Gifting	Contact information			
9	Conversational AI	Contract and e-signature	Call tracking and intelligence			
10	Social engagement	Sales quote and proposal	Visitor identification and tracking			
11	Mobile and field engagement		Web social prospecting and monitoring			

These pitfalls are also echoed in Vendor Neutral's whitepaper, which outlines six challenges that companies wrestle with:[9]

- Navigating an overly complex sales tech landscape
- No sales tech, the wrong sales technology or complacency with the existing tech
- Too much money spent on tech
- Low buy-in and poor adoption
- Overly influenced by third parties about which technology to adopt
- No selection strategy

You might well have experienced some of these issues personally. Perhaps a sales director you know went to a trade show, saw a sales technology demo, and was so impressed that they decided to implement it in their organisation without really figuring out if it was the right choice. The net result was poor adoption, and then management threatened to use the system or else!

Building a clear digitisation strategy

How, then, can SMEs and start-ups build an effective strategy for their sales technology? A clear and logical approach to this challenge has been developed by Paolo Guenzi and Johannes Habel in their California Management Review article, *Mastering the Digital Transformation of Selling*.[10] They advocate defining your transformation goals by systematically reviewing your:

- Pre-selling
- Selling
- Post-selling activities

and looking for opportunities to increase:

- Effectiveness and/or
- Efficiency

in two areas:

- Internal processes and/or
- Customer interaction processes

Using their '6S' approach, you can use six digital pathways to re-engineer these areas:

- *Substitute* (e.g., using a chatbot to answer customer questions).
- *Supplement* (e.g., adding extra channels that customers can interact with).
- *Simplify* (e.g., make it easier for customers to place an order).
- *Share* (e.g., transferring best practices between salespeople).
- *Support* (e.g., providing customised sales collateral on tablets).
- *Service* (e.g., giving customers access to digital resources they value)
- Figure 12.1 Summarises the approach.

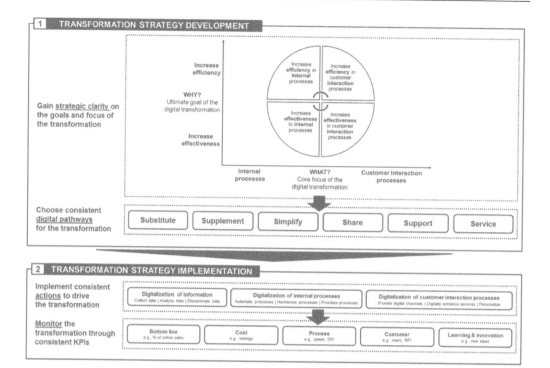

Figure 12.1 The digital transformation of sales

If you have created your *sales strategy, growth model, sales process, sales methodology* and *lead generation* approach, then you will have plenty of activities to review and decide if one of the '6S' approaches can help you.

The 6S approach is especially helpful when you are in 'sales process design mode' (Chapter 3) because it enables you to systematically look at the phases and dream up new ways of managing them.

For example, many large organisations use content management systems (CMSs) to curate content that salespeople can use in the discovery phase of B2B selling. They might have sector-specific content that *supports* salespeople in front of a customer. They might *simplify* the proposal phase using automated *configure-price-quote* (CPQ) software and tools like DocuSign to manage contract paperwork.

Having an appreciation of the sales technology universe helps here because we know roughly what 'ingredients' are available to support sales efforts.

Sales technology for the end-to-end commercial process

Don't forget to think about all the commercial activities your team is involved in as you look for opportunities for sales technology, from lead generation to account management.

Perhaps the most obvious example of this is when *inbound marketing* is used as a lead generation approach. Many businesses will have some kind of *marketing automation* in place (of which HubSpot is perhaps the best-known provider) that tracks website visitors and encourages them to download content in exchange for contact information, such as an email address. This process generates leads for sales teams to contact. Systems like this also act as a CRM for all your customer and contact data, with new prospect data being automatically transferred to its database. In this case, one technology solution may straddle 'pre-selling' and 'selling' activities.

As discussed in Chapter 3, the handover of leads to your sales team must be professional and slick if you want to maximise conversion rates. Similarly, when a sale is closed, there should be a very smooth handover to whoever manages the account (if not the salesperson who closed the deal).

Pay attention to data

One of the challenges that all organisations must address is how to have accurate customer data in all the areas where they need it. Carl Mela and Brian Cooper note that many organisations fall into the trap of *data hoarding* when they deploy technology.[11] This means having lots of data that's not useful and is not in the right place.

They suggest mapping out the flow of data across your sales and marketing processes and ensuring it's possible to transfer what you need between the various platforms. Today, software solutions do exist to help connect systems together (Integration Platform as a Service [iPaaS]).[12] However, these will add cost to your solution, and checking compatibility between systems makes sense.

Customer data can increasingly create the potential for competitive advantage,[13] and so thinking carefully about what data you collect and how you might use it wisely will pay off.

Depending on your operating countries, you must also pay attention to legislation regarding the use and storage of customer data, which in many territories is regulated by legislation.

Three key stakeholders

Whenever technology is considered an option, it's important to keep sight of three key stakeholders. Unfortunately, many systems have been designed by *managers* with a focus on giving *managers* what they need (especially CRM systems). When this happens, salespeople get frustrated with data entry, which they see as an annoying chore, existing purely so their boss can print off a report.

The tech stack design should help three key stakeholders:

1 Customers
2 Salespeople
3 Management

Customers can really appreciate good tech. Research by Othman Boujena identified four types of value customers perceive when salespeople use effective technology,[14] namely:

- Salesperson's professionalism
- Customer interaction frequency
- Salesperson responsiveness
- Salesperson-customer relationship quality

According to McKinsey, "The majority of B2B companies want both human and digital interactions on their buying journey"[15] and so customer focus is essential when thinking about sales technology.

Sales technology should also help salespeople sell. Brandon Bruce, a specialist in CRM adoption, quotes Forrester Research, showing 49% of CRM projects fail, and also CSO research, finding less than 40% of organisations achieve full-scale end-user adoption.[16] Mainly, this happens because the CRM offers nothing but data entry for salespeople. Instead, good tech should be motivating for salespeople because it helps them sell and gives them useful insights about how to sell more (see Chapter 9 case history for an example of how this works in practice).

Finally, insights for management are, of course, vital *if* they use them.

If these three stakeholder groups are kept front and centre of mind during selection, it will help a lot in the long run.

Using external agencies to help you with sales technology selection

Organisations like Vendor Neutral also have their own proprietary methodologies to advise clients on which technologies will best suit their sales context,[17] which again is based on defining sales processes clearly and then deciding which tech will add the most value. A good methodology defines the category of sales tech that is likely to be effective, not the vendor. This approach avoids 'shiny object syndrome' and forces a strategic view of what is actually useful.

Is there a short cut for SMEs and start-ups?

It's easy to be put off by the vast range of sales technology options. To simplify the selection process, many start-ups tend to benefit from a core sales technology stack.

One very useful perspective to consider is the approach taken by venture capital (VC) firms, because they tend to be experts in helping start-ups drive high growth, as they take an active role in supporting their portfolio companies to achieve it.

Craig Rosenberg, Chief Platform Officer of Scale VP, a West Coast VC firm, has vast experience in both sales technology (having worked in the space for most of his career) and specifically what helps start-ups the most.

He advises[18] high-growth companies to typically focus on four main sales technology applications:

- CRM,
- Contact data source
- LinkedIn (basic or navigator)
- A sales engagement platform

The combination of these four technologies assists their portfolio companies to rapidly build their pipeline, and they can then refine their tech stack over time, adding in new applications as required.

For SMEs where hypergrowth is *not* the main focus, different sales technologies might make more sense. Table 12.2 considers these two basic scenarios to help you short-cut your sales technology selection process.

Table 12.2 Two core approaches to sales technology for start-ups and SMEs

Scenario	Hyper-growth with substantial new customer acquisition	Mainly account management with some new customer acquisition
Typical example	SaaS company with a proven product, looking to grow rapidly	Established IT services firm, where account management is the main focus
Core technologies	CRM (customer relationship management) MA (marketing automation) Sales engagement platforms Data enrichment Adverts and PR SEO (search engine optimisation) Social LinkedIn Navigator ABM (account-based marketing)	CRM (customer relationship management) MA (marketing automation)
Optional extras	CMS (content management) IPaaS (integration as a service)	ABM (account-based marketing) Website and blog management tools CPQ (configure price quote) LinkedIn Navigator Sales enablement

Each technology will be reviewed in detail to help you decide if it could help your business. I have also included some typical providers to help you get started on searching in the category. The inclusion of a sales technology provider in the text should not be considered a recommendation. No commercial arrangement exists with Routledge for any of these providers.

CRM

According to the category leader, Salesforce.com,[19] organisation should consider CRM when:

- You have no single source of customer information.
- You have no visibility of what is happening to your customers.
- Reports are hard to share.
- You don't have a mobile solution for salespeople.
- Resale/up-selling opportunities are lost.
- You lack a plan to scale fast.

CRM is often the 'single view of truth' for sales organisations, with many interested stakeholders, including management, marketing, operations and investors. CRM is often the first system that start-ups invest in. Your CRM will track all your customer contacts, interactions, sales and sales potential as a minimum, meaning if a salesperson moves on, you still have all the key information.

Martech guru Darryl Alfonso notes that "marketers use CRM for targeting, analysis and reporting. It is the starting point of many of their marketing campaigns".[20] For this reason, it is likely to be your prime sales technology.

Current providers include:

- Salesforce.com (the market leader with many integrations possible)
- HubSpot (Easily customisable and a favourite among SMEs)
- Microsoft Dynamics 365 (compatible with other Microsoft products and embedded in 365 packages)
- Pipedrive (popular with start-ups because of its competitive pricing and ease of use)

Customer Relationship Management, by Francis Buttle and Stan Maklan, gives a detailed understanding of what CRM can do from an operational point of view.[21] As technology is rapidly evolving, you should research CRM solutions online to find which is the best fit for your organisation.

Marketing automation

Inbound marketing and marketing automation go hand in hand. According to Trust Radius, "Marketing automation helps to automate and scale repetitive marketing tasks and the subsequent analysis of those efforts".[22] HubSpot, perhaps the best-known marketing automation provider, has specific products for small businesses and explains inbound marketing in this way, "inbound marketing is about using marketing to bring customers to you".[23]

Marketing automation can be deployed across all parts of your core sales processes to attract, engage and retain customers. Most systems are easily programmed by users to set up targeted email campaigns by segment, landing pages and customised content based on customer behaviour. For example, if a customer downloads one of your whitepapers, the system could be programmed to send a follow-up email with sequential, relevant content.

Well-designed campaigns using marketing automation can help to nudge a potential customer to contact you when they have a need for your services. Systems can also track the route customers take when they visit your website, enabling you to enhance its content.

Current providers of marketing automation include:

- HubSpot
- Marketo (an Adobe product)
- Customer.io
- Pardot (A Salesforce product)

Sales engagement platforms

While marketing automation focuses on inbound lead generation, sales engagement platforms focus on outbound/outreach.

They are very popular in organisations with sales development reps (SDRs) because they provide a single interface for a wide variety of tasks that SDRs do every day.[24]

Specifically, they help plan, enable and evaluate *outreach sequences*, as discussed in Chapter 6. Given the repetitive work required by sales reps to effectively implement sequences, anything that can be done to automate this and incrementally improve it is hugely welcome.

Leading organisations in this space include:

- SalesLoft (the market leader)
- InsideSales
- Outreach

Data enrichment

Nearly all organisations experience the curse of 'missing fields' in customer data. Simply put, data enrichment applications help you automate the filling of these missing fields. This can save time and make your sales teams' lives a lot easier if you are doing a lot of prospecting. It can also make it more convenient for potential customers, as you will need to request less information from them when they sign up for your content.

The current providers of these applications include:

- ZoomInfo
- Clearbit
- Salesgenie

Adverts and PR

Paying for adverts to be put in front of your customers is not new. But the technology to enable ad-serving has increased in complexity significantly over time, with *real-time bidding* and a whole ecosystem of ad-buying possibilities.[25]

Advertising platforms help you place your ads across a variety of channels. The decision whether to invest in one will depend on how important advertising is generally in your business. If your sales process involves a lot of personal selling, then adverts will typically be less important. If reaching new customers without human intervention is a key part of your strategy, then AdTech will make sense.

Current providers include:

- Google Ads (a good start point for SMEs)
- LinkedIn Ads (sensible to amplify your social media efforts)
- Adroll (useful for Facebook)

SEO

For many start-ups and solopreneurs, SEO and website building go hand in hand. You want your wonderful new site to be found by as many people as possible, don't you? Often, external support is useful for this (see Chapter 6). Platforms that can be used to support SEO include:

- Google Search Console (familiar and intuitive)
- SEMrush (preferred by more sophisticated users)
- Moz (an alternative choice)

Many SEO platforms have now broadened out into other sales and martech areas, such as campaign management and ads. Keeping your sales strategy front and centre will help you avoid being tempted by 'shiny objects'.

LinkedIn navigator

This variant of LinkedIn was discussed in Chapter 6 as a key lead generation tool. It will help you find and contact potential buyers for your product/service, as well as facilitate all of LinkedIn's usual network functions.

Sales enablement platforms

These tend to be more relevant for SMEs that have a wide range of products and new releases that require regular communication and training for their sales teams. Sales enablement systems provide a streamlined way to manage content, training and coaching. They support the sales enablement philosophy of providing sales teams with what they need, when they need it, so they can implement your sales strategy effectively.

It is worth bearing in mind that they stand or fall based on the content that you can feed into the system, so you will therefore need existing content to get the most from these systems, which must be continually evolved. This implies that you will also need personnel to invest time in these activities and the development of these resources so that you don't end up with a white elephant.

Good systems facilitate *closed-loop marketing*, meaning that you will get feedback on how engaged customers are with your marketing content. If, for example, a salesperson shows a customer content on a PC or tablet, then the system will tell marketing which sections were most interesting for them.

Current platforms that provide a wide range of functionality are:

- Seismic
- Allego
- Salesloft
- Showpad

Account-based marketing (ABM)

If your business primarily involves managing a portfolio of stable and large accounts, then account-based marketing is a technology worth considering. Similarly, if retention is very important, then ABM makes sense.

ABM essentially hopes to engage each customer with tailored, specific content relevant to specific roles. Systems like LinkedIn Navigator can support ABM by helping you identify key contacts at your account and update you on what they are posting about, enabling you to better target messaging. If used well, ABM should help penetrate and retain your best accounts.

ABM platforms include

- Demandbase (perhaps the best-known ABM)
- HubSpot ABM (good choice if you are already using HubSpot)
- Marketo Engage (an Adobe product popular with tech companies)

Website and blog management

If you are actively managing the content on your website, then you are probably already using a tool for this. While larger organisations might require a full-on CMS many SMEs and start-ups will only need relatively basic content creation and editing tools.

These applications help you store, edit, and serve up website content. Your choice of which platform to use will depend on the complexity of your content changes and how many people are involved.

Typical platforms for this service include:

- Google Suite
- WordPress (used by many start-ups and solopreneurs as it is very intuitive)
- Wix (simple to get started)
- Adobe Experience Manager (for more advanced users)

Configure-price-quote CPQ

A lot of time can be lost when you have to create separate pricing proposals for customers. Accordingly, a large category of sales technology addresses this need. Many platforms simply facilitate the creation of proposals, track their progress, and facilitate signing by customers. Their stated ROI is to increase revenues.

Care needs to be taken in the implementation of CPQ platforms to ensure they do not decrease your conversion rate. Recall from Chapter 4 the added value of presenting a proposal to a customer rather than just sending it. Saving time on creating proposals is a good thing, while reducing the number of those that convert to closed opportunities is not good!

Common CPQ platforms are:

- Proposify (one of the more well-known smaller brands)
- Salesforce revenue cloud (Logical choice if you use Salesforce)
- Dealhub.io (a popular alternative to the above)

Integration platform as a service iPaaS

Despite best efforts to design good data flows and transfer between technology applications, many organisations find themselves with tricky integration challenges. This can result in frustration for your sales team, from duplicated data entry to the use of complicated spreadsheets to extract and upload data.

Fortunately, iPaaS platforms can potentially solve your data issues by acting as the 'go-between' for your data siloes. iPaaS systems extract data from one source, store it in a defined format and then serve it up to other systems in the format they require, thus enabling you to get the most from your valuable data.

Providers include:

- Workato
- Tray.io
- MuleSoft

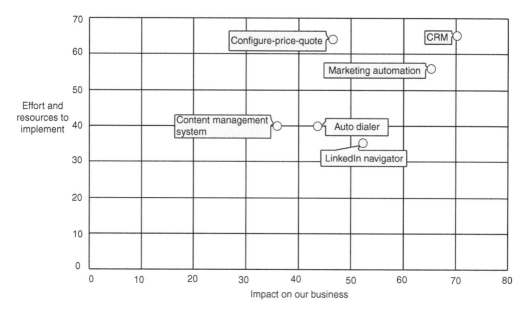

Figure 12.2 An example of an impact effort matrix for sales technologies

Making choices and prioritising your sales technology roadmap

Having defined all the potential areas where sales technology could help you, it's possible that the cost and time involved in all the solutions on your wish list will be prohibitive. Many organisations solve these challenges by building a one-to-three-year technology roadmap, starting with the essential tech first and then adding in 'nice to have' stuff later.

To help you define your roadmap, it is useful to build an impact vs. effort matrix. Figure 12.2 shows an example.

To build the matrix, you will need a working group of key stakeholders who rate each technology option according to:

1 The expected impact it will have on your business
2 The amount of effort and resources required for successful implementation

The process to arrive at the matrix is:

Reach alignment with your colleagues on the evaluation criteria to use: How will you assess each dimension? Table 12.3 shows some examples.

Weight each criterion: Allocate 100% between the assessment criteria. In this example, 'potential to grow sales' scores the highest weighting at 40%, as any money invested should show an ROI.

Score each measure: Using a scale of 1 to 10, each member of the working group gives each criteria a score.

Multiply out the scores using the method in Table 12.4, calculate the weighted score for each technology, and arrive at a percentage for impact and for effort (e.g., 45% impact, 60% effort).

Table 12.3 Example scoring criteria for impact and effort

Measure	Typical examples of evaluation criteria and weightings	Scoring for each dimension (1 = low/10 = high)
Impact	Potential to grow sales (40%)	1–10
	Improves customer journey (30%)	1–10
	Positive effect on the sales team (30%)	1–10
Effort	Budget required (60%)	1–10
	Disruption to the business (30%)	1–10
	Time to implement (10%)	1–10

Table 12.4 Calculation of the weighted scores

Criterion	Weighting (%)	Individual score for the tech	Weighted score
Potential to grow sales	40	6	$0.4 \times 6 = 2.4$
Improves customer journey	30	4	$0.3 \times 4 = 1.2$
Positive effect on the sales team	30	3	$0.3 \times 3 = 0.9$
Total	**100**	**13**	**4.5** (out of 10 maximum)
Score			**45%**

Take the averages of the working group to arrive at a balanced view of each tech.

Plot the scores for each technology on the impact/effort matrix to arrive at your version of Figure 12.2. In this example, we can see that CRM, while high effort, should deliver the most impact, while CMS is not a priority right now.

Discuss the output with the working group: Scoring systems like this should form the basis for further discussion and alignment, rather than being relied upon to make the 'final decision'.

If you are on a rapid growth curve, then it is likely that you will need to drop some technology along the way and replace it with more sophisticated software. It is not uncommon for start-ups to 'get by' with basic 'out of the box' systems and then replace them with a more expensive but more effective version to suit their needs.

Evaluation of vendors

Part of finalising your roadmap will be meeting with the potential technology providers to confirm that they can indeed meet your needs. It is essential to have a clear scope of what you require from the solution, because it is easy to be seduced by flashy demonstrations, but if the system does what you need it to, it's likely to cause frustration.

You should also check out these aspects:

- Upfront and ongoing costs
- Training provided
- Helpline and fault resolution
- Customer success approach – do they have personnel to help you get the most from the tech?

- Longevity and stability of the organisation – Are they likely to be here next year?
- Compatibility and integration – how will the system work with your other technologies? How will data be exchanged/synched?

Rollout and adoption

IT rollouts have a bad press, as stories abound of poor implementation and adoption. Brandon Bruce's book *The Shelfware Problem* reminds us that "adoption is tricky because people are tricky".[26] Therefore, to avoid sales technology becoming shelfware, we must pay attention to good *change management* principles.

A lot of good work has been done in this area over time. A landmark piece of research is *the unified theory of acceptance and use of technology, UTAUT,* developed by Viswanath Venkatesh and his colleagues.[27] They identified seven key drivers of adoption, outlined in Table 12.5.

The first two of these drivers will be heavily influenced by how well you have selected and adapted sales technology to your context and considered the three key user groups alluded to already in this chapter. It will also depend on how proactive and well-crafted your change communication has been. When introducing any changes to a sales team, it's important to set out:

- Why are you doing it? (The case for change)
- What's in it for the sales team? (Appeal to personal values and growth)
- How will you make it possible? (Set out the implementation and training plan)

Social influence is another important driver to pay attention to. As far back as 2002, Scott Widmier and his colleagues found that having an 'initiative champion' within a sales team makes a difference to tech adoption.[28] If one of your well-respected reps is an advocate for your tech, peer-to-peer influence can be very powerful.

Training is a very essential part of the mix to provide *facilitating conditions* and drive *habits*. Brandon Bruce warns against trying to cover training in one event[29]; instead, arrange regular, short sessions (part of sales meetings?) to focus on one or two key areas at a time. Training should be fun, regular, and help make your tech part of the fixtures and fittings.

The building blocks of a scalable sales organisation (Figure 1.1) also provide ways to embed sales technology as a habit. The specific tech usage points should be written into your sales process and methodology so that the proper usage of tech in your way of selling is continually reinforced.

Table 12.5 Drivers of technology adoption

Driver	Explanation
Performance expectancy	How much will it help me to sell?
Effort expectancy	How much work do I need to put in to get the result?
Social influence	What do my peers think of the technology?
Facilitating conditions	Does my organisational setting encourage me to use it?
Hedonic motivation	How much do I enjoy using the software?
Price value	Am I getting value from my investment in technology?
Habit	Does regular use of the technology mean its use is 'automatic'?

Where you are implementing AI solutions, you might need to pay attention to extra factors. This is because we are in a phase of transition where AI use cases are growing rapidly, but users don't always understand the underlying algorithms and therefore don't trust them.

Johannes Habel and his colleagues have studied the adoption of predictive analytics among salespeople.[30] They have found that it takes time for users to build trust in the analytics and therefore, apply them. Also, 1:1 support in working with the algorithm output is helpful for salespeople to apply the predictions in practice.

For many organisations, the adoption of AI solutions will require a culture shift towards tolerating and encouraging experimentation. Jim Dickie and his colleagues writing in the Harvard Business Review recommend[31]:

- Optimise your processes first.
- Ensure top managers visibly support the AI strategy.
- Provide the resources for success (people, systems and training).
- Establish a data-driven culture.
- Start small and generate short-term gains.

AI use cases are covered later in this chapter. In general, a core question for all sales organisations to ask today is "How will we evolve our sales team to be digitally competent?".

Artificial intelligence

In July 2018, Harvard Business Review published an article entitled *How AI is changing sales*,[32] already listing several use cases, including price optimisation, lead scoring and up-selling/cross-selling. Roll on to 2023 and Chat GPT, among other AI applications, has substantially added to what AI can do for sales. A later article in the HBR, *Can AI really help you sell?*[33] lists applications from simple chatbots to "cutting edge technologies that generate deep insights".

There is no doubt that AI will further transform sales, and I won't try to predict how this will look in one, two- and three years' time. For start-ups and SMES who might not have tested the water yet, the good news is that you can start small and free today. Applications like Chat GPT and Bing AI have free basic accounts that enable you to augment and automate some basic sales tasks. For example, in preparing for a sales meeting, you could enter prompts like these:

- What are typical challenges for customer X in managing Y?
- What criteria would customer X take into account when choosing a vendor like us?
- What questions can I ask customer X to uncover their needs?
- What objections might customer X raise when speaking to a salesperson selling Z?
- How can we manage typical objections from customer X?
- Create a table comparing our business A versus our competitor B based on criteria 1, 2 and 3.

The quality of responses you will receive depends on the quality of prompts you use, and a little practice will enable you to get high quality responses in seconds to substantially aid call preparation.

Beyond these 'entry-level' uses of AI, there is a world of possibilities to explore. Well-respected consultants McKinsey describe how AI can help at all points of the customer journey[34]:

- AI algorithms can leverage multiple data sources to segment and target customers.
- A/B testing can optimise lead generation, suggesting changes to content to increase conversion rates.
- Hyper-personalised chatbots can provide support to large numbers of customers with no human intervention.
- Real-time insights and assistance can be provided for pricing and negotiation to help increase profits.

A quick search on the internet (no doubt using AI) will soon throw up many more ways in which sales organisations can use this exciting technology.

Summary

We started this chapter by exploring the universe of possibilities for sales technology. This gives us enormous possibilities for how we can go to market. It also reminds us that high-quality thinking and evaluation are required so that we don't fall prey to shiny object syndrome and the other risks associated with all IT implementations.

Into action

Revisit your sales process and try taking the 'disruptor's view.

If you were new to the industry, how could you design a completely new way to buy and sell?

How could technology make personal selling redundant? How could you reduce the cost or friction of transactions for your sector?

If you conclude that personal selling is still essential, then use the 6S method outlined earlier in the chapter to see how technology could enhance your core sales processes (*substitute, supplement, simplify, share, support and service*).

Try building an impact/effort matrix with your team to align on the best way forward.

Expert view: Sales technology adoption at Aspire Active Education

Aspire Active Education has a very exciting mission, which is to help the nation's children become physically active. At a time when obesity is an ever-present risk in developed countries, the value of exercising cannot be overstated.

Aspire works with schools to deliver physical education programmes, including some very innovative approaches. For example, its 'Maths on the Move' programme helps children who struggle with mathematics find a new way to learn through physical play. Aspire also works with teachers to develop their knowledge of physical education and effective ways to deliver it.

Working with so many schools creates both opportunities and challenges in terms of business development. Retention of schools into the programme is essential to building a foundation for further growth. Because Aspire has quite a few programmes to offer, there are opportunities for cross-selling and up-selling, and so the management of school data, sales and sales activities is critical to success.

Aspire adopted CRM early on in their growth journey, and its use has been heavily championed by Dan Hays, who is responsible for business development.

What types of sales technology do you use at Aspire?

We use HubSpot for three main areas:

- *Business CRM system used to coordinate sales, marketing and customer care*
- *Website building and performance analysis linked to the above*
- *Inbound lead generation via online Scorecards*

How has technology helped you as a small business to grow?

We have automated a lot of our sales processes, so we can handle more enquiries and customers with the same size team. This has increased our sales while also making each sale more profitable in comparison.

The system also analyses our sales, marketing and care data live. This helps us make informed business decisions daily rather than just quarterly, helping us to be more agile in our approach and shifting/pivoting exactly when needed to ensure we are focusing in the right area at any given time.

How did you decide which providers to use for your sales technology needs?

With the CRM system, we were already using one but had lots of headaches. We began by listing the headaches we currently have and the systems we would be able to implement in the 'ideal future state'.

From this list, we conducted research ourselves to identify systems that could solve our headaches, following which we engaged with organisation that had used the systems to gather further relevant information. We then engaged with the system that stood out and invested in their onboarding support to ensure it functioned exactly as we needed it to, so that the whole company would buy into it.

The website building linked nicely to the system we are now using and ticked all our boxes for customer journey analysis.

The scorecard for lead generation was a recommendation. We trialed this with a simple scorecard and a select target audience, which gave great results for us, and we average an extra 1,000 leads per year without much effort at all from this inbound marketing method.

What is your main advice to other SMEs/start-ups thinking about using sales technology to support growth?

A common barrier for SMEs jumping into using sales technology is either the initial outlay or ongoing cost. Either way, there is always a financial barrier, which, understandably, scares most SMEs away from the benefits they bring. I would encourage any SME leaders to address how they are viewing this, from a barrier to an opportunity.

For example, think about the roles, automation and processes the sales technology can take on rather than using their team's very valuable time, investing in more wages or everyone having to work twice as hard to achieve the same results.

From our experience, we're able to automate a lot of big processes, ongoing tedious tasks and even new customer care and sales processes to actually save us a lot of time, increase professionalism, customer care and efficiency for our customers, leading to more sales, more profitable sales and an increase in retention, all without having to increase our personnel overheads.

Where best to start? Begin by identifying below-the-line tasks. Map out every single task you and your team undertake in a normal day, week, month and quarter, then associate a weekly amount of time for that task (if it's a monthly task, then allocate a quarter of the time per week, for example). What you can then do is highlight the value of your time per hour and make that the line, then list all the high-pay off/value tasks that fall above this. These are the ones you should retain, and the lower-value tasks below the line are those that are taking up your time and are below your value to the business.

After you and your team have done this, you will have enough below-the-line tasks, mapped out with their relevant times, to most likely identify that a new employee is needed to take these off your hands so you can focus on the higher-value tasks. Instead of rushing to employ someone, review these tasks and research which sales technology could in fact automate them for you. I guarantee there will be a lot!

Finally, once you have all of these listed against the ideal technology, you can compare the cost of the technology to accomplish those tasks automatically and the cost of hiring, training and continuing to employ and manage a new employee. This is where the sales technology will show how impactful it can be for you.

Notes

1 Allegedly a phrase coined by David Bowie to promote Heroes https://blogs.bath.ac.uk/iprblog/2016/01/14/tomorrow-belongs-to-those-who-can-hear-it-coming/
2 T. Baumgartner et al "Why salespeople need to develop 'machine intelligence'" *Harvard Business Review* June 2016
3 https://vendorneutral.com/salestech-landscape/
4 The salestech landscape can be found at https://www.cacubeconsulting.com/p/salestech-market-landscape
5 Based on an interview with Dan Ciley, CEO, in October 2023
6 D. Alfonso *The Martech handbook* Kogan Page 2022
7 Interview with Vendor Neutral founder, Dan Cilley in August 2023
8 D. Alfonso p12 Kogan Page 2022

9 Vendor Neutral whitepaper https://resources.vendorneutral.com/guide-digitally-transform-your-sales-organization

10 P. Guenzi & J. Habel "Mastering the digital transformation of sales" *California Management Review* vol. 62 (2020), 62–71

11 C. Mela & B. Cooper "Don't buy the wrong marketing tech" *Harvard Business Review* July 2021

12 D. Alfonso p64 Kogan Page 2022 (referring to the Martech 8000 produced by Scott Brinker)

13 V. Govindarajan & V. Venkatraman "The next great digital advantage" *Harvard Business Review* May 2023

14 O. Boujena et al "The benefits of sales automation: A customer perspective" *Journal of Personal Selling and Sales Management* p137–150 vol. XXIX (Spring 2009)

15 C. Angevine et al *The secret to making it in the digital sales world: The human touch* McKinsey whitepaper 2018

16 B. Bruce *The shelfware problem* p1 Cirrus Insight 2016

17 Vendor Neutral use the 5 E approach as set out in the "ultimate guide to digitally transforming your sales organisation" 2023 whitepaper https://vendorneutral.com/

18 Interview with Craig Rosenberg of ScaleVP September 2023

19 Salesforce.com "Your complete guide to SRM" 2018

20 D. Alfonso p59 Kogan Page 2022

21 F. Buttle & S. Maklan *Customer relationship management* p211 Routledge 2015

22 E. Tomac *The Buyer's guide to marketing automation software* Trustradius 2016 edition

23 "Digital marketing for beginners" Whitepaper downloaded from HubSpot 2023

24 https://www.gartner.com/en/articles/sales-engagement-the-definitive-guide-for-platform-selection#:~:text=The%20sales%20engagement%20platform%20is,across%20multiple%20touches%20and%20channels

25 D. Chaffey & F. Ellis-Chadwick *Digital marketing* p433 7th ed Pearson 2019

26 B. Bruce p4 Cirrus Insight 2016

27 V. Venkatesh et al "Consumer acceptance and use of information technology: Extending the Unified acceptance and use of technology" *MIS Quarterly* March 2012

28 S. Widmier et al "Keys to implementing productive sales force automation" *The Marketing Management Journal* vol. 13, no. 1 (2002), 195–196

29 B. Bruce p14 Cirrus Insight 2016

30 J. Habel et al "Effective implementation of predictive sales analytics" *Journal of Marketing Research* vol. 13, no. 1–24 (2023), 34–54

31 J. Dickie et al "Can AI really help you sell?" *Harvard Business Review* November 2022

32 V. Antonio "How AI is changing sales" *Harvard Business Review* Reprint July 2018

33 J. Dickie et al *Harvard Business Review* November 2022

34 R. Deveau "AI powered marketing and sales reach new heights with generative AI" *McKinsey blog* May 2023

Chapter 13

The vital importance of sales training

What does good development look like for sales teams?

Can't we just hire salespeople with the right skills?

Don't SMEs and start-ups have enough to worry about without trying to pay for and organise training as well? Surely, there are 'ready to sell' staff out there who can just hit the ground running. Finding the right salespeople to begin with is most definitely important, and this will be covered in Chapter 16. Even when you recruit effectively, training and coaching are still essential activities in all sales organisations, large or small. Why? There are many reasons:

To grow effectively Bryon Matthews and Tamara Schenk cite the example of Mereo, who implemented a specific sales training programme and saw team target/quota attainment increase from 60–70% to 110–120% in just one quarter.[1] Similarly, sales organisations that add 'dynamic coaching' to the mix, on average improve their win rate of forecast deals by 28%.[2] Good training and coaching can and will help you grow.

To implement your sales strategy: If you buy into the logic that every product/service/market combination is unique, then new salespeople will need to be trained in *your* strategy, sales process and methodology (Chapter 5). And this will need updating when the strategy changes. This is a core purpose of *sales enablement* teams.

To be the best: Abraham Lincoln famously said, "Give me six hours to chop down a tree, and I will spend the first four hours sharpening the axe." For any of us to stay at the top of our game, we need to invest time to challenge ourselves, practice and 'stay fit', through continued professional development.

Imagine a physician who didn't bother to stay up to date with medical advances. We would take a dim view of them. Why, then, should a profession like sales be any different? If your sales strategy, markets, products or competitors change, then this will most likely require a change in your selling approach. Training is the vehicle that enables you to help the team win in a new context.

Because 'natural' salespeople do not exist There exist many myths about sales being a kind of 'gift'. Nick Lee at Warwick Business School argues that most skills are malleable and that perpetuating the idea that sales is a kind of special talent that cannot be developed is unhelpful.[3] Training respects the fact that everyone can improve their competence when it comes to working effectively with customers.

Staff retention It is well known that personal development both serves to engage and retain employees, and so if you want to keep your A-players, then it is wise to invest in them.

Time to competence: If you have ambitions for high growth, then it will be essential not only to recruit at speed but also to help salespeople sell according to your sales strategy as

DOI: 10.4324/9781003449614-13

quickly as possible. Effective training is one of the core processes you will need to master to make your organisation scalable.

Coaching versus training

Coaching as an essential sales management routine was covered in Chapter 9. You may then wonder how it differs from training and whether you need to offer both to your sales team. So, let's deal with these two broad options upfront without submerging into a long debate about definitions. For the purposes of this discussion, I will define training as learning to apply the core skills necessary for the role and coaching as individualized, ongoing support to help your staff perform better in their role.

Great sales organisations use both, often starting with substantial amounts of 'must-have' training early on in the life of a salesperson and then providing regular coaching to fine-tune performance later on. Training is often considered a 'mass learning method', while coaching is an 'individual learning method'.

With this in mind, a 'typical' career training path for a new sales hire could be:

1 *Induction training* in the first six months of an employee's joining to help them understand *the way we sell.*
2 *Refresh training* every year or so to 'sharpen the axe' concerning the use of your sales process and sales methodology.
3 *Product- and market-specific training* when required to learn and practice how to sell in a new context, for example, a new sector.
4 *Professional development training* at least annually to add to the basic training and keep your more senior reps engaged and growing (e.g., negotiation skills, resilience management, time and personal organisation).

Coaching should be a continual activity throughout this journey to work on individual development areas so that employees can perform at their best.

Some organisations set annual targets for training and coaching to ensure that there is a continuous focus on salesperson development. Coaching, for example, is often mandated monthly or weekly, with systems in place to ensure it gets done.

How is good sales training designed?

Effective sales training is built using the same principles that are used to build any effective organisational training. Starting with the end in mind is a good approach, and Figure 13.1 sets out a simple process you can use to design and deploy training.

Defining learning objectives for training

Good training design starts with deriving *learning objectives* or *learning outcomes* from your *sales strategy*.[4] To see how this works, suppose your sales strategy requires selling to financial services organisations, which is a new sector for your organisation. The relevant sales strategy goal could be:

Achieve $X of sales to financial services companies by year end.

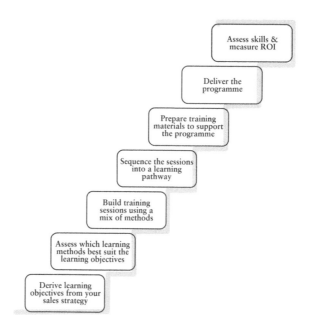

Figure 13.1 Design and deployment of sales training

The derived learning objectives from this strategy could be:

Salespeople are able to ask questions to discover finance sector-specific pain points.

Salespeople are able to share examples of how our solution can benefit finance sector customers.

Notice that learning objectives typically use the phrase "participants are able to", because the implication is that training will fulfil this goal. Focusing on observable skills and behaviours is useful, as in most cases, the trained skill should be visible. Here are some further examples of learning objectives that are quite typical for many sales roles and illustrate the point:

Participants are able to listen actively to fully understand customer needs.

Participants are able to present the value of our solution X.

It is very good practice when you think, "My team need training" to write down the learning objectives that will solve the problem. It forces us to be very clear about what skills/behaviours/attitudes/routines are required, and this makes designing training a lot more effective.

To add further rigour to your learning design, you can also think about how you will assess each learning objective. This helps to sharpen the value of the learning objectives and avoid them becoming unmeasurable.[5]

Assessing which learning methods fulfil the learning objectives

Once you've defined your learning objectives for training, you can then figure out which methods will most likely achieve them. For many start-ups and SMEs, buying in training from external providers might be the only viable option initially, until someone in your team shows promise to take training on as part of their role. Chapter 4 identified some of the typical proprietary sales methodologies that you could use to build the foundations of your approach.

Even if you invest in training, defining your learning objectives is good practice because it will help you assess whether potential training providers can actually deliver what you need. Bought-in training will most likely need to be supplemented with your own internal training because of your unique sales process/methodology logic. In this scenario, it is best to play to your strengths. For example, your external training provider could teach your salespeople generic B2B behavioural skills that need practice and feedback, such as:

- Call preparation
- Questioning
- Listening
- Objection handling
- Presenting
- Negotiating

Your internal resources, by contrast, could then train the very specific aspects of your sales process that are more 'content-led', and require less training in delivery skills, for example:

- Technical needs assessment
- Product demonstrations
- Key needs of specific buying roles and sectors
- How to overcome specific objections

As you reach greater scale, it is helpful if you have internal resources to train all aspects of your sales process and methodology whenever you need to do it, so that training does not become a choke on growth. Not only will you be able to deliver on demand, but you can also ensure the training is fully aligned with your sales strategy without re-educating an external provider every time. At this point, you will pretty much have a *sales enablement function*, which will be covered later in the chapter.

With clear learning objectives and a decision on internal vs. external delivery, it's then possible to choose the most suitable learning formats and start to build a training programme. Specific learning objectives often suggest learning formats. For example, if the learning objective is "to be able to deliver an effective product demonstration in front of a customer", then an element of practice is indicated. Either classroom or virtual classroom training would work best for this, so participants can practice in the environment they would naturally use. Alternatively, a learning objective based on "to be able to identify pain points a CFO experiences" could be trained using a PDF with issues and related questions.

Table 13.1 shows some of the common formats and when they are most suitable for a sales development programme. For a fuller, more in-depth treatment of the pros and cons of each approach, "Learning and Development Practice in the Workplace" is an excellent resource, endorsed as it is by the Chartered Institute of Personnel Development.[6]

Build training sessions using a mix of methods

Having worked through your learning objectives and selected activities that fit them best, the next job is to figure out a sequence of activities that will form the basis of your training session. Taking the example of "being able to do a product demonstration", the activity could be as follows:

Table 13.1 Choice of training media for sales

Format	Description	When to use
Classroom	Training delivered face to face, usually facilitated by a specialist in sales training	To create motivation, energy and social connection Where extensive practice and behavioural feedback are paramount
Virtual classroom/web meeting	Interactive training using group meeting software such as TEAMS or ZOOM	For quick, content-led topics, saving travel time/costs is useful
e-learning	Guided online learning with differing levels of interactivity and assessment	Where the same topic has to be repeatedly trained to large groups of people
PDFs, word documents	Custom-created documents giving content/how-to knowledge	For quick, low-cost knowledge transfer solutions
Workshop	Face-to-face or virtual sessions, where the aim is to use group intelligence to solve problems	Where high levels of interaction are required and knowledge resides in the many, not the few
Video	Short instructional content on shared platforms like YouTube or your own internal file sharing systems	Where an element of seeing a skill take place is valuable (e.g., demonstrating a product)
Activities	Often outdoor or team games, designed to provide fun and/or physical challenges	To boost morale, increase energy levels and build a team
On the job training	A learn-by-doing approach, centred around your employees' daily workflow	For skills where it is best for salespeople to learn in situ, for example, using new software
Peer-to-peer learning	Small groups of salespeople who help each other learn through mutual coaching and knowledge sharing	To reinforce the learning already given To provide coaching where managers may not have enough time
Social media/ chat forum	Usually, a private group set up to ask questions and share knowledge in real time	To share and diffuse best practices quickly To solve problems/answer questions from your sales team
User-generated content (Wikis)	Either online or face to face, a learning format specifically designed to capture sales best practices and diffuse them	As a way to extract and codify expert knowledge in your sales team

10 minutes: Read the product technical description and customer benefits PDF

5 minutes: Prepare to demonstrate the product using a 'typical customer' case

20 minutes: Several reps have a go at doing with demonstration, while another salesperson takes the role of the customer. The whole group gives feedback after each practice session

10 minutes: Group discussion and actions. What can the team do to make sure every demo is as effective as it can be?

Note that training blocks like this do not need to be overcomplicated with expensive e-learning or external trainers. They just need a bit of clear thinking to align the activity with the learning objective.

By working through all the learning objectives, you will arrive at one or more training sessions to help achieve them.

Good training programme design both optimises the media for the message and uses a mix of delivery styles to create variety and suit different types of learners.

Clearly, a mix of learning methods as outlined in Table 13.1 will make for a richer learning experience for your sales teams.

Personally, I have found that highly interactive, practical, action focused training works well with sales teams. Too much reflection and analysis often lower the energy levels, even though these skills do need to be trained for some sales roles.

Sequence the training sessions into learning pathways

With your individual training sessions built up, you should be in a position to sequence training sessions into a *development programme*. One way to do this is to build a *learning pathway*. This is simply a sequence of learning activities that combine to increase the chances of delivering effective development.

They can be particularly useful for SMEs and start-ups that might not yet have internal trainers, formal training or glossy materials because you can signpost existing resources, no matter how basic they are, with learning outcomes in mind. You can check in with learners from time to time to make sure they are getting what they need.

The learning pathway shown in Table 13.2 demonstrates this and is a good way to capture the various steps and think about the best sequence/structure.

If you have a learning management software (LMS) software in place, you can often set up learning pathways in it, enabling you to track and manage their usage. If you don't have an LMS, then it is a good idea to use a spreadsheet to track what training has been given to whom, so you can ensure everyone is trained in all they need to be.

Preparing the training materials

With the learning sessions and pathway defined, the next job is to build the training materials to support them. Specifically, this means you will need:

- *Training notes*: To ensure that the delivery of training is consistent for all sales staff, training notes can be beneficial. Training notes set out the learning objectives, timings for

Table 13.2 A sample learning pathway

Step	Activity	Learning objectives
1	Meet with the product manager	Be able to articulate our product range to a new prospect
2	Read "our solutions" on the website	Be able to explain the typical operational pains experienced by our customers
3	Read the technical specifications products A, B and C	Be able to explain how each product helps our customers
4	Present selling benefits to the sales director	Be able to confidently link needs to benefits in a simulated customer meeting for products A, B and C
5	Visit customer X with a senior sales rep	Be able to explain the typical operational flow to one of our customers

each module, the activities to be carried out, and references to any key slides or handouts that will be used.

- *Support slides*: Many programmes will require slides for agenda, objectives, content, and to guide activities. It's worth investing time to prepare these professionally, using your company branding template, so you set the tone correctly and help salespeople feel part of a high-quality organisation.
- *Handouts*: Aide-memoires for the key points in your training are a very good idea, especially if you think about practical 'Use back at work' content. For example, you could have a handout with ten great questions to ask during a sales call. These should also be high-quality company-branded products to keep standards high. If you have built your sales methodology as outlined in Chapter 5, then your sales playbooks will most likely be the handouts you'll use. Indeed, a good output from sales methodology exercises is a set of 'trainable' resources that you can use in multiple development situations.
- *Online resources* Essential learning materials should be available online, either using a content management system or simply as PDFs if you want to keep it simple.

Delivering the programme

If you have ever experienced dull, irrelevant and uninspiring training, then you will appreciate how important delivery is. If you have a good internal trainer, then you can delegate delivery to them. If you are the founder or sales leader and have to deliver the training yourself, then I would advocate paying attention to the following areas:

Interactive Good trainers ask a lot of questions to their groups to engage them and make them think. Poor appreciation scores from training nearly always stem from limited interaction and 'death by PowerPoint'.

Practice-focused Where possible, give salespeople the opportunity to practice a skill. For example, how to open a meeting or how to use follow up questions based on customer responses. Practice sessions should be short, relevant and involve feedback at the end. Involve the group in commenting on what was done well and what could be improved. Keep the energy levels high, with many people having a go, and avoid long debates and discussions. Favour action over discussion.

Based on your sales methodology: This is your ultimate definition of what good looks like, so ensure that you refer to it often to reinforce it and make it a habit.

Phased delivery Training tends to be more effective when we learn a small number of skills and then put those skills into action on the job straight away. You might train questioning and listening, and then bring everyone back together after a week/month to report back on how they applied these skills. Ask each participant to do a short report-back on their experiences, applying the principle, "What gets inspected gets respected".

Bring the best out of people: Establish a climate of psychological safety[7] where it's ok to make mistakes and try new things. If your intention is to help your team develop and not to judge/criticise them, this will show through in their levels of openness and willingness to try new approaches.

Set the bar high: French writer Pierre Corneille once said, "where there is no peril in the fight, there is no glory in the triumph". This classic wisdom is now understood to be a manifestation of *effort justification*. If your sales team has to work to achieve high standards of professional sales skills, then they will feel pride in their efforts. Going through an intensive training programme typically increases staff retention because salespeople feel they are part of an "elite outfit' and will be less tempted to join your competitors. Research by McKinsey found that training certification, where sales teams have to work to a high standard to achieve defined outcomes, was correlated with higher overall sales performance.[8]

Focus on transfer: Because people inevitably forget some of what they learnt, it is important to put in place effective mechanisms to encourage them to put what they have learned into practice. As already mentioned, phased training helps with this.

Other ways to increase transfers are:

- Explain the why behind each training module and how it supports sales strategy.
- Explain the results you expect if your team masters the skills.
- Show the sales KPIs and metrics that the training should impact.
- Have written action plans for each learning session.
- Coach the skills in the field.
- Consider adding the application of your sales methodology to annual appraisals
- Repeat key themes, and practice them often, to show they are important.
- Put up posters, screen savers and coasters in your office to help recall.
- Talk about training concepts in sales meetings and 1:1s
- Use technology to nudge behaviours (CRM, for example).

Assessing and measuring the impact of training

Because training is time-consuming, potentially costly, and critical to the success of sales teams, it's important to measure the impact of what you are delivering. A good place to start is with Kirkpatrick's four levels of evaluation.[9] Table 12.3 shows the levels and a brief description of what they measure, adapted for a sales context.

Although other models of evaluation do exist, Kirkpatrick's model is an excellent go-to for SMEs and start-ups. If you have done a good job of aligning your learning objectives with your sales strategy, then level 4 measurements of the results you are hoping to impact should be clear. Regular evaluation of your training, at the very least, will help to take on board employee feedback and also enable you to enhance and improve training delivery.

Having looked at the design and delivery of effective sales training, let's now turn to the other types of training identified earlier in the chapter that support lifelong learning and sales career development.

Induction training

This is one area that is vitally important to get right. The CSO Insights 2017 Sales Enablement Optimisation Study identified "decreasing new hire time to full productivity" as the

Table 13.3 Kirkpatrick's four levels of evaluation

Level	What is measured	Typical questions
1	Participant's reaction	How well was the training received? Did your team enjoy and value the time invested?
2	Participant's learning	How much have they learned as a result of the training? What do they now know?
3	Participant's behaviour	What have they changed? What is observable in their behaviour?
4	Organisational results	How has the training improved their sales KPIs?

second most important concern of sales leaders.[10] When setting out the number one sales enablement goal for new hires, Cory Bray and Hilmon Sorey express this quite colloquially "Aggressively reduce new-hire ramp time. Get them on the phone on Day 2 and in a full-time selling role as soon as humanly possible. No excuses".[11]

It's worth bearing in mind that good induction programmes typically last one year to ensure that new hires become fully integrated and do not get frustrated, leaving their new employer.

Induction and onboarding will be covered in Chapter 16. For now, it is important to ensure that you have a solid training and coaching programme for new starters, and a learning pathway as outlined above is a very good start.

New product/sector training

Whenever you make a major shift in what/how you sell, it's seriously worth considering developing training sessions to help your sales team excel in what can be quite a new environment. Given that new products or decisions to focus on a new sector are likely to be strategically important decisions, it's worth setting up for success. The idea of the *sales learning curve* was introduced in Chapter 9. Effective training will help accelerate sales by reducing the time to competence.

Often, new products or sectors can be addressed with short workshops or bite-sized training blocks. Let's consider an SME that launches a new food ingredient, perhaps a novel type of protein that could be added to improve the texture and flavour of a ready meal. The salespeople are competent at selling, but not this particular product. A workshop agenda could be as shown in Table 12.4:

Table 13.4 A typical workshop flow for product launches

Agenda item	Activity	Output
Product manager technical introduction with Q+A 30 minutes	PM shows the new features of the product, typical application cases and approvals/test results	Sales team understands the new product and what it can do
Team ideation session 20 minutes	Sales team generates a list of USPs/benefits for typical customers	The sales team internalise the product features and gets excited about how they can help them sell
Generate questions to lead sales meetings 20 minutes	Sales team generates questions that they can use to open discussions with customers, identify potential needs, and create curiosity	A tool kit of useful questions to use at customer meetings
Practice meeting 40 minutes	Short customer-sales role plays to practice introducing the new product	Increased skills and confidence in selling the new product
Action planning 10 minutes	Define a list of target customers to meet in the next month to introduce the product	Concrete action plan to introduce the product

Note: A two-hour workshop for the new product launch.

Research presented by professors Thomas Steenburgh and Michael Ahearne in the Harvard Business Review[12] showed that training sessions are particularly useful for salespeople some time after the new product launch, when progress starts to slow down.

Typically, it's easy to get customers to meet with you to learn about a new product, but getting commitment and traction after this initial excitement may be more challenging. Training should then focus on objections that have surfaced, technical challenges with your product/service and solving any other problems that may have arisen. Having product managers and marketing specialists involved in training is really productive at this point, as tweaks may need to be made to your offering once this 'contact with the market' intelligence starts to flow in.

You don't need all the answers to run new product training. Your salespeople can help you create the knowledge during training. After all, they are the specialists in the craft of selling, and they have contact every day with customers. A workshop format helps to establish a climate of "This is our new product…how can we best sell it?".

Staff retention and lifelong learning

Salespeople will stay with you if they feel they are continually developing and using their potential to the best effect. Because effective recruitment can be expensive and challenging, especially if you need highly skilled people, it is far better to provide a structured career development track where successive training and development engages your 'gold collar workers'.

It is a wise move to sketch out what a typical career track could look like for salespeople that stay with you for two, three, five and ten years. How will you keep them stretched and growing? What training and support could help them stay with you?

Typical development programmes offered by sales organisations are:

- Sales methodology refresh training ('Stay sharp')
- Negotiation skills
- Time management and personal organisation
- IT and sales technology skills
- Wellbeing and resilience
- Personality profiles such as the MBTI,[13] DISC[14] and INSIGHTS[15]
- Key account management
- Coaching skills
- First-line management for high potentials
- Sales excellence specialist training
- 1:1 executive coaching
- CRM deployment and development
- Sales operations management
- Sales enablement management
- Digital marketing strategy

Secondments and special projects are also excellent vehicles to develop your senior, experienced salespeople. Not only do they seriously stretch and develop your team, they also help you get work done that would otherwise involve outsourcing or additional headcount. According to their preferred development track, you could ask them to:

- Get involved in building a sector development plan in conjunction with marketing
- Create sales collateral to support a product launch
- Mentor and coach a new colleague
- Help create your sales methodology
- Manage one of your largest accounts

What is sales enablement, and do I need it?

Over the last ten years or so, more and more sales organisations have set up sales enablement functions. This is especially true in software and SaaS businesses, where growth is constrained mainly by the ability to sell, not the ability to produce products.

The trend has rapidly accelerated in the USA and is diffusing to other countries as well, often via international corporates that have global sales enablement teams.

So, what actually is sales enablement? A great definition is provided by an early pioneer of sales enablement, Sharon Little, who led sales enablement functions at VMware, Oracle and Cadence. She explains it in this way, "Sales enablement means having the ability to reliably transform your sales team, no matter what happens in the market".[16]

A fuller definition is provided by Byron Matthews and Tamara Schenk, "Sales enablement is a strategic collaborative discipline, designed to increase predictable sales results, by providing consistent, scalable enablement services that allow every customer facing professional and their manager to add value in every customer interaction".[17]

Typically, sales enablement teams help salespeople have the best content, training and coaching to implement a sales strategy. In this way, they help move from good (making the numbers) to great (selling a chosen product to a chosen customer base in a defined time period).

So, is it something for start-ups and SMEs to worry about? Potentially yes, if any of the following conditions apply to you:

- You have very high growth targets that will often involve recruiting and training salespeople.
- You have external funding where expectations for growth are high.
- You have a lot of product/service complexity, meaning salespeople are confused about who to listen to internally and what sales efforts should be prioritised.
- Your sales involve a lot of technical information that changes quite frequently.

Sharon Little eloquently describes sales enablement teams as the 'gateway' between front-line sales and all the internal functions that vie for their attention: marketing, product teams, technical, sales operations and sales leadership. By brokering the key priorities and supporting salespeople to sell according to the strategy, they reduce noise and drive focus.

Start-ups and SMEs might allocate sales enablement to an existing manager, who coordinates the activities of others in the business, to ensure that salespeople are 'enabled to sell'.

A key part of sales enablement is content. In this context, we mean the messages and collateral that salespeople receive to help them sell. Using the example from earlier of an organisation selling into the financial services sector for the first time, this could mean developing:

- A sector insights PDF
- An ideal customer profile
- Typical personas in the ideal customer profile

- A list of their operational pains that your product solves
- Questions to ask linked to these pains
- Use-case examples and testimonials
- Product/service benefits linked to financial services
- Common objections and ways to manage them

A salesperson trained in all these aspects is likely to achieve more success in selling into the new sector in this way.

In conclusion, elements of sales enablement can well be of value to start-ups and SMEs if intelligently applied.

Into action

Start by auditing what you already have in place for training. Ask your team how they feel about the training they have received. Ask them how much they use what they have been trained in. This will enable you to continue training that is useful and discontinue training that is not.

To prioritise where to start, typically, SMEs and start-ups should build training solutions in this order.

1 Sales methodology (Chapter 5) training programme for existing salespeople
2 Career track training for existing employees
3 Induction training for new hires

This logic is based on developing and retaining your existing team before tackling the new hires. However, if you are doing a lot of hiring in the near future, then induction training may need to take priority.

For each programme:

1 Define the learning objectives from your sales strategy.
2 Choose the best learning methods to meet the objectives.
3 Build the training sessions and associated learning pathways.
4 Pilot and review

Expert view: Investing in training at Jumar

Jumar specialises in helping clients find people and technical solutions to their complex digital transformations. The company has won an impressive array of awards, thanks to its singular focus on creating an excellent environment for employees to flourish in. Recently, it was awarded the prestigious "Great Place to Work in Tech" status, which is only achieved by a few companies that really pay attention to employee development.

Jumar provides training in a wide variety of areas for its employees, including sales training. Eleanor Sheehan, People Advisor, has been instrumental in the company's employee engagement plans.

Why have you put so much focus on employee engagement and development?

It's a cliché, but engaged and happy employees do the best work and stay with the company for long time. Investing in additional support and development opportunities demonstrates our commitment to every individual and, in turn, helps us reduce turnover and burnout. Employee feedback is incredibly important for shaping our strategy and has contributed to our overall success. We encourage regular 121's to understand our employees both on a personal and professional level and listen to what they need.

What type of training do you offer employees?

We offer a variety of training opportunities for our teams. Our training budget is generous, and we don't tie our employees to specific providers or courses. We have built a library of recommended technology and soft skills courses and exams which fit in with our company strategy, but we are keen for our employees to own and build their own training paths to help them achieve their personal career goals.

Many SMEs find working on projects like this quite challenging because of time and resources. What is your advice to other SMEs concerning how to make a success of employee programmes?

This will always be a challenge, but adapting your mindset as a senior team member is vital. Don't look at training opportunities as a drain on time and resources; this is an important investment in your future. Taking the time and money to invest in the right software for your business is a no-brainer, so why would you look at the development of your teams any differently? Plan ahead and understand your employee's medium- and long-term career goals, which will help you shape a programme that offers maximum benefit for everyone.

You have a very experienced business development team, so how do you develop them when they may well have attended several sales trainings earlier in their careers?

Fostering a culture of self-development and continuous learning throughout the business encourages a positive learning mindset among most employees. This should be encouraged at all levels of business. In the words of our Chief Operations Officer, "the day I think there's nothing left to learn is the day I'm no longer useful to this business". We always ensure company-wide shout-outs for achievements, and we hold appraisals twice per year for the teams to set their own work and learning objectives.

Besides core sales training, what other development do you think is useful for sales teams?

Exposure and short secondments to other teams and areas of the business can often help to build confidence and understanding in the company and the services on offer. Strong internal relationships build trust between teams. Internal mentoring is a must. For technical sales roles, some basic certifications in Agile can also help to establish credibility with clients.

Notes

1 B. Matthews & T. Schenk "Sales Enablement" p94 Wiley 2018
2 Ibid., p108
3 N. Lee "Natural salespeople do not exist" *The international journal of sales transformation issue* 2.1 (2016)
4 K. Beevers et al *Learning and development practice in the workplace* p102 Kogan Page 2020
5 Ibid., p106
6 Ibid
7 I. Nembhard & A. Edmondson *Psychological safety: A foundation for speaking up, collaboration and experimentation in organisations* The Oxford Handbook of Positive Organisational Scholarship August 2011. This paper explains the areas managers can focus on to create psychological safety
8 W. Decherd et al. *The difference between good and bad sales training: A closer look at certification* McKinsey whitepaper February 2019
9 K. Beevers et al p299 Kogan Page 2020
10 B. Matthews & T. Schenk p100 Wiley 2018
11 C. Bray & H, Sorey *The sales enablement playbook* p20 Bray & Sorey 2017
12 T. Steenburgh & T. Ahearne "How to sell new products" *Harvard Business Review* November 2018
13 MBTI is the short name for the Myers-Briggs Type Indicator, which is a registered trademark of the Myers-Briggs company www.themyersbriggs.com
14 DISC assessments are run by various companies and are based on the work by psychologist William Moulton Marston https://en.wikipedia.org/wiki/DISC_assessment
15 Insights personality profiles are based on the work of Carl Jung. Various versions exist, with perhaps the most popular being the Insights Discovery profile which is copyrighted https://www.insights.com/products/insights-discovery
16 S. Little *The enablement advantage* p10 Halo Publishing 2015
17 B. Matthews & T. Schenk p28 Wiley 2018

Chapter 14

Account management

What can we do to make sure our hard-won customers stay with us?

When do you need an account management strategy?

Hands up if you want to lose customers! Ok, there are maybe one or two that you wouldn't mind losing, but for the rest, you probably want to keep them. And, since new customer acquisition is famously more expensive and difficult than selling to existing customers, most Small and medium enterprises (SMEs)/start-ups will benefit from an account management strategy to drive retention.

The need becomes more acute when you have 100s or 1,000s of accounts, because then the cost of servicing them all is high, and you will face choices about which ones to prioritise for the best return.

Similarly, if you have a handful of large accounts that make up a substantial percentage of your turnover, then the risk of losing one or more of them indicates that a *key account strategy* would be wise too.

What are the goals of an account strategy?

There are many outcomes that might be important for your business, for example:

- Increase retention rates as part of your growth model.
- Increase revenues by up-selling and cross-selling at your accounts.
- Fuel word-of-mouth marketing and advocacy through happy customers.
- Motivate customers to give testimonials/feature case histories for your marketing efforts.

With these aims in mind, it's clear to see that a good account strategy can make a real difference to your bottom line.

Prioritisation of your customer base

The case for customer prioritisation was laid out in Chapter 2 as part of your growth model and sales strategy. Since not all customers present you with equal opportunities for growth, the simple question answered by customer prioritisation is, "Where are the best opportunities to invest your valuable sales time?".

Customer prioritisation is used by many large organisations to direct their sales teams to the best customers to work with. Often this is strongly steered by CRM systems, targets and bonuses, because, if done well, it is a proven lever of growth.[1]

DOI: 10.4324/9781003449614-14

Even if you have a relatively small account list, an understanding of customer prioritisation principles can help you make smart choices about where to focus your efforts.

Customer prioritisation models

How is it best to assess where to focus valuable sales time? This question gets to the heart of what makes a customer attractive. Here are some typical customer assessment criteria used in sales organisations:

- Growth potential
- Profit margin
- Expected customer lifetime value
- Size (revenue)
- Quality of relationship
- Ability to trial/sell new products
- Brand cache (will the customer's brand help us sell to others?)
- Number of products sold
- Loyalty

Thus, there is no one 'silver bullet' measure that we can use to answer this question, as it depends to a certain extent on your product and service.

Some companies keep it very simple and do an ABC analysis, as shown in Figure 14.1.

While this quick and crude method is, well, quick, it is also crude. Just because an account is big does not make it attractive, nor does it always mean time invested is time well spent. Some large accounts can be demanding, unprofitable and painful to work with. For this reason, although it is useful to know the spread of spending for your account base, more sophisticated measures are required to be clear on where to prioritise time.

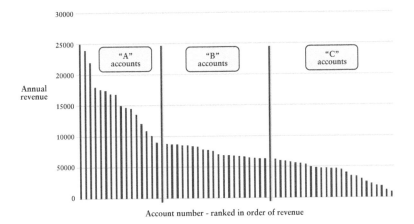

Simple ABC analysis of accounts by revenue

Figure 14.1 An ABC analysis of customer account revenues

To offer greater clarity in how to manage accounts, many organisations build a portfolio model using two or more dimensions to categorise their accounts. Figure 14.2 shows such a model, along with the high-level strategic approach for each category.

This example maps growth potential against attractiveness. The simple principle is that it's best to invest time and resources in attractive customers who have high potential for growth. Customers who are not that attractive and have low potential for growth are best served by 'hands-off' methods, for example, telesales or self-serve through e-commerce.

Other prioritisation matrices are possible. To explore more options, I recommend *Customer Relationship Management* by Francis Buttle and Stan Maklan.[2] The authors discuss a wide variety of methods that you can use.

A vital ingredient of the *portfolio approach* to account management is that you free up time from some accounts to invest in others. Therefore, reducing time or cost to serve on some accounts so it can be used elsewhere is vital to success.

Assessing attractiveness

As already mentioned, there are a number of measures that we can use to assess attractiveness. Many companies will use a weighted basket of measures to arrive at an overall score. This is done in a similar way to assessing technology, as outlined in Chapter 13. Table 14.1 shows an example of how the criteria might be constructed:

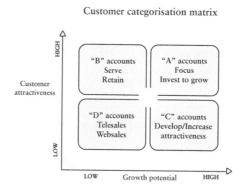

Figure 14.2 A portfolio categorisation model

Table 14.1 Example customer attractiveness criteria

Customer attractiveness Criteria and weightings	Growth potential Criteria and weightings
Profit 40%	Expected customer turnover growth rate 20%
Size revenue 30%	Options for volume increase 40%
Quality of relationship 20%	Options for cross-sell 40%
Brand cache 10%	

By using pre-specified levels, you can score each account objectively to arrive at a weighted overall score for each criterion. Table 14.2 shows how this could be done, using the assessment of account profit (gross margin) as an example.

By developing scoring levels for each criterion in your assessment list, you should end up with a percentage score for each account (see Chapter 13 for more detail on the working method).

When this has been done for all your accounts, for both axes of your prioritisation matrix, you will be able to plot them on a 'starry night' graph, as shown in Figure 14.3.

Setting the boundaries

Figure 14.3 sets the boundaries between A, B, C, and D accounts using 50%/50% lines, which is an obvious start point; however, it is not necessarily the end point. Recall that categorisation answers the essential question, "Where are the best opportunities to invest your valuable sales time?". Depending on the resources available to you (number of sales roles, time and cash), you might shift the boundaries so that you end up with a *manageable* portfolio of opportunities.

Jason Jordan and Michelle Vazzana, maestros of metrics, state it like this, "The ultimate goal of account management is to maximise the long-term value of a select group

Table 14.2 Example of scoring criteria

Profit (gross margin)	<20%	20–24%	25–28%	29–32%	>33%
Score		1–2	3–4	5–6	7–8	9–10

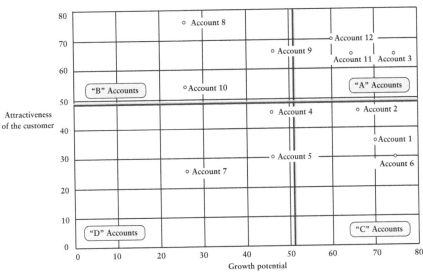

Figure 14.3 An example customer attractiveness portfolio

of customers".[3] Therefore, setting the boundaries is a demand-supply balancing exercise. Realistically, how many A-category customers can you manage with kidgloves? Do you have a way to drastically reduce the cost/time-to-serve for D-category accounts? Allocation of workload to teams is never easy to figure out, but the 'build-up method' covered in Chapter 9 on structures is a useful guide for account allocation.

It is normal, therefore, to shift the lines on your grid away from 50%/50% to arrive at a practical, workable categorisation scheme. This should enable you to reduce time spent at unattractive, low growth accounts and invest it where there is high potential to grow attractive customers.

Setting metrics for account management

With your accounts categorised, it's time to set metrics for each category. These should, of course, reflect the differing levels of time and resource investment. Typical metrics that firms use are:

- Visit/interaction frequency (for example, x calls per year)
- Penetration/share of wallet
- Up-selling/cross-selling targets
- Price levels
- Account development plans in place
- Progress versus the account plan
- Business review meetings
- Sales of new products/technologies

Setting metrics helps to make the expected level of service to each account clear for everyone. CRM systems can help operationalise account management by providing prompts, checks and reports for expected activities. Indeed, once you have a base of over 100 accounts, it is probably essential.

Key accounts

If you have several large accounts that make up a substantial percentage of your turnover, then it is wise to implement a *key account strategy*. What is a key account? This is a question that comes up time and again. Mark Davies, author of *Infinite value,* offers this practical definition, "A key account is an existing or prospect enterprise customer that has the potential to generate significant commercial opportunity".[4] By corollary, a key account has the potential to cause pain if you lose it too!

While you may have several key accounts, it's important to recognise that they are not all created equal. Key account experts Diana Woodburn and Malcom McDonald explain that "our research revealed that about 85% of Western European companies do not know whether they make or lose money from their biggest customers".[5]

This is one reason why it's important to carry out a special categorisation for your largest accounts. There are other reasons too: Key accounts, by their nature, involve a lot of time investment from your direct sales team and internal roles too. Is this time investment justified? Also, if your key customer does not see you as an important/attractive supplier, then there is a risk that you *over-invest* in them. Woodburn and McDonald call this *supplier*

Table 14.3 Mutual attractiveness permutations

Scenario	Description	Strategy
Customer is attractive to us We are attractive to them	Strategic customers	Invest to grow Build a joint account development plan
Customer is attractive to us We are not attractive to them	Star customers	Reposition ourselves to be more attractive Find new contacts and develop a new value proposition
Customer is not attractive to us We are attractive to them	Status customers	Implement a simple retention strategy Work on increasing profitability Be careful not to overinvest
Customer is not attractive to us We are not attractive to them	Streamline customers	Reduce cost-to-serve Don't give them a reason to leave

delusion,[6] and it is a real risk when you work with a 'big name', that everyone sees as unquestionably attractive.

The authors recommend that to avoid supplier delusion, we need to assess how attractive we are to our key customers, not just how attractive we are to them. This gives rise to the concept of *mutual attractiveness* and to four simple scenarios, shown in Table 14.3.

Generally speaking, we don't want to lose key customers (unless they are really unattractive to work with!). So, the key account categorisation is another version of prioritising time at the best opportunities.

Assessing mutual attractiveness

To figure out how attractive we are to customers requires a mirror image of the approach we use to assess their attractiveness to us. Woodburn and McDonald recommend looking through your customers' eyes to assess how attractive you are compared to your competitors.[7] This is done by asking them what factors are important to them, weighting these and then scoring yourself against the criteria *compared to your competition*.

This method ensures we take a customer-centric approach, that is benchmarked against our competitors. You will use exactly the same method to end up with a percentage score for assessing customer attractiveness. This will enable you to categorise your accounts using the logic in Table 14.3.

Be aware that assessing mutual attractiveness is fraught with human bias. There is a natural tendency for salespeople to avoid scoring individual accounts as unattractive because this has implications for support and their career prospects. It is therefore essential to reassure your sales team that you will take care of any downgrades or substantive changes to their account portfolio and status.

When you have scored your accounts, they can be categorised into *stars, strategic, status* and *streamline* customers, as described in Table 14.3.

The strategic approach is outlined for each category in the table.

Because power and status are at stake with key account categorisation, it's important to involve your sales team in the process. Simply using the raw data to make the classification won't cut it. You will need to discuss each individual account and be prepared to adjust the scoring and/or classification if 'extenuating circumstances' are revealed. The core question has not changed; it is "Where are the best opportunities to invest your valuable sales time?". If you keep the team focused on this, you will reach a sensible portfolio of accounts that everyone buys into.

Remember that it is not just sales time that is invested in key accounts; it's all your internal roles as well.

Key account strategy

Good key account management is a 'whole enterprise endeavour', meaning everyone involved in serving your accounts needs to be involved. This is because, as you develop plans for your accounts, you will be making commitments to customers that involve the work of many. It's important to make sure that they can commit and to engage their creativity in serving customers. A good account plan will also involve your internal team having contact with key people in the account.

Taken together, it implies good stakeholder mapping and change management to ensure your key account strategy can take flight.

For a much more detailed view of good strategic account management, *Key Account Management*, already alluded to, is an excellent resource.[8]

Key account plans

The subject of account plans has come up several times already. What are they, and why do we need them? Jordan and Vazzana again explain "that winning strategy can only be brought to life if you develop a plan outlining the required tasks".[9] At the most basic level, an account plan is a mid- to long-term living document of key activities, timelines and responsibilities. More sophisticated account plans can be much more comprehensive. They can be separate documents (Word, Excel and PowerPoint) or part of your CRM/other salestech.

Firstly, not all accounts should have an account plan. Recall a key principle of customer categorisation: It's to reduce time investment in low-grade accounts and deploy it elsewhere. If you ask your sales team to do an account plan for every account, you will end up with low-grade account plans for ALL your accounts.

Therefore, the type of account plan you require should be adapted according to the customer category. For example, a strategic account should have a comprehensive account plan that is co-created with the customer. On the other hand, a streamline account should have just a few lines to outline core objectives.

What should be in an account plan?

This will, of course, depend on the significance and complexity of your account. A checklist is shown in Table 14.4, followed by a description of each element.

Customer profile

In Howard Stevens and Theodore Kinni's extensive research into 'what B2B customers want', the second most important thing (out of a list of 7) was "you must understand our business".[10] Credible key account managers cannot walk into their customers' premises

Table 14.4 A checklist of potential sections in a key account plan

	Strategic account	Star account	Basic account
Customer profile	✓	✓	
Opportunity analysis and growth targets	✓	✓	✓
Decision making unit	✓	✓	✓
Macro-environment analysis	✓		
Competitor analysis	✓	✓	
Power analysis	✓		
Procurement type	✓		
SWOT	✓	✓	
Strategic objectives	✓	✓	✓
Roadmap/action plan	✓	✓	✓

without a solid understanding of how their business works. The customer profile section of an account plan covers things like:

- Ownership
- Financial structure
- Revenue and profits
- Number of employees
- Operating sites and territories
- Your customer's customers
- Their business model and drivers of profit
- Vision/mission/values
- Sustainability policies

Understanding the basics of your customer's business allows you to anticipate trends and be the first supplier to help your customer address them.

Opportunity analysis

Think of this section of an account plan as figuring out the growth model (Chapter 2) for the relationship. Sometimes good opportunities get missed. The exact framework should be adapted to your product/service. Some areas to focus on are:

- How much extra share of wallet can we go for?
- What opportunities exist for up-selling?
- What opportunities exist for cross-selling?
- How much can our prices be increased by?
- Which new products could we sell/develop?
- What new geographies/sites could we sell to?
- What new business model could we think of?

A thorough analysis of how much you can grow your business will go a long way towards understanding how attractive a customer truly is.

Decision-making unit analysis (DMU)

Recent research has shown a trend for more and more 'influencers' getting involved in B2B purchasing. Figures quoted in 2015 in the Harvard Business Review article, *Making the Consensus Sale*, suggested the average number was 5.4,[11] although this has likely risen due to economic and geopolitical uncertainties weighing heavily on organisations' collective confidence.

Therefore, a core disciple of key account management is to map the decision-makers and those who influence them so that you can try to win them over. This involves finding out:

- All those involved in influencing buying decisions for your product/service.
- Figuring out their role in the buying decision.
- Understanding their level of credibility and influence in their own organisation.
- Understanding their support for your product/service.
- Finding any hidden influencers.

Once you have a map of your current network and contacts, you can use political nous to extend your influence and thus, your likelihood of success. Table 14.5 shows an example of such a map for an organisation that is looking to buy sales training. In the table, a *technical influencer* is one who sets specifications/parameters for a purchase but cannot sign off on the purchase. They can say no to a supplier's offer, but they cannot give a yes. That privilege is reserved for the *budget holder*. An *advocate* is one who wants you to be successful, normally for reasons of personal status/gain within their organisation (if you are lucky enough to have one).

Note that in the table, question marks exist where information is missing. This is quite normal when mapping decision-making units. Of course, there will be information we don't know. And finding it out is often a key takeaway from this exercise.

Strategies to improve our influence on a customer's decision-making unit include:

- Using an advocate to introduce you to new influencers
- Encourage those who are positive about your solution to influence those who are not.
- Connecting with missing influencers.
- Working along the lines of power and politics in an organisation to improve your position of influence.

There are many iterations of decision-making unit mapping. John McMahon, for example, strongly advocates looking for *champions* and *economic buyers*[12] when engaging with

Table 14.5 A map of a customer decision making unit

Contact	Title	Role in buying process	Level of influence	Support for us
Sheema	Sales director	Budget holder	High	??
Tamsin	HR business partner	Technical influencer	Medium	Neutral
Arun	L&D manager	Technical influencer	Low	Negative
Howard	Sales manager – North	Advocate	Medium	Positive
?	Sales manager – South	?	?	?

customers. Essentially, economic buyers make the final decision, and champions can give us access to them.

Decision-making unit analysis (DMU) mapping is essential for *strategic* and *star* accounts. For star accounts, DMU mapping helps us identify which new people we might engage with to change how we are perceived as suppliers.

Macro-environment analysis

Good account managers understand what is going on in the wider world and how this *macro-environment* affects customers. Recent years have reminded us why this is so important (The COVID pandemic and the invasion of Ukraine). If we are not aware of the unique pressures our customers face, then it is difficult to be a really effective partner for them. Worse still, we might be blindsided by changes that make us obsolete as suppliers.

For many businesses, doing a macro-environment analysis for the sector is enough. It does not necessarily need to be account-specific. Historically, PEST was used as a tool to do this (assessing political, economic, social and technological factors). PEST has steadily expanded over time to encompass more elements. Accordingly, you can use an ESTEMPLE analysis for a really thorough check,[13] as shown in Table 14.6.

Macro-environment analysis does not need to be overcomplicated: Even 20 minutes spent reflecting on our customer's situation is time well spent.

Competitor analysis

A very important theme in key account strategy is the need to develop a *competitive advantage*. Without it, suppliers become *price-takers* in a perfectly competitive market (affectionately known as *strategic hell*). If we do have a competitive advantage, then we can charge higher prices, and it is less likely that we will lose business to competitors.

For key accounts, this is especially important because it is not just the time of one salesperson that is at stake, but the time and cost of internal resources too.

How do we then ensure we have a competitive advantage? Basic *competitor analysis* was covered in Chapter 2, and the key output we are looking for is to find a *distinctive positioning* that customers value.

Table 14.6 Estemple factors applied to key account analysis

Macro factor	Description
Economic	How is the economy affecting your customers?
Social	What social trends are affecting their business?
Technological	How is technology transforming the way your customer operates?
Ecological	How are issues of sustainability and the environment affecting customers?
Media	What is the impact of social influence, media and PR?
Political	What government policies, trade and taxation factors are important to understand?
Legal	Which legislation, now and planned, could affect our customers?
Ethical	What acceptable ways of doing business do we need to be aware of?

Solid account plans should include a competitive analysis, which helps define what your competitive advantage could be. The potential sources of competitive advantage are:

- A unique product or service
- A unique process or technology for the buy-sell transaction.
- Specialist knowledge or expertise.
- Geography – that is, your locations are preferential to customers.
- Data, for example, *product-in-use, customer behaviour* and *market information.*
- *Economies of scale* that enable low costs.
- *Network effects* that make you the de-facto choice for new users.

A quick look at any industry will reveal that any competitive advantage is *transient*. As Michael Portor advised us many years ago in his Five Forces model, if you are making good profits, customers, suppliers, competitors, substitutes and new entrants will be vying to disrupt your position.[14] For this reason, a key account development plan should continually seek to find new ways to maintain competitive advantage so that you de-risk your revenues.

Power analysis

This theme was covered in Chapter 7 as part of our value proposition and pricing. For key accounts, the stakes are even higher, as the size of revenues involved will likely attract the attention of your customer's procurement teams, who will look to maximise value for their firm.

My experience with working with key account managers is that this is an absolute game changer for their confidence in negotiations and the ability to say NO to unreasonable requests from large customers. Alternatively, if you have very little power, there is more realism about what can be negotiated.

Your account planning document should include a power analysis, plus objectives for increasing your power over time.

Procurement type

One of the frustrations I hear a lot from account managers is working with procurement. Often this is expressed as "It's difficult to get meetings with the buyer" or "The buyer is really difficult to deal with".

Understanding how procurement views you as a supplier is a good starting point for decoding the behaviours you experience. Consider that many of your customers will have to manage a long list of suppliers. Given that headcount is always under pressure, procurement departments will have to prioritise which suppliers they invest most time with. This is the mirror image of *customer prioritisation* already covered in this chapter.

Peter Kraljic addressed this challenge by developing a framework for working with suppliers according to their potential to affect profit and the risk of supply (or difficulty in finding reliable suppliers).[15] He identified four categories, as shown in Table 14.7.

Looking through the eyes of procurement can reveal a lot about how you are managed and what the next steps should be to develop your account strategy.

Some account managers can feel a bit deflated when they realise they are 'just' *routine* suppliers, and their boss wants them to co-create an account development plan. In fact, being a routine supplier can be a great place to be. If you give good service and don't cause

Table 14.7 Supplier management categories

Category	Description	Example and typical supplier management approach
Critical	High potential to impact profit High risk to source	e.g., PC makers buying processors Expect lots of meetings, close management and regular negotiations
Leverage	High potential to impact profit Low risk to source	e.g., Book publisher buying paper Expect RFPs, reverse auctions, and endless tough negotiations
Routine	Low potential to impact profit Low risk to source	e.g., Car maker buying stationary Expect very little contact from procurement
Bottleneck	Low potential to impact profit High risk to source	e.g. Bank buying specialist coding services Expect to be treated as a 'partner' and be aware that buyers may actively search for substitutes to de-risk

problems, then you will likely be left alone, with less risk of being displaced. Buyers simply don't have the time or bandwidth to negotiate with you!

For a more thorough understanding of the working methods of professional buyers, I recommend *Procurement Principles and Management*, by Peter Baily and his co-writers[16] and *Negotiation for Procurement Professionals* by Johnathan O'Brien.[17]

SWOT analysis

For account planning, you can use the SWOT format (strengths, weaknesses, opportunities and threats) to summarise all the inputs from the previous sections. It is a way to make the current view of the account clear for all to see.

We are using SWOT from the perspective of our *current relationship* with the customer. We are not doing a SWOT for their business or our business. The SWOT should have no more than five to six points per quadrant, prioritised in terms of importance. Table 14.8 shows an example.

Using SWOT as a summary tool enables us to see the big picture for the account and forms the springboard to develop strategic objectives.

For a quick account development approach, we can build a SWOT without too much detailed analysis. This approach can make sense for your less attractive opportunities, so you can spend more time on your priority accounts.

Strategic objectives

When you have worked through your analysis work and summarised it in SWOT, the next logical step is to derive *strategic objectives* for developing the account. These should flow directly from SWOT.

In the example in Table 14.8, potential strategic objectives could be:

1 Use our advocate (factory manager) to introduce us to new product development, procurement and technical buyers.
2 Negotiate a 12-month supply agreement.
3 Convince customers to trial 2 of our best products to increase their dependence on us as a supplier.

Table 14.8

Strengths	Weaknesses
Our product is performing well	We only interact with two people today
Good relationship with factory manager	We don't have a long-term
Our supply point is very convenient for them	supply agreement

Opportunities	Threats
Sell to their other factory	We know competitor X is active on site
Cross-sell new lines	New procurement director started this month
Develop a new product for their new launch	

Strategic objectives are typically mid to long term and should help you advance your position with your key customers. They form the basis of how progress is measured for your account.

This is a crucial point to understand for *star accounts*, where you don't yet have a commanding position. Sales directors sometimes set unrealistic growth targets for star accounts where the foundations are not in place to secure that level of business. It is more sensible to focus on building influence and a sound value proposition before setting crazy growth targets.

Roadmap/action plan

As Jason Jordan and Michelle Vazzana put it so eloquently, "There's the pesky chore of flawlessly executing the plan".[18] With your strategic objectives defined, they need to be given timelines, responsibilities and follow-up. The "what gets inspected gets respected" approach applies again here.

A simple format of key milestones, with who, what and when, will help you stay on track *if and only if* you regularly review your plan. Technology can, of course, help, with many CRM systems facilitating this too, with calendar reminders.

You can also aid this by having regular review dates hard-baked into your annual calendar. 1:1 and group sessions to go through account development plans can help to drive real progress.

Account plan formats

One of the issues organisations wrestle with is: what format should an account plan take? Questions like how many pages, which document type, where it is stored and who can access it can all arise.

Generally speaking, it should be as simple and pragmatic as possible. Once you have decided which sections are required for your account plan (Table 14.4), try to create a basic template using a Word or Excel document.

The account plan should be easy to read and easy to update. If done well, a key account development plan is great to stay focused on what should be a well-thought-out strategy. Paying attention, particularly to the strategic objectives, can help when you or your team are time-poor and in the heat of the sales action.

Business review meetings

The cornerstone of account development is a business review meeting. This is typically conducted quarterly or annually with your key account, depending on its categorisation (e.g., strategic, star, business as usual and streamline).

The purpose of a business review meeting is to:

- Review performance and action plans
- Seek feedback
- Give feedback
- Review and build joint development plans
- Secure new opportunities for the future
- Extend your network

Customers' willingness to enter into business review meetings is a good indicator of your importance as a supplier and the quality of your relationship.

Customer success philosophy

The incessant rise of SaaS businesses and the need to secure good retention rates have seen the role of *customer success* rapidly become more prominent. Essentially, the role of customer success is to help buyers get maximum value from your product/service. This has led to a whole new way of thinking about post-sales customer management.

Taking responsibility for your customers' success (and therefore satisfaction) is an excellent attitude for account managers to have in a sales organisation. It is also likely to lead to benefits beyond pure retention. Aaron Ross and Jason Lemkin call customer success "a core growth driver"[19] because happy customers tell their friends and generate word-of-mouth marketing for you.

This theme was also picked up by Stevens' and Kinni's research, as already mentioned. The number one factor predicting world-class status for B2B salespeople from a buyer's point of view was "Personally manages my satisfaction".[20]

Account-based marketing

This was first mentioned as a potential tool to help SMEs in Chapter 13. Sales technology can help support your account management efforts by automating and personalising contact/engagement with your significant accounts.

Relationship management

"People buy from people" is often thrown around by salespeople as 'sales wisdom 101'. What does this mean for account managers? As customers, it certainly helps when we like and trust the salespeople we do business with. Indeed, if you have strong relationships between your team and your customer's team, this can be a source of competitive advantage. How then can we build good, solid relationships with customers?

Deliver on your promise: First and foremost, be a great supplier. It's difficult to build rapport with a customer when you're letting them down, so stay focused on getting the work done.

Professionalism As outlined in Chapter 4, setting our standards higher than customers means they are unlikely to ever be disappointed.

Be interested in them Showing genuine interest in customers' work, pastimes and passions is the best way to become liked. Who doesn't like to talk about their interests?

Make each meeting an event If you are able to make your customer meetings unique, interesting, stimulating, fun, useful and generally valuable, then it won't go unnoticed.

Social time and entertainment Respecting principles of bribery and corruption, inviting customers to social and sporting events can be a good way to deepen your relationship.

Remember that your competitors are probably doing their best to take your business, and therefore a little bit of healthy paranoia goes a long way for account retention.

The management of relationships can be systematised, by considering who should talk to who. Woodburn and McDonald identify four types of relationships that exist between buyers and sellers[21]:

Basic relationships are where you have one point of contact in an account and are typical for transactional sales.

Co-operative relationships involve more contact between different roles in yours' and the customer's team, while the key account manager is still the central point of contact.

Interdependent relationships have many structured interactions between your team and your customer's team, with the key account manager acting as the 'conductor'.

Integrated relationships involve fully embedded cross-functional/cross-boundary teams working together.

Relationship types should be in tune with the categorisation of your trading relationship. For example, independent and integrated relationships make more sense for *strategic* accounts, but less so for *streamline* accounts.

Summary

Customer centricity is often paraded as a 'silver bullet' strategy for growth. This chapter has hopefully shown that not all customers are created equal, and it is important to invest time and resources where the best opportunities lay, by categorising your account base intelligently, and then deliberately managing your time to support your chosen growth strategy.

Into action

Have you categorised the relative attractiveness of your account base?
If not, start by doing that, either by

a Using the weighted evaluation method in this chapter
b Discussing the accounts and using a consensus approach

When you have categorised your accounts, define the high-level strategic approach for each category:

- The service-level agreements for each category
- Visit/interaction frequency targets

- Account planning requirements
- Use of technology (CRM) to enable your categorisation model
- The measurement and follow-up strategy

Ensure that you involve your sales team in the process so that you have buy-in for the end result.

Expert view: Account management at Essentia Protein Solutions

Essentia is a global protein specialist, providing high-quality products to the food industry. All around, the nutritional value and taste characteristics of our food are enhanced by Essentia's range. For account managers at Essentia, this means working with major household names to develop food solutions to exacting standards while keeping costs under control.

As part of a long-term drive to enhance its customer centricity, Essentia began to look at its account management strategy. This initiative was led by Søren Moller, Director, who has been involved in the programme from the start.

Q1 Why did you decide to put extra effort into your account management strategy?

Following a re-organisation of our company, we took the opportunity to initiate a thorough strategy development process, leading us to embrace customer centricity as a guiding philosophy for the company, on both a strategic and cultural level.

With corporate initiatives circling around delivering better value to our customers, we realised how our insights into the needs and strategies of our individual customers were too general-based and not systematically grasping the different customer needs and growth strategies across the customer base. Driven by our commercial team, we designed a strategic account planning process with new tools and processes, securing structured selection, categorisation and in-depth business plan development for each key account across the group.

Q2 What did you learn along the way?

There were numerous "Aha" moments that turned assumptions into facts. For example, the mapping of decision-making units led to the realisation of why and where projects were stalled and where we needed to focus. It was a great help internally to share customer strategies with cross-functional teams. Also, we learned about the great variance of customer strategies – even within the same industry segments – which made most of the "one solution fits all" initiatives irrelevant, while a selected mix of services targeted to meet individual key account needs has boosted loyalty.

We realised that consensus on which key accounts to focus on truly matters, and this enabled us to focus senior management resources on the right players, leading to strong lock-in on a high strategic level. This has led to joined-up innovation processes with a more strategic-oriented business approach, which removes focus on price.

Q3 What advice do you have for organisations that want to introduce account plans?

As for account plans, I would highly recommend these reflect the customer category: long and deep plans for star accounts and short, opportunity-oriented plans for high potential. Streamline and business as usual accounts should have very short plans to enable more time to spend on high-priority opportunities.

There should be champions and a clear top management commitment, but tools and processes should be developed bottom-up by the key stakeholders.

It is important to involve internal virtual teams in the plan development, as this greatly adds to understanding the width and depth of the customer touchpoints. A lot of crucial knowledge sits with the team dealing with everyday transactions, for example, customer service and quality departments.

It is also important to get going: Practice on a few accounts before rolling out the full program. We hot-housed four accounts during programme development and embedded the learnings into the final account management strategy.

Q4 How do you think your customers have benefited from your account management strategy?

While every customer is treated in a professional manner, there is no doubt we have become conscious of where to spend our time and resources. We now direct our efforts to customers where there is a clear strategic fit, an openness to engage in co-creation processes, and long-term business development. This opens up access to our technical services. At the same time, I see that our opportunity management focus has led to a much broader use of our product range, meaning cross-selling for mutual benefit.

One of the consequences of account planning is that it involves saying no. If streamline accounts experience less access to our time and services, then this is part of the exercise.

Notes

1 C. Homburg et al *Sales excellence* p34 Springer 2012; M. Johnson & G. Marshall *Sales force management* 13th ed Routledge 2021
2 F. Buttle & S. Maklan *Customer relationship management* p142 Routledge 2015
3 J. Jordan & M. Vazzana *Cracking the sales management code* p119 McGraw Hill 2012
4 M. Davies *Infinite value* p151 Bloomsbury 2017
5 D. Woodburn & M. McDonald *Key account management* p4 Wiley 2013
6 Ibid., p57
7 Ibid., p42
8 Ibid
9 J. Jordan & M. Vazzana p120 McGraw Hill 2012
10 H. Stevens & T. Kinni *Achieve sales excellence* p40 Platinum Press 2007
11 K. Schmidt et al "Making the consensus sales" *Harvard Business Review* Mar 2015
12 J. McMahon *The qualified sales leader* p283 John McMahon 2021

13 D. Angwin et al *The strategy pathfinder* p5 Blackwell Publishing 2008
14 J. McGee *Strategy: Analysis & practice* p149 McGraw-Hill 2005
15 P Kraljic "Purchasing must become supply management" *Harvard Business Review* Sep 1983
16 P. Baily *Procurement principles and management* 11th ed Pearson 2015
17 J. O'Brien *Negotiation for procurement professionals* Kogan Page 2016
18 J. Jordan & M. Vazzana p121 McGraw Hill 2012
19 A. Ross & J. Lemkin *From impossible to inevitable* p52 Wiley 2016
20 H. Stevens & T. Kinni p39 Platinum Press 2007
21 D. Woodburn & M. McDonald p54 Wiley 2013

Chapter 15

Compensation, incentives and prizes

How do we ensure we have competitive, motivating incentive schemes in place that align to our sales strategy?

Truth and lies about sales compensation

There is a perception among some that salespeople are only interested in getting their commission for a sale. As in any career, there are those who are extremely motivated by money, but there are others that find fulfilment in a sales career for a whole variety of other reasons.

Detailed research has been done by Dr Monica Franco-Santos and Dr Javier Marcos to find out what actually motivates salespeople,[1] and their data revealed a number of factors important to salespeople. Table 15.1 summarises some of the more important areas:

While money is clearly a factor, there are many other sources of motivation that you can use to encourage performance.

What is known is that variable compensation has been shown beyond reasonable doubt to motivate salespeople to perform.[2] Indeed, in the USA, 40% of salesforce remuneration is compensation-based,[3] demonstrating its widespread use. So, while it might not suit everyone, at the organisational level, it does work.

Aside from questions about motivations, one thing that is fairly clear is that the compensation scheme you implement sends a message about what your organisation wants to focus on (or not). Mark Roberge (already a familiar sales leader in this book) puts it a little stronger: "one of the biggest lessons I've learned involves the power of a compensation plan to motivate salespeople not only to sell more but to act in ways that support a start-up's evolving business model and overall strategy".[4]

There is a belief that there is a perfect sales compensation package out there, if only we could discover it. The truth is that all reward schemes can have unintended consequences, so getting it right is more of a journey than a destination, especially as new product launches or competitive moves can disrupt the status quo at any point.

What elements does compensation include?

When you design a compensation package for your sales team, there are five core elements you can play with[5]:

- The base salary
- Commission
- Bonuses
- Sales contests
- Other benefits

DOI: 10.4324/9781003449614-15

Table 15.1 Salespeople motivators

Extrinsic monetary factors	Extrinsic, non-monetary factors	Intrinsic factors
A reasonable annual salary	Advancement opportunities	A job I find meaningful
Annual salary increases based on experience/seniority	Coaching/mentoring	A supportive manager
Organisational incentive pay	Job security	Autonomy to decide what I do in my work
Retirement benefits	Workplace flexibility	Supportive peers
Individual incentive pay	Recognition	Autonomy to decide how best to do my work

Note: Salespeople's top five motivators are ranked in order of importance for each area.

Table 15.2 Compensation design process

Step	Activity	Description
1	Set the pay level	First and foremost, you have to be an attractive employer compared to who else a salesperson could work for
2	Balance salary and incentives	Your type of sale will guide your choices here
3	Design the plan	Design elements are considered in this chapter
4	Choose payout periods	Timing does affect psychology
5	Consider additional elements	Since the COVID pandemic, non-monetary benefits have assumed a greater role in attracting and retaining talent

The sum of these constitutes the remuneration you offer and, ultimately, what salespeople will use to evaluate you as a potential employer.

How to design an effective compensation package

Doug Chung, writing in the Harvard Business Review, offers a pragmatic five-step approach to building your compensation plan, summarised in Table 15.2.[6]

Let's look at these steps in turn.

Step 1: Set the pay level

It's wise to do your research to consider what employment options salespeople have compared to working for you. This will help establish the total remuneration package you should offer to be a winner in 'the war for talent'. If you want to offer less than the market rate, you will need to lean more on the non-monetary benefits to attract applicants.

Step 2: Balance salary and incentives

Industries vary massively in the proportion of fixed basic compared to bonus/commission. There are several drivers that you can consider in making this choice:

The length of the sales cycle: If it takes months/years to close a deal, then increase the ratio of fixed salary vs. variable salary to keep people motivated.

The degree of relationship-selling involved[7]: If customer service and follow-on support are important, then increase the ratio of fixed salary vs. variable salary to keep people motivated.

The amount of teamwork involved in bringing in the sale If multiple individuals are involved to win a sale, then a high variable proportion is likely to cause conflict and dissent.

Ethical perceptions Many pharma and medical device companies have publicly stated that they have removed variable pay to send a clear signal that salespeople's actions will not be biased by potential financial gain.

What are the norms for balancing fixed and variable? Frank Cespedes, author of *Aligning Strategy and Sales,* quoting a VP of Sales, uses these benchmarks:[8]

If variable compensation is 10% or less, salespeople will barely notice it

Between 10% and 25% you get their attention

Between 25% and 50%, it affects behaviour and management can control a few things

More than 50%, management loses control over salespeople, who operate with a 'make quota or quit' mindset

A whitepaper by international consultancy Deloitte recommends that for every dollar taken off the base salary, 2–3 dollars should be offered if the target is achieved.[9]

You also have the option to link incentives to profit performance. This has the advantage that salespeople won't be tempted to slash prices so that they can get deals over the line. The challenge with this method for many organisations is that measuring actual profit can be difficult.

To a certain extent, compensation schemes act as informal performance management systems. If a rep does not earn their OTE (on-target earnings), it will be very visible and create tension for them and their manager. The flip side of this is that where you have a low percentage of variable pay, you will need a strong performance management system based on non-quantitative factors to weed out 'social loafers'.

Step 3: Design the plan

There are a number of options you have for the variable element of salespeople's compensation.[10] They are:

Introduce straight-line compensation, where salespeople receive a fixed percentage of sales, regardless of how much they sell.

Alter the slope of the payout line/curve to determine the actual percentage they get paid for each sale.

Introduce floors where commission is only paid once a minimum level of sales is achieved.

Introduce caps where commission is not paid over a certain level.

Include steps/accelerators in the payout curve where the percentage paid is increased once sales reach a certain ambitious level.

Add bonuses, which are paid when specific targets/metrics important to your sales strategy/organisational goals are achieved.

Much research has been done to assess the effects of varying these factors, and the evidence behind these choices is reviewed later in this chapter.

Figure 15.1 shows some of the variations that are possible using these variable factors (Figure 15.2).

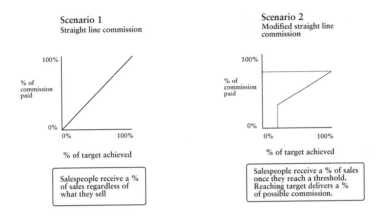

Figure 15.1 Compensation payout curves

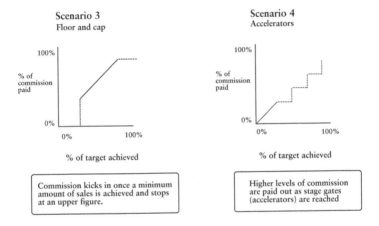

Figure 15.2 Compensation payout curves

Step 4: Choose the payout periods

When should you pay commissions and bonuses? Unsurprisingly, timing does make a difference, and the psychological influence of timing is considered in the next section.

Step 5: Consider additional elements

As already hinted at, not everyone is motivated solely by money. You can offer a wide range of other benefits that could be very valuable to salespeople. These include:

- Remote working/hybrid/co-working spaces
- Flexible hours/work arrangements
- IT devices and equipment
- Car/transport options
- Healthcare/wellbeing packages
- Retirement benefits

- Holiday allowances/sabbaticals/unpaid leave
- Perks (gym membership, travel discounts, etc.)
- Training and development

We stray into good HR practices here. A little research and creativity will help you figure out what employment benefits are likely to be attractive/affordable.

What research/evidence can guide our choices of compensation schemes?

Beyond the five-step method outlined above, Doug Chung explains in his article some of the findings from research into compensation schemes.[11] Of particular interest are the following points:

Complicated schemes tend to encourage 'gaming' Salespeople slow down or hold back sales to maximise their personal gain.

Introducing caps to commission schemes can hurt overall sales by as much as 8%. Caps should be avoided.

Cumulative bonuses work: If a salesperson misses a quarterly target, they can still get their commission if they meet the cumulative target for all missed quarters.

Non-monetary gifts of the same cash value are perceived as more rewarding: Consider replacing a cash payout with a gift of value to the sales team/individual.

Ratcheting up a target so that overperformance is rewarded with an even higher target in the following year is demotivating for salespeople.

Other researchers have also discovered useful insights into the design of compensation schemes. Tobias Kuntner and Johannes Voester, writing in the NIU Journal of Sales,[12] discovered some of the same effects mentioned above and also advised:

The payout curve should either be straight-line or have small steps only: This is because salespeople might engage in detrimental behaviour to 'get to the next level', for example, giving discounts to accelerate a sale.

Set ambitious but realistic targets: Targets or steps that are perceived as 'too difficult' are likely to be demotivating.

Given that salespeople have different motivations and competencies, should compensation be universal (i.e., the same for everyone) or personal (i.e., adapted to the individual)? There are two schools of thought in this area. Some argue for fairness and consistency so that you don't have to face awkward conversations such as "Why wasn't I offered that package?". Others have experimented with different schemes to test their effectiveness.

One interesting study in this area was done by Thomas Steenburgh and Michael Ahearne,[13] that recognised most sales teams consist of a mix of abilities and labelled *stars, core performers* and *laggards*. They discovered that applying a universal commission scheme to all these three groups was not effective. For example, stars do not appreciate caps because they are habitual overachievers and see them as demotivating. Also, laggards need more coaxing and 'stick', as well as 'carrot' incentives.

Accordingly, they differentiated their approach for each group, using the principles shown in Table 15.3.

With the rapid advancement of AI and machine learning, it will most likely become easier for sales managers to segment sales teams and motivate them more appropriately.

Table 15.3 Different reward approaches based on current performance

Group	Approach
Laggards	Implement pace-setting bonuses (i.e., commissions are paid out more regularly)
	Use the "man on the bench" principle: Salespeople are told that a new trainee is entering the team and will replace the lowest performer
Core performers	Introduce multi-tier targets to boost efforts as each increment of a target is reached (provided it does not encourage excessive discounting)
	Offer differentiated prizes for this group so that the stars don't win them all
Stars	Remove any ceilings on commissions
	Allow multiple winners in competitions if you have several stars
	Introduce the accelerator/overachievement commission

After all, personalisation is a social 'macro-trend'. We come to expect it more and more in our personal lives.

How about the timing of payments? Research by Doug Chung and his colleagues published in 2014 in *Marketing Science*[14] echoed what was found to motivate laggards, namely that increasing the frequency of payouts increased performance. The increasing frequency of payouts did not affect high performers.

Core checks for your compensation scheme

When you design your scheme, there are some general checks and guidelines to consider. Some key themes suggested by Dr Christian Homburg are:[15]

- It must be *transparent*, i.e.; salespeople can understand it.
- It should be *flexible* to allow for changes in strategy.
- It *motivates* salespeople to achieve the desired outcomes.
- The scheme must be *cost-effective*, i.e., paid for from extra sales, and not detrimental to your finances.
- The scheme limits *compensatory effects*, i.e., non-achievement in one area cannot be compensated for by achievement in another area.
- *Consistency* across sales teams i.e., your scheme should not create envy in individuals, because equivalent roles experience markedly different compensation schemes in your organisation.

It is also important to be clear when a 'sale is a sale'; in other words, do you pay out compensation when an order is received or when an invoice is paid? This decision will depend on your cash collection cycle. If the timing is wrong, you could upset your working capital position.

Above all, remember that the core purpose of compensation schemes is to align sales behaviours with your sales strategy. Frank Cespedes, the already-mentioned author of *Aligning Strategy and Sales*,[16] puts it this way: "Sales incentives have three allied purposes... (1) Communicate management's goals and direct sales efforts towards the most strategically attractive opportunities... (2) Increase the ROI in the firm's sales capacity...and (3) Motivate".

For a great description of how this has been applied in practice, Mark Roberge's account of how HubSpot adapted their commission scheme is a good read.[17] Initially, the focus was on the acquisition of new customers, but while salespeople enthusiastically signed up new customers, the attrition rate was too high. Roberge changed the bonus to include rewards for signed-up customers that stayed for a full year. In this way, salespeople's behaviours were altered to better qualify potential customers as HubSpot learned about the market and how it responded to their new product.

This insight is especially important for start-ups, who are often in a rapid learning phase with their product/service.

Continual experimentation

As was mentioned upfront, the perfect scheme probably does not exist, and therefore you may well have to experiment with different approaches to get the best fit. It is wise to 'stress test' a potential compensation system. What could you do to maximise your personal gain? How would that affect your sales strategy?

Competition and prizes

If you have worked with salespeople for any length of time, you will often detect an inherent 'competitive nature' in them. It's normally pretty easy to see this in action during a team day involving sports or games – there are sure to be a few individuals with a 'win at all costs' attitude.

Competitions and prizes have been used for some time in sales organisations to drive results, and they offer a useful extra lever to accelerate sales. If the competitions and prizes are well designed, then they can also generate team spirit and a culture of fun and positivity.

Mark Roberge puts it this way, "*Contests bring a fun, dynamic aspect to a sometimes mundane, daily routine*".[18] He gives the following advice for designing a good competition:

Align the contest with a desired short-term behaviour change, e.g., to prevent a summer sales slump.

Make the contest team based as this helps to build team culture, and avoids the 'every man for himself' attitude.

Make the prize team based, e.g., go-cart racing for the winning team, again to build a team-wins-together culture.

Send out the contest standings out daily so that the contest is front of mind.

Competitions can work well in call centres because they help to create a culture of fun and winning that is visible to all and can thus raise energy levels and pace, which can be contagious.

Putting it all together

Designing compensation systems can be daunting. Start-ups might benefit from external HR support to draw up contracts and stay on the right side of local employment law. More and more, enlightened employers are asking their own staff what they want, to ensure that their compensation scheme actually motivates as it is supposed to, while taking care to align incentives with sales strategy.

Recall that a world-class sales organisation delivers predictable, sustainable revenue growth and is agile enough to adapt sales strategies, knowing that the sales team will implement them. Your compensation plan is an essential element in supporting this agility, so it is important to build in the flexibility to make changes.

If designed well, it will act as a lever you can pull to drive your sales team in the direction you want them to go. It is an essential part of the 'sales system' that good VPs of sales build to grow their revenues.

Into action

A benchmarking exercise can be a good thing to do with your compensation scheme. What are competitors/equivalent organisations offering? Try to find five job adverts to benchmark your own scheme.

What do your employees want? Ask them without promising that you will deliver everything they ask for!

Check your existing scheme. Does it encourage people to implement your sales strategy? Can you see any aspects that would cause your employees to act against the interests of your organisation?

What would you change?

Expert view: James Hutchings – Sales director animal health medicines

James has worked for a wide range of global animal health brands and has extensive experience in building winning sales teams. During his career, he has designed many incentive schemes for salespeople.

What kind of incentive schemes have you found to be most effective in motivating salespeople to sell?

It's a subject very close to my heart because it's easy to get them wrong, and it's very impressive and rewarding when you get them right! You really do remember those years you got it bang on, and try to think, why did I get it right on those occasions?

Bonuses, incentives, commission and objectives often get bundled together. The commission is simple: you sell X, and you get a percentage of the sale Y. This usually replaces part of the salary. A bonus is usually related to salespeople being rewarded for achieving sales over target. I truly believe that a decent incentive plan for a sales team is a stand-alone inspirational scheme that drives the very best performance from your salespeople and the sales team.

I think objectives should be kept separate because they are a whole different subject. They are important measures for your team. Objectives should set the direction, linking to SFE and performance management.

Incentives and incentive plans tend to appeal to the top percentile of your sales team. In an ideal world, every salesperson will achieve 100% of their year's target and everyone's happy. You've sold what the production has made. The marketing team has spent the budget they had. But it never happens that way. You know that one or two of your sales team members are going to be 10% over, and you hope they make up for the underperformers. These top performers are the ones that you're trying to encourage. You're trying to inspire them to do even more, realising their true potential and keeping them engaged, motivated and, most importantly, on the team.

The best incentive scheme is often the simplest scheme. But it must be fair. I don't think enough time gets spent on creating incentive schemes. For example, if you've got a team that works as a team and you want to encourage that to create a top-performing-winning team, then your incentive scheme must be a team-related incentive scheme. That team will encourage each other to achieve, utilising the different strengths of individuals to maximise the opportunity they have as a team.

If you've got a team of individuals and you are happy for them to work individually, the incentive scheme should not be related to team performance. It is a bad move to penalise a top performer due to the poor performance of other individuals when they are not interacting as a team.

I think it's important to give incentive schemes a name as well. I used one in the past called 'Spectrum 5', because it was about getting people to cross-sell five products. If possible, give it a name related to what you want to achieve. This will help make the scheme come alive.

It should have frequent measurements and reporting. If salespeople don't know where they stand on their incentive scheme, that's a problem. Nor should you change it mid-year. I did that once and regretted it! You might please some people, but you will inevitably upset those who are really working hard towards that scheme.

It's important to know your individuals inside out as a sales manager so that you know what motivates them. Sometimes it's money, but not always. One great example was a vet practice that had very little parking, so staff had to park in a public car park 1/2 mile away. The employee of the month got a parking space right outside the practice, giving them an extra 10 minutes in bed in the morning! Incentives could include extra day's holidays, a better car, corporate recognition, or a new job title. Be creative!

If you've got more than one team, creating competition between teams is always good. You can have a prize for the winning team. It doesn't have to cost very much, as it's often about the recognition and accolade of winning.

One scheme I did that worked well was a trip abroad. It was a team-based incentive, and on achieving a certain level of sales, they were given a budget for a trip abroad. They decided where they went and what they did as a team, which gelled them even better as a cross-functional unit.

To me, it's about knowing your people and creating the best incentive scheme you can to drive them forward and realise their true potential.

Do you have any advice about how to link incentive schemes to sales strategies effectively?

Often, senior management/founders will want to see an incentive scheme that provides them with what they want. As a sales manager, linking to the sales strategy is part of the sell to get the funding you want for your incentive scheme. It can be difficult to link an incentive scheme to a company strategy unless it is a sales-related strategy. For example, if part of the overall strategy is to focus on securing sales through three key accounts, I would put in a scheme that offers more cash for sales through these accounts; this will automatically focus the salespeople on those key accounts.

You can link incentives to individual objectives, so your objectives have to be achieved; otherwise, you only get a certain percentage of your incentive money. Those objectives must be aligned all the way up. Make sure the objectives are SMART; otherwise, this will lead to conflict.

A decent incentive stays simple because there is a risk of overcomplicating things.

What pitfalls should new sales leaders be aware of with incentive schemes?

Singling out individuals is a dangerous thing to do. If you put someone on a pedestal because they're doing really well, you can actually breed contempt from others within the team. This can generate a lot of excuses; for example, that person's done really well because they've got more opportunities on their patch. You have to manage that and nip all excuses in the bud.

Decent incentive schemes should not have a ceiling. If it is working, why stop it? Some companies say when salespeople get to 20% over target, that's it – no extra reward. Good salespeople will get to 20% ahead of target, then sandbag sales for next year. In fact, I would try the opposite approach and accelerate sales after 20% to encourage them to go to the next level.

The other thing to be careful of is punishing high performers. If a rep overachieves target by 30% and you whack up next year's target by 30%, there is a chance that you might well be working against them in the future because they will just walk. De-motivating top performers is the last thing you want to do.

Be careful as well around the individual and team situation. It can happen that you have a couple of excellent reps who earn really good commissions, and the rest of the team is struggling for whatever reason, meaning that overall, the team doesn't make its target. Underperformance and overperformance go hand in hand, and both should be managed. Some sales leaders will try to keep the incentive results quiet for fear of upsetting individuals, but success should be celebrated, and everyone should know about the incentive scheme. Similarly, poor performance has to be managed so good performers don't get disgruntled.

Finally, watch percentages because it's easy to make a mistake. Usually, the better reps have higher targets or bigger customers. For example, a rep with a target of £1,000,000 has to find £100,000 for 10% growth, whereas a rep with a target of 500,000 only has to find £50,000 for 10% growth. Immediately, you've got a conflict. In this case, absolute value makes more sense, if the reps have the same opportunity to grow by the same value. So, I would always try to link an incentive to value rather than a percentage.

Overall, it is important to think carefully about your scheme well in advance for the following year, so you can get targets and incentives right. Overperformance needs to be recognised and rewarded if you want to motivate and keep your best salespeople.

Notes

1 M. Franco-Santos & J. Marcos Cuevas "Motivating and rewarding the sales force" *The International Journal of Sales Transformation* Issue 3.4 (December 2017), 45–48
2 D. Banker et al. "An empirical analysis of continuing improvements following the implementation of a performance based compensation plan" *Journal of Accounting and Economics* vol. 30 (2000), 315–350
3 A. Zoltners et al "Breaking the salesforce incentive addition: A balanced approach to salesforce effectiveness" *Journal of Personal Selling and sales management* vol. 32, no. 2(2012), 172–180
4 M. Roberge "The right way to use compensation" *Harvard Business Review* April 2015
5 M. Johnston & G. Marshall *Sales force management* 13th ed p342 Routledge 2021
6 D. Chung "How to really motivate sales people" *Harvard Business Review* April 2015
7 M. Johnston & G. Marshall 13th ed p346 Routledge 2021
8 F. Cespedes *Aligning strategy and sales* p179 Harvard Business Review Press 2014
9 R. Miller *Sales compensation challenges and points of view* Deloitte whitepaper 2017
10 T. Kuntner & J. Voester "Principles and success factors of effective B2B salesforce compensation" *NIU Journal of Selling* vol. 16, no. 1 (2016), 48–54
11 D. Chung "How to really motivate salespeople" *Harvard Business Review* April 2015
12 T. Kuntner & J. Voester vol. 16, no. 1
13 T. Steenburgh & M. Ahearne "Motivating salespeople: What really works" *Harvard Business Review* July 2012
14 D. Chung et al "Do Bonuses enhance sales productivity? A dynamic structural analysis of bonus based compensation plans" p24–25 Harvard Business Review Working Paper 13-066 2013
15 C. Homburg et al *Sales excellence* p134 Springer 2012
16 F. Cespedes p180 Harvard Business Review Press 2014
17 This account is covered in "The right way to use compensation" *Harvard Business Review* April 2015 and Mark Roberge's book *The sales acceleration formula* Wiley 2015
18 Contests are covered in page 93–94 in *The sales acceleration formula*

Chapter 16

Recruitment and onboarding

How do we find the best salespeople and set them up for success?

The A team

"Recruiting high quality, committed staff is seen as central to best practice HRM (Human resource management)", so say Mick Marchington and Adrian Wilkinson, authors of *Human Resource Management at Work*.[1] In the context of start-ups and SMEs, the already familiar scale-up specialists Aaron Ross and Jason Lemkin state, "People always matter, but when you're doing something new, the first hires make an even bigger difference".[2]

You might already recognise some 'A-Team players' in your company: those individuals that you can fully rely on to make their numbers and drive the business forward when you introduce new ideas. Jim Collins, author of *From Good to Great*, went a stage further, famously stating that it is better to get the right people on the bus before deciding where to go.[3]

We have all seen examples where excellent staff make all the difference in our experience as customers, and therefore the importance of getting recruitment right is clear to see.

Also, for start-ups, the first hiring decision can be especially daunting, particularly where boot-strap funding is being used.

The good news is that, with some clear thinking, solid recruitment practices are within reach of the smallest firms.

Equally important is that once we have found good staff, we help them become competent as quickly as possible and encourage them to stay through good *onboarding* processes.

Let's look at these two key areas in turn, beginning with what an effective recruitment process looks like, how to source candidates, and how to design an excellent onboarding process.

Bringing rigour to recruitment

Somewhere in the ether of business management, the expression "hire slowly, fire quickly" has emerged. It's a reminder of the importance of taking your time to find the right people, but if they don't work out, move on quickly! How then can we design an effective recruitment process for salespeople? Figure 16.1 shows the simple, high-level steps we can use.

Step 1: Build your job description

If you have worked through the preceding chapters, you will have a good sense of your *sales strategy*, *sales process* and ideal *organisational structure*. Recall that one of the details of good organisational structure design is that you have job descriptions in place for each role.

DOI: 10.4324/9781003449614-16

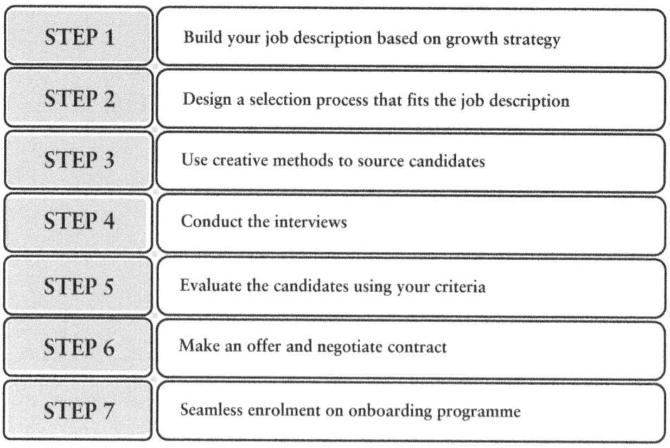

STEP 1	Build your job description based on growth strategy
STEP 2	Design a selection process that fits the job description
STEP 3	Use creative methods to source candidates
STEP 4	Conduct the interviews
STEP 5	Evaluate the candidates using your criteria
STEP 6	Make an offer and negotiate contract
STEP 7	Seamless enrolment on onboarding programme

Figure 16.1 A sales recruitment process

Table 16.1 Key sections in a job description

Key area	Description	Example
Knowledge	What potential hires need to know	Industry-specific information (e.g., how a manufacturing plant works) Qualifications (e.g., MBA for a strategy consultant)
Competence	What a candidate is able to do	Enact your sales process (e.g., uncover customer needs effectively) General role competencies (e.g., manage time and workload)
Responsibilities	The sales work to be done	Sales process (e.g. deal with new enquiries) Account management (e.g. retain current customers)
Outputs	The targets and deliverables for the role	Sales metrics (e.g. achieve sales of $x in year one) Qualitative (e.g. implement an account management process)

For effective recruitment, this is a truly essential starting point. I have lost count of the number of start-ups I have worked with. Who believe that just hiring a 'cold caller' will solve all their problems. You need to be very clear about what the 'sales work to be done' is. That is why this book starts with figuring out the likely best approach for your particular type of sales and growth ambitions. This will give you clarity about what a new hire should be doing.

Job descriptions should be clearly linked to the work to be done, which is derived from your sales process and sales methodology. So, what is in a sales job description? Table 16.1 shows the four key areas it should cover:

The easiest way to build your job description is to work directly with the aforementioned sources. For example, your sales strategy will give you a clear indication of who you are targeting and how you will reach them. Your sales process will give you all the activities that a salesperson should follow. For each activity in your sales process, you can derive the knowledge and competence required.

For example, if you are a consultancy selling operational improvement programmes to manufacturing customers, you will likely have a step in your sales process based on *engaging* (see Chapter 4). This could require salespeople to facilitate workshops with factory managers to scope out production challenges. You might therefore decide that you need:

Knowledge: An understanding of lean production and process improvement techniques.

Competence: Candidate is able to design and facilitate workshops for senior managers.

Working through your sales process methodically will help you build the required competency and knowledge profile for the role.

For more 'standard' sales roles, The Association of Talent Development has created an excellent resource, *Success in Selling*, by Reza Sisakhti, which gives a broad range of competency profiles for sales[4] that you can use as a base.

Responsibilities and outputs are derived from your growth targets and the work to be done for the role. These are essential components of performance management, and it's vital that these are made clear up front to potential candidates so they know what they will be responsible for.

To make the job description useful and appealing, Ross and Lemkin recommend "write authentic, interesting job descriptions...rather than the boring, generic descriptions most companies use".[5] This will help you attract people to apply. They also recommend including a video that describes the role in a more humane way. Trish Bertuzzi echoes this point "A job description should sell the job. If you can't capture attention and interest, who the hell cares about the fine print".[6] Her book, *The Sales Development Playbook*, gives great examples of sample texts you can draw inspiration from.

Step 2: Design the selection process

Clear thinking at this stage will enable you to screen out the pretenders and the misfits for your organisations. Unfortunately, because the craft of sales involves convincing others to buy from you, salespeople can be good at interviewing but not necessarily good at delivering once in a role. Therefore, your selection process should be rigorous to make sure you hire good staff. The days of "oh they will be a good fit with our company" based on one interview are hopefully resigned to history!

What constitutes a thorough recruitment process? Ideally, it will give potential candidates a chance to demonstrate many of the skills that will be required in the role, and importantly, it will give you the opportunity to assess them against the role description you have just built. There are a wide variety of methods that you can use to build your selection process, shown in Table 16.2.

The exact selection of methods you use will depend on the seniority of the role you are recruiting for and the resources and time you have available for the task. As a minimum, your process should include:

- CV check
- Two interviews, one of them competency-based
- A sales task to allow the candidate to demonstrate their sales skills
- Reference check

Anything less than this is likely to result in a biased hire.

It is also vital that you ensure your interview process is *inclusive*, encourages *diversity* and does not break discrimination legislation. Process-based methods such as structured interviews go some way to help this by presenting all candidates with the same questions

Table 16.2 Assessment methods for sales recruitment

Method	Description
CV review	A basic check on the claimed experience Useful to 'read between the lines' about a candidate's history and to prepare questions for interviews.
Personality test	Whilst personality profiles can offer insights into the preferences of potential hires, caution must be applied in their use. Firstly, the evidence is sketchy about their validity for predicting sales performance.[7] Secondly, firms in certain jurisdictions (USA, for example)[8] must be able to demonstrate that no bias or discrimination is introduced by the use of the test.
Writing test	Giving a written assignment as part of recruitment serves two purposes: Firstly, it screens out time wasters, and secondly it gives an indication of the candidate's writing skills (provided you prevent AI tools being used).
Video test	Producing quick videos for customers and social media is becoming more and more an important tool for salespeople, so this can be a useful test of creative storyboarding and 'in the field' video production skills.
Aptitude test	Where an element of cognitive skills is required in your sales process (e.g. data analysis), it makes sense to test this. You could, for example, ask candidates to prepare and interpret an Excel sheet based on the data you give them.
Social media scan	Checking how a salesperson presents themselves on LinkedIn and other platforms will give you an indication of their personal brand and social savvy, both important aspects of modern selling.
Screening interview	Short 15–30-minute video interviews can help to whittle down your long list of candidates to create a short list to enter the next stage.
Structured competency-based interview	A non-negotiable component of any interview process is to ask candidates to give concrete examples of where they have applied the competencies you are looking for. You should create a score sheet for this task so that you can objectively assess each candidate. You will need to prepare specific probing questions such as, "What examples can you give me where you demonstrated skill X?"
Assessment centre	This is the gold standard of recruitment practice. Candidates complete a number of individual and team exercises, directly based on their role competency profile. They are observed, and the observers aggregate their feedback to arrive at consensual scores. It is rigorous, but also time consuming and expensive.
Presentation/pitch	Since sales involves presenting, advocating and explaining benefits to customers, it is often a good idea to test candidates' ability to do it. Typically, you can send details of your product/service and then ask for a presentation as if you were 'customer X'.
Time with your sales team	Interview processes should be two-way, so potential hires can assess your organisation and culture as a place to work. Giving candidates time with your sales team enables them to do this, and you will gain interesting feedback from your sales team too.
Role-play exercises	Short exercises to see candidates' sales skills in action form a useful tool during a longer interview. The recruiter takes on the role of a potential customer with a clearly defined sales scenario. Give candidates time to prepare, then do the exercise for a maximum of ten minutes. Ensure the exercise is realistic for your sales environment.
References	References are a much-disputed tool for hiring, but speaking to two references will nearly always yield useful insights.

and evaluation methods, but manager bias is notoriously difficult to crack. An HBR article entitled *Why subtle bias is so often worse than blatant discrimination* by Eden King and Kristen Jones[9] gives the example of non-job-related chit-chat outside of the formal interview process, which already helps bias form.

For a comprehensive list of methods that you can use to build inclusion, *Inclusion Nudges* by Tinna Nielsen and Lisa Kepinski is a good source of ideas.[10]

Finally, but very importantly make your recruitment process fast, fun, timely and interactive. Because of the 'war for talent', you will likely be competing against several other employers. It is really normal for salespeople to apply to several companies when looking to change employers. If they find your recruitment process engaging, with the chance to have a two-way conversation early on and some unexpected moments of fun and surprise in it, they are much more likely to choose you than their competitive offers.

Step 3: Use creative methods to source candidates

I'd like to start this section with a 'health warning'. Over the 20 plus years I have been involved in sales training and consulting, I have noticed that there is a significant proportion of salespeople who move roles every 1–2 years without making any meaningful progress in their careers. They are great at getting through the interview stage and making all the right noises, but as time goes by with their new employer, they don't meet the promises they made and decide to 'move on' because of a lack of fit with their employer. They repeat the cycle at a new organisation. The real problem? They cannot sell. They don't have the right mindset to succeed in a sales role.

When you go searching for new hires, there is a real risk that these 'candidates' show up first, as they are likely to be in a 'grass is greener' state of mind in their current role. Of course, a good recruitment process will help to screen them out, but how can you go about finding better candidates?

Mark Roberge, again, already familiar to readers, explains his damascene moment in this regard: "Great salespeople never have to apply for a job…truly great salespeople have multiple job offers at all times, even if they are not in the job market".[11] This means you will need to work hard to find good salespeople; they won't necessarily be the ones that instantly apply to your open position.

So, what are the methods that you can use to source candidates?

Recruitment agencies An obvious route to finding good candidates is to outsource this job to a professional recruitment agency. The quality of agencies varies enormously, from excellent and indispensable to downright useless. To increase your chances of success, some factors to check are:

- Do they specialise in finding salespeople?
- Who else are they recruiting salespeople for?
- What process do they use to select candidates?
- What support do they provide post hire?
- What are their fees?

It clearly helps if they specialise in recruiting for sales, with the proviso that, if they are currently recruiting for your competitors (in the broadest terms), they may not prioritise the best people for you.

Some agencies are set up not only to recruit salespeople but to ensure they are successful by providing ongoing training and support for their candidates, and this might be appealing to you if you have limited resources to develop them 'in role'. See the interview with the founder of Venatrix, Elaine Tyler, for an example of a UK company doing this type of placement.

Develop an internal referral scheme: Depending on the employees you currently have and their networks, a brilliant way to find good salespeople is to ask your own employees to put candidates forward. This will help to draw out stars who are not in the job market at the moment. You can offer a decent referral bonus for this because it will nearly always be cheaper than using an agency.

LinkedIn Recruiters have used LinkedIn for years to source candidates. Even the free version enables filtering by job title, region and education. The company also provides a recruitment-optimised version (LinkedIn Talent Solutions) that provides many other recruitment-specific tools to assist you. If you are using LinkedIn Navigator as your prospecting tool, you could even use it to contact potential candidates directly via its in-mail feature.

Researching excellent sales development organisations in your vicinity/sector One sales director I worked with was a genius at recruiting salespeople from a large organisation that trained its salespeople exceptionally well. By keeping your ear to the ground, you can work out who the good sales teams are in your universe of selection. Sometimes large organisations are too restrictive and bureaucratic for certain personality types, and moving to a more nimble, agile start-up/SME might be just what they need.

School/university open events Very few 'institutions' make their students aware of sales roles. Maybe they will cover marketing as a career or professions like medical, legal, engineering and consulting, but sales often gets missed. By forming close links with career support personnel, you can run an open evening where you excite students about what a career in sales can mean. Since many schools/universities are targeted with placing their students into meaningful work, this arrangement can be win/win.

Adverts/job boards Multiple websites exist in each geography to advertise job roles. These can help you increase your reach but will almost certainly attract the 'do two years and move on' crew already alluded to.

Internal advertising Don't overlook the current staff in your firm who may be motivated to move into a customer-facing role. Promotion from within is nearly always a smart HR strategy, and some roles, such as *account management*, lean more heavily on *management* skills and less on front-end *cold calling*, which can turn some non-sales roles off.

A word on getting the numbers of applicants right. Mark Johnston and Greg Marshall, in their book Sales Force Management, explain that "too many recruits can overload the selection process, forcing the manager to use less thorough screening and evaluation procedures".[12] Therefore, the aim of a good recruiting process is to find fewer, high-quality candidates.

Many organisations have turned to web-based application processes that enable potential hires to self-screen. The inclusion of some relevant hurdles (e.g., record a video or write a marketing advertisement) is one simple way to reduce time wasters.

Step 4: Conduct the interviews

One complaint I hear time and time again from applicants for sales roles is the *black hole syndrome* and lack of feedback during the application process. Often, this leaves candidates with a bad taste in their mouth. Whatever the decision you make about a potential candidate, they should always leave the process as a positive advocate for your organisation. Why? Because they can become either an informal salesperson for your brand or they can badmouth your brand. Since the aim of this book is to help you sell, make sure you are not the organisation running an awful recruitment process that detracts from this!

This effectively means treating interviewees like potential customers in the way you communicate with them. It doesn't mean any reduction in rigour: If candidates don't get hired but see you as a 'high-standards sales organisation', that will only be to your benefit. Just make sure you take time to give rejected candidates reasonable feedback that they can use.

Having designed the selection process in step 2, follow it! Ensure that you document the results of your interview process, especially the scoring for the competency-based interview element, so that you can compare candidates objectively, side by side.

Ideally, several of you will be involved in the selection process, so you can compare notes and reach a consensus decision.

Step 5: Evaluate the candidates

There is a good reason why we develop job descriptions and assessment tests up front. It is so that we don't fall prey to *halo effects/confirmation bias*.[13] If you have stuck to the interview process, then you will have sufficient data to review and make a decision.

If you have several candidates for whom you can't make a decision, you can always request an extra interview to probe deeper.

Step 6: Make an offer and negotiate the contract

For start-ups and microbusinesses, it can be helpful to get specialist HR/legal advice on your employment contract and job offer to ensure you set things up right from the start. As was mentioned in the chapter on compensation and incentives, you will want to ensure you have the right clauses for flexibility in case you want to change the commission/bonus scheme.

You can expect good salespeople to negotiate terms when you offer them the role: The best candidates will not be afraid to do this, and it should augur well for contact negotiations with your customers if they are not fazed by this type of conversation! It is wise to build your matrix, as developed in Chapter 7.

It is also wise to pay attention to the demographics that you are targeting so that you can make yourself an employer of choice. For example, Gen Z, having worked mainly through COVID, may well appreciate *work-from-home* initiatives and also be less likely to be drivers or own a car, so factoring this into your offer might well help.

Step 7: Seamless enrolment to your onboarding programme

Just as soon as you have a 'yes' from your desired candidate, contact them to explain to them the process of how they will be welcomed into your organisation. I recently saw the powerful impact of this when someone in my network joined a new firm. Although she was apprehensive up front, the degree of organisation for her first week gave her confidence in her new employer. After her first day, she was absolutely buzzing with excitement about the company.

What should be in a good onboarding programme? We will cover that next.

What is the case for effective onboarding?

Ron Carucci, a consultant who has worked for many Fortune 500 companies, notes that 20% of staff turnover occurs in the first 45 days of employment.[14] In times when it is difficult to recruit good salespeople, clearly losing them so quickly is not good news. Carucci goes on to recommend that onboarding should be planned for a *whole year*.

Time to competence is another compelling argument for excellent onboarding. Since the productivity of salespeople is so visible (via their targets), helping them raise their sales game as quickly as possible has a clear return on investment. Indeed, reducing time to competence is a key driver of value in a sales organisation. McKinsey research estimates that the average time to breakeven for a salesperson is nine months,[15] and so it is critical to get onboarding right.

What should onboarding achieve?

In the context of sales organisations, onboarding should achieve the following goals:

Connect them with a buddy: Do you remember how scary and daunting starting a new job can be? One very simple way to reduce this anxiety for new hires is to connect them with a more senior salesperson who is a good role model for your organisation on the day they join. The buddy is their 'go-to' person for all the left-field questions they need answering.

Show them how things work: In any new company, there is a multiplicity of new systems, codes, information sources, procedures, IT rules and other things to learn. By planning short sessions with the relevant person, they will at least know who to ask for specific information.

Give them the tools: There is nothing more frustrating than having no phone or problems with your new laptop when you join an organisation. Make sure your new employee gets the tools they need to do the job as soon as possible.

Start customer contact straight away: According to the experience of the people you've hired, you might either need to provide them with sales training or get them to start selling right away. Cory Bray and Hilmon Sorey, authors of *The Sales Enablement Playbook* recommend that you get experienced senior hires selling on the phone on day 2 of their induction programme,[16] while junior hires benefit from sales training first.

Introduce your sales process and methodology in the first week: Even for experienced salespeople, it's important to show them *your* way of selling (Chapters 3 and 4), as people tend to be most malleable in their first few weeks at a new company. If you have put in the work to design your sales approach well, then make it clear to new hires that you expect them to use it. Training should be ongoing over the first year, because study after study shows that employees value this and gives them a key reason to stay.

Provide them with structured products and technical training: For new hires to have confidence and credibility in front of customers, they will need to know your sector, customer challenges and how your product/service adds value to customer operations. If at all possible, allow your salespeople to be users of your product/service so they 'practice as they preach'. At the very least, ensure they know enough to be taken seriously in front of the most demanding customers.

Steep new hires in your culture: Developing a culture your team can be proud of is essential for staff retention, and in sales it is even more critical because if employees are proud of where they work, customers will notice it. Research done by the Great Place to Work organisation estimates that employees who feel proud of their company are two times more likely to stay.[17] Explaining your values with conviction, stories of 'culture heroes' and team events can all make new employees feel connected to their employer.

Provide ongoing sales coaching: One of the biggest omissions I see in sales organisations is that a pretty reasonable induction programme is followed up with...nothing! Looking at the financial services sector, Zahed Subhan found that while sales training is a critical aspect of onboarding at the start, coaching takes over as a vital activity in higher-performing organisations.[18] Regular 1:1 check-ins are strongly recommended to stay in touch with how new hires are feeling and to provide adaptive performance coaching to help them succeed. Carucci recommends setting short-term goals that you know new hires can achieve so that you can boost their confidence early on.[19]

Help connect them with others Sales can be a lonely job, and it is important that even if salespeople are not required to work as a team, they do feel part of one. Engagement gurus Marcus Buckingham and Ashley Goodall have discovered that being part of a team substantially increases engagement with an organisation.[20] This is why so many sales managers organise 'team events', because they see the value of being part of something bigger.

Resourcing onboarding for SMEs and start-ups

There is a lot to be done, isn't there? How do you manage it within a busy, growing organisation? One short cut is to jot down a list of learning objectives for induction, and for each item, note down where to find answers. You can then charge the new hire with arranging to meet key people, reading source documents, telephoning customers and so on, in a kind of 'self-directed learning' project (see Chapter 13 for a more detailed explanation of this approach). Just be sure to have weekly check-ins of at least one hour, so you can make sure they are happy and on track.

Remember, under-resourcing onboarding is likely to be a false economy if your new hires walk out the door after all the hard work you put in to recruit them!

Into action

Are your current recruitment and induction programmes fit for purpose?

Either ask a recent recruit(s) for their feedback on what they liked and what can be improved, or map out your current process.

How can it be improved?

If you were considering joining your firm, what would motivate you?

What recruitment process could you use to attract and select A-Grade players?

Same with onboarding:

How is the current process?

What knowledge/skills/attitudes would help new recruits succeed?

How best to phase activities over one week, one month or one year?

Expert view: Elaine Tyler is the CEO and founder of Venatrix, an international high-growth SDR recruitment agency

When should companies use a recruitment agency?

There are two major reasons that motivate leaders to partner with recruitment firms:

1   Lack of time. When the leaders feel like they don't have the bandwidth in their own schedules or that of their teams, and they feel like time spent on delivering key business activities could create more value than the cost of a recruitment fee, it can make sense to have a dedicated party covering ground in the candidate market on your behalf.

2   Lack of expertise. Candidates' expectations change around many different factors (salary, benefits and working arrangements), and recruiters are having a volume of conversations with candidates on a weekly basis, so they will be able to give you valuable insights into that can help you to attract the candidate you are seeking. A professional recruiter will offer you a service which spans their tenure in recruiting in that market; they can therefore headhunt on your behalf and open the candidate pool to include passive as well as active candidates. You want to meet enough candidates to have a choice, but not so many that your search becomes long-winded and diluted. Recruiters can also vet candidates for you, and as they are doing this consistently, they may have a stronger benchmark than you if this is a role you only hire for occasionally.

When choosing a recruiter to partner with, ask for referrals in your network. If you can't find a suitable suggestion, ask your potential recruiter to connect you with a client they have worked with to understand how they operate.

What kind of sales recruitment does Venatrix specialise in?

Venatrix specialises in placing salespeople and sales leaders in Software-As-A-Service companies. A typical client of ours will be 50–100 people, most likely have achieved a level of funding, have a proven product or service and will be looking for a strong sales team to help take the proposition to market. The calibre of the salespeople and sales leaders can then dictate how quickly the firm is able to monetise, achieve breakeven after borrowed capital, become liquid or even achieve an exit event.

What do you think is important when building a job description to use in recruitment?

A job description to use for recruitment purposes is an augmented version of what the role involves. Start with the basics, i.e., job title, salary, bonus if applicable, who the role reports to and the location/working arrangements. If you are using this document to share with candidates to "sell" the role, the first part of the document can then describe how the candidate can benefit professionally from joining the business in the role. This is a hook to capture their interest, as people make career moves typically to benefit themselves. From there, introduce the company's mission or vision to inspire and list any notable clients/awards/projects to add credibility. Next, a description of the role: be clear and transparent about the different facets of the role, and don't be afraid to list the challenges the candidate may encounter if they join. Detail the skills and experience you are seeking in the ideal candidate; some of these might be mandatory, and some might be preferred but not essential. The more prescriptive you are, potentially, the smaller the pool of candidates. Next up, depict the potential progression opportunities for successful hires before sharing any additional benefits and the application process.

What is your advice for start-ups and SMEs in designing a solid interview process?

Start by gathering the stakeholders to discuss the profile sought so it is clearly understood by all parties. Identify the key skills and experience you are looking to identify throughout the process, and therefore, the questions and topics you will discuss with the candidates. Create a scorecard and define the gradings that you will use to describe the suitability of the candidate. Decide on the process and the number of stages. This is normally 1–3 stages for more junior roles and 3–5 stages for more senior positions. A typical process would include an initial screen as a first stage where the interviewer might sell the role to the candidate while assessing suitability, a second stage involving more role/experience-specific questions or perhaps a case study or task and then a final culture stage that may explore matched candidate and company values, allow a candidate to meet a future peer and clear up any final questions. A successful process will be well designed, avoid duplication of topics/questions in the different stages and be timely so as not to rush but also reduce the risk of "losing" the candidate to another opportunity.

For SMEs and start-ups who have limited budgets, do you have any advice about how to source good candidates?

Start with your known networks. Ask your current team, investors, partners, non-execs, suppliers, etc. if they have any connections who could be a good fit for the role. You can offer a small incentive to encourage people to think deeply about who they know. Write a job description and post it as an advertisement on free sites such as Indeed and LinkedIn. Once you have created a job advertisement, promote it! Continue to post about the role on social channels if you use them such as LinkedIn, Instagram and Twitter. The key with these channels is consistency and not being disheartened if the first post doesn't yield results. Attend networking events and constantly be opening up conversations and scouting for talent. Continue to do this even when you are not actively hiring; keep notes on people who have impressed you and store their details as a first port of call for when you are hiring again.

Notes

1 M. Marchington & A. Wilkinson *Human resource management at work* 3rd ed p76 CIPD 2007
2 A. Ross & J. Lemkin *From impossible to inevitable* p134 Wiley 2016
3 https://www.jimcollins.com/article_topics/articles/first-who.html
4 R. Sisakhti *Success in selling* ATD press 2016
5 A. Ross & J. Lemkin p134 Wiley 2016
6 T. Bertuzzi *The sales development playbook* p65 Trish Bertuzzi 2016
7 E. King & K. Jones "Why subtle bias is so often worse than blatant discrimination" *Harvard Business Review* July 2016
8 T. Nielsen & L. Kepinski *Inclusion nudges* inclusion Institute 2016
9 M. Roberge *The sales acceleration formula* p 25 Wiley 2015
10 M. Johnson & G. Marshall *Sales force management* p290 Routledge 2021
11 Halo effect is where we are too swayed by initial positive impressions to critically evaluate participants later in the interview process
12 R. Carucci "To retain new hires, spend more time onboarding them" *Harvard Business Review Article* December 2018
13 E. Buesing et al "Maximise the lifetime value of your salesforce" *McKinsey Marketing & Sales Practice* March 2019
14 C. Bray & H. Sorey *The sales enablement playbook* p20 2017 Create Space Independent Publishing Platform
15 https://www.greatplacetowork.co.uk/resources/workplace-pride
16 Z. Subhan et al "Running an effective induction programme for new sales recruits: Lessons from the financial services industry" *NIU Journal of Selling* vol. 14, no. 1 (2014), 24–29
17 R. Carucci *Harvard Business Review Article* December 2018
18 M. Buckingham & A. Goodall "Engaging employees - The power of hidden teams" *Harvard Business Review* May 2019
19 M. Johnson & G. Marshall p304 Routledge 2021
20 Ibid

Chapter 17

Working with partners and resellers

When should we sell through other organisations and how can we best manage these relationships?

Why work with partners and resellers?

The ecosystem of partners, agents, resellers and distributors is huge and exists across multiple sectors. Why do so many companies build and maintain networks of partners? Here are some of the reasons it can be worth considering selling through/with other organisations:

- To access new markets (for example, other geographies).
- To leverage others' skills (for example, selling products through technical specialists).
- To build your sales capacity (where recruiting your own team would be too expensive).
- To offer unique value (for example, through holding stock local to a customer's site).
- To accelerate learning (for example, working with an experienced partner).
- To convert fixed costs to variable costs (by not having to employ salespeople).

While the attractions of working with partners can be very tempting for start-ups and SMEs wishing to scale quickly, there are a number of challenges to factor into your decision to build a successful partner network.

Some industries have complex supply chains, meaning several intermediaries are involved between the 'producer' and the end customer. Figure 17.1 shows a typical example that many of you will be familiar with when you need to replace a tyre on your car. Each actor in the chain provides unique added value enjoyed by you, the end consumer.

Looking at your own business, therefore, you could be selling to a distributor, who in turn supplies channel partners who actually sell to the end customer.

Let's begin by exploring the types of partners you could work with and the pros and cons of each. Table 17.1 outlines the main types of partners that you can look for as part of your go-to-market strategy.

What is the best partner structure for your business?

Mark Davies, author of *Infinite Value*, recommends addressing four fundamental questions in assessing your supply chain and route to market:[1]

- Who is your customer?
- What do they value?
- Where is value created?
- Where is value destroyed?

DOI: 10.4324/9781003449614-17

Supply chain

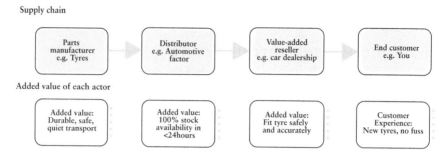

Figure 17.1 An example supply chain

Table 17.1 Types of partners

Partner type	Description	Pros and cons
Sales agent	A lone agent, often a successful ex-corporate salesperson, who has a good network within your target customer base.	Pros: Easy to set up, low barrier to entry/exit Easy to manage Cons: Unlikely to set the world alight. May have only a few contacts
Referral partner	A complimentary organisation to your own that might work with similar target customers as you but does not compete. A referral fee is paid for any leads.	Pros: Can form a regular, pain-free stream of leads Cons: Likely to be passive rather than active
Distributor/ Wholesalers/ Stockist	Typically a larger player with sophisticated warehousing/distribution facilities and an extensive customer network.	Pros: Good partners may have an attractive customer list They may be the de facto choice for your customers Cons: They can wield uncomfortable amounts of power Because they often stock a wide range of items, there may be little incentive to push yours
Added value resellers	A specialist in a sector or application who has strong technical knowledge of how to use and apply your product.	Pros: They can provide technical skills you lack, helping you better serve end customers They often have great relations and reputation with your target customers Cons: They will need plenty of support and training They can command high margins on your product
Outsourced salesforce	A specialist organisation that can provide you with a contract salesforce, dedicated or part-dedicated to selling your product	Pros: A flexible labour force Good for getting scale with new product launches Cons: Not cheap and will require extensive support to sell as you'd like them to
On-line platforms	Specialist online traders who can promote and distribute your product/service online. Specialists in online marketing and trading	Pros: Potentially huge scale-up potential Cons: As intermediaries, they can gain too much power for comfort.

Using the example of changing your tyres (Figure 17.1), as a customer, you probably value:

- A local garage (minimal time to drive to)
- Quick service (less time waiting)
- No issues with the tyres (safe, durable and fitted properly)
- Fair price (not feeling ripped off)

It's easy to see how each partner in the chain helps deliver these outcomes. The automotive factor helps your local garage get access to a vast range of tyres quickly without having to stock them, which would involve a lot of extra space and cost. The dealer has a workshop and skilled technicians to fit the tyres according to their specifications, and it is near your house.

Each actor in the chain has an effective, useful role to play that serves the end consumer. Would there be space for an additional player in this supply chain? Only if they could demonstrably add value. If not, they would destroy value by charging a fee which does not serve the end consumer. Where partners in a supply chain do not add value, there is a high risk of 'disintermediation', where suppliers bypass them and sell directly to the next 'link in the chain', or to the end consumer.

What does this look like in your sector/industry? When you think about the customers you are trying to reach, what do they value? What value could potential partners add? Davies advises organisations to figure out what they need from a distribution/partner network first, then segment and classify potential partners according to how well they could fulfil their needs.

Selecting and engaging potential partners

"All good commercial relationships start with understanding the other party", is the advice given by channel specialists Julian Dent and Michael White.[2] It is essential to understand the business strategy, ownership and financing of potential partners. This will enable you to check for a good fit with your sales strategy and brand and to sell your proposition to the potential partner.

One of the biggest challenges in working with partners is competing for attention with the other priorities they have. If there is not a strong "What's in it for me" for a partner, they are unlikely to push and promote your product/service. Therefore, understanding what their focus is will be essential to making a long-term relationship work.

Pragmatic considerations are also important:

- Can they access your target market?
- Are they operating in your desired geographies?
- Will there be conflicts with your other channels/channel partners?
- Do you have the resources to support your proposed distribution/partner structure?

Partner enablement

A common mistake made by many start-ups is to assume they can present their product/service to a partner and then sit back and wait for the sales to roll in. This mindset is almost

Table 17.2 Categories for partner enablement

Tools	Resources to help specify your product/service, assess customers and find opportunities
Content	Product information, marketing assets and sales aids that can be forwarded or used to sell
Training	Technical knowledge about your offering, sales arguments and ordering processes
Insights	Tips and tricks to support selling activities

certain to result in failure! The purpose of *partner enablement* is very similar to *sales enablement*; in this case, it is to support partners to sell your product/service.

Simon Hall, author of *Innovative B2B Marketing*, believes partner enablement falls into four main categories,[3] summarised in Table 17.2.

A good mindset is to treat your partners as you would your sales team; in other words, to train them effectively and provide them with ongoing motivation and insights so that you keep them on-side for your offerings. Hall calls this "Gaining channel partner mindshare",[4] and suggests the following activities to achieve this:

- Sales incentives (to motivate salespeople to promote your products)
- Great content (that salespeople will engage with and use)
- Lead generation (to help partners win)
- Marketing development funds (to help partners invest in marketing your offering)
- Partner programmes (to motivate achieving pre-specified levels of sales and activities)
- Awards (to compete against other partners, thus stimulating activities)

Setting all this up will involve considerable effort and resources, and you will need to think about structure, roles and responsibilities to make it work. The vast majority of organisations that work successfully with a partner network have dedicated roles for partner enablement.

For start-ups and SMEs, this could materialise as one of your teams being responsible for all partners. As you grow, you will most likely need more people to manage your partner network. Large organisations go as far as having one dedicated manager for each key partner.

Should you implement a tiered partner programme?

Many software organisations have implemented a *tiered partner programme*, for example, with 'gold' and 'platinum' providers. The tiered model has diffused into other sectors too. Essentially, it works by offering special perks to partners according to their commitment levels to your brand. An example of what this could look like is shown in Table 17.3.

In many sectors, the partner status is made visible in all marketing communications, meaning end customers know which partners are the highest rated. This can provide a strong incentive for up-and-coming partners to 'raise their game'.

Tiering makes sense when you have multiple partners, and it is clear some are more committed than others. It has parallels with *customer prioritisation*, covered in Chapter 14, because it addresses the fundamental question, "Where best to prioritise your valuable time

Table 17.3 Example partner tiers and benefits

Tier	Typical partner commitments	Typical partner benefits
Platinum	Generate x leads per month Generate y sales per year Attend z hours of training per year	Receive leads from supplier marketing Maximum marketing development fund Individual partner development manager Involvement in product development Corporate hospitality
Gold	Generate 0.5x leads per month Generate 0.5y sales per year Attend 0.5z hours of training per year	Moderate marketing development fund Shared partner development manager
Silver	Generate 0.25y sales per year Attend 0.5z hours of training per year	Dedicated helpline

and resources?". It has the potential to create a meritocratic system where sales efforts and results by partners lead to more support, investment, development and growth.

In many sectors, deep mutually beneficial relationships exist between supplier and partner. It is not unusual for suppliers to provide cash, expert support, and considerable resources to their distributors.

Sales and marketing channels (Julian Dent and Michael White's book) make the case for a deep understanding of the financial dynamics of your distribution network[5] because it will enable you to support partners in the best possible way. Each actor in a supply chain will have unique challenges (working capital management, thin margins, profit optimisation of range), and if you know them, you can provide tailored support to build this type of strong, enduring relationship.

Managing partners

As already alluded to, you will need to put considerable effort into managing your partners if you want them to thrive. Typical activities to think about are listed below.

Regular communication To stay on partners' agendas, regular communication is essential. You can use all the channels you would think of when working with customers: e-mail, newsletters, videos, podcasts, webinars and face-to-face events. And it is worth applying the same care and attention to make sure that the right content gets to the right people. Marketing automation platforms can help with this.

Content management To support partners effectively, they will need access to a wide variety of content. This will include marketing assets that can be customised/co-branded, as well as product information, sales aids and up-to-date insights. A content management system can help you keep control of this, ranging from a basic password-protected Dropbox/OneDrive folder to more sophisticated platforms like WordPress, Drupal or Squarespace.[6]

Events and conferences To build connections, relationships, commitment and communities, face-to-face events are an important element in your partner management mix. Major brands tend to stage lavish events to launch new products, with hospitality, team building, high-profile guest speakers and awards, to encourage partners to support them and not competitors. SMEs and start-ups can use creativity to design events that get the same buzz without deep-pocket budgets.

Conflict resolution It is extremely rare not to have conflicts in a partner network. These can arise because:

- One partner perceives another as 'stealing their customers', for example, where geographical territories are allocated.
- Partners end up competing on price because a canny customer plays two distributors off against each other.
- Your direct sales force believes they should be dealing with an end-customer, while a partner believes that the customer 'belongs to them'.
- Partners are not happy with the margin/discount levels they are receiving from you.
- Partners perceive that other partners are on better deals than they are.
- You are not happy with a partner's performance/added value, and you would like to take on a customer directly.

Having clear written agreements and being consistent and fair in your enforcement of them can go a long way towards preventing conflict. However, conflicts can and do arise, and each one has to be treated on a case-by-case basis. In my experience, good partner managers tread a fine line between 'sticking to the rules' and working with individual partners to accommodate their unique situation.

There is definitely a role for 'holding the line' on some issues and saying no to requests, which would compromise your position overall.

Many partners and distributors are entrepreneurial by nature, being SMEs and start-ups themselves, so you will probably 'get' their mindset. Often there is the 'cult of the individual' syndrome to manage, where leaders of partners have a Zeus-like status in their business, and effective partner management means accommodating this type of personality while at the same time playing fair with other partners.

A special note on platforms and online resellers

Depending on what you are selling, there may be an option to sell it through an established platform such as Amazon, an App Store, e-Bay or, indeed, a lesser-known specialist platform in your sector/target market. As Andrei Hagiu and Julian Wright spell out in their excellent article "Don't let platforms commoditize your business",[7] "Large digital Multi-sided Platforms...have made it much easier for sellers to reach new customers, but as thousands of companies, large and small have discovered, conducting business on them carries significant costs and risks".

Concerning selling on Amazon, Ayelet Israeli and her colleagues warn that while "Amazon ships to 130 countries and is the dominant retailer in 28...brands face real challenges when selling on the platform – from competing products, third-party sellers and even from Amazon itself".[8]

Platform strategy is a book in its own right, and if you are serious about selling through others, I would advise deep diving into this area. Selling through Amazon is particularly a specialist area. Ayelet Israeli and colleagues' HBR article offers a useful scorecard to assess which channel is the right one for your business.[9] There is also an ecosystem of consultants, agencies and advisors with expert knowledge of how Amazon works who can help you set up product listings in the right way. If you go down this route, do your due diligence to check that the specialist actually has the knowledge required and can show you examples of where and how they achieved success.

Some general principles to help you navigate platform strategy are listed below.

Product/service suitability: Is it actually practical to sell your product/service through an online reseller platform? For example, is it complex? Does it need extensive customisation?

Competitor landscape: How many of your competitors, or product/services substitutes, appear when you search for your category on the reseller's platform? If there are 100s, then it is going to be difficult to stand out.

Margin calculation: Does the margin taken by the reseller work for you?

Customer data and relationship: One of the biggest issues with reseller platforms is that they own customer relations and customer data. These assets are extremely valuable for sales and marketing. Is there a way you can still get customers to sign up with you so you have permission to contact them? Practical ways to achieve this are to offer customers the chance to join a community or a special benefits/latest updates club. In terms of power dynamics, ownership of customer relationships is often the trump card of effective resellers.

Build your own platform: While this may be an ambitious option for SMEs and start-ups, if you can attract customers directly to your own platform, you will avoid the risk of losing power to a reseller. There are some fine examples to draw inspiration from around the world. Julian Wichmann and his colleagues give some great examples and strategies for this in their HBR article, Building Your Own Brand Platform.[10] Brands like Nike and Garmin have done a great job of building platforms that offer real value to end consumers by facilitating the activities that are most important to them.

Into action

If you don't use resellers or distributors today…

1 Start by listing all the potential organisations/individuals/websites that might have an interest in selling your product/service.
2 How might these actors add value to your target customer?
3 What might be their gain from working with you?
4 What would be the practicalities of setting up a partner programme over the long term?
5 What does this mean for your resources/structure/focus?

Make a decision on what to do next.
If you already have a reseller network in place…

1 What are the strengths and weaknesses of your network today?
2 What is the added value of each actor in the supply chain, from producer to end consumer?
3 If you started with a clean sheet of paper, how would you ideally design the supply chain?

4 What would you change in the activities and roles of each actor?
5 What gaps and duplications exist in your partner network?
6 What persistent conflicts arise, and how could you solve them?
7 How effective is your partner enablement programme, and what would you change?
8 How effective are your partner management routines, and what would you change?

Expert view: Partner enablement at Aspire

Aspire Active Education Group is featured in Chapter 11 as a proactive user of sales technology. For an SME of 60 people, they have also built up an impressive partner network of 50+ organisations. Partners resell high-quality educational programmes, like Maths on the Move and Swim: ED, to the schools in their local area.

Aspire supports its partners in a highly impressive way, with a structured programme of market support, educational workshops, bespoke training, collaboration events and other services to help them be successful.

The partner network is led by Paul Griffiths and Luke Johnson, who ensure they are enabled to sell and grow with Aspire.

Aspire started working with like-minded sports coaching organisations in 2016. Our network takes forward-thinking sports coaching businesses to the next level and produces results that include increased market share, greater activity engagement, higher turnover, enhanced staff retention and improved profitability.

What made you decide to deliver services via a partner network rather than sell your services directly to schools?

Aspire is based in the West Midlands and has a 40-mile radius to deliver directly to schools and communities, predominantly in the Birmingham area. We had considered growing our delivery area and branching into new areas; however, we had the following considerations: the increased travel for our team members, our brand awareness in new regions and the logistical headaches of trying to engage more children and young people in physical activity over a larger geographical area. By partnering with organisations with a similar mission and ethos, we could indirectly help engage children and young people by helping other organisations succeed.

How did you go about finding suitable partners?

We believe that collaboration in the children's activity sector is crucial to improving physical activity levels across the nation, and we look for like-minded organisations to join the network. Many organisations in the sector feel other organisations are 'competitors', whereas we believe by that collaborating and sharing best practices, we can all achieve our goals, make the sector attractive to work in and have a huge impact.

Our communication is all about collaboration, and those who resonate with this message often reach out and want to find out more. Through initial conversations and meetings, both parties decide if the network is the right fit for them.

What do you think are some of the success factors that have helped you build such a large partner network?

Managing and facilitating the activities within the network can be challenging, and as the network continues to grow, more challenges appear. At Aspire, we have a fantastic team to support what we do and how we care for our partners, including sales, marketing, recruitment, delivery and operational support from Aspire team members. We also build relationships with consultants and business experts from outside our sector who can offer new and innovative insights into the workshops and training events our partners take part in.

Some of our key values include being transparent and honest, having fun and not taking ourselves too seriously, doing the right thing and communicating effectively and informatively, all of which contribute to the running of the network and its success so far.

What advice would other SMEs/start-ups give to keep partners engaged and actively selling for them?

For other SMEs or start-ups wanting to keep partners engaged, I would suggest keeping to your core values, even when you start to grow. For example, if you offer marketing support to partners when you have five partners in total, you still need to offer that same support when you have 50 partners...if not more! As your network of partners grows, the internal processes are tested and strained, so being innovative with process management, technology and AI can be a game-changer. Our network has grown over time; however, our internal team hasn't grown at the same rate, as we've embraced technology and AI to help us streamline processes and increase output without increasing people's input.

Notes

1 M. Davies *Infinite value* p194 Bloomsbury 2017
2 J. Dent & M. White *Sales and marketing channels* p120 Kogan Page 2018
3 S. Hall *Innovative B2B marketing* p194 Kogan Page 2017
4 Ibid., p207
5 J. Dent & M. White p53 Kogan Page 2018
6 D. Alfonso *The Martech handbook* p51 Kogan Page 2022
7 A. Hagiu & J. Wright "Don't let platforms commoditize your business" *Harvard Business Review* May 2021
8 A. Israeli et al "Should your company sell on Amazon" *Harvard Business Review* September 2022
9 The scorecard is contained within the HBR article
10 J. Wichmann et al "Building your own brand platform" *Harvard Business Review* September 2022

Chapter 18

Evolving your sales organisation

How can you ensure your sales organisation
adapts to a changing environment?

Builders and architects

Working with a wide range of sales leaders over the years, I have noticed some have a bias towards 'architecture', that is, designing great sales organisations, and some have a bias towards 'building', that is, getting on with the daily work of sales management and seeing what emerges.

We need both sets of skills to create world-class sales organisations, and the closer these two mindsets can be integrated, the better. We don't want 'analysis by paralysis', any more than we want 'senseless action'.

Hopefully this book has shown you the building blocks of a world class, scalable sales organisation and also some very pragmatic things you can do today to increase sales. You can also hopefully see the interconnectedness of the building blocks and that changing one element can influence other blocks. So, if we change our sales process, the metrics to manage it should change too. And if we change the metrics, we might need to think about the compensation and incentives that go with it.

This 'sales as a system' view reminds us that, in trying to diagnose issues, we might need to look beyond the problem in front of us to fix them. For example, as a training consultancy, we often get requests for 'closing skills', because conversion rates are poor. Often, this is because the sales process is either poorly defined, plain wrong, or not executed well.

Professor Nick Lee has long advocated that sales leaders should think like scientists in finding out what works rather than relying on 'fake news and sloppy thinking'.[1] With the abundance of data, sales leaders more than ever have the opportunity to do this.

Evolving your sales system

As your start-up/SME grows, you will undoubtedly need to change the system. An often-encountered example of this is moving from one generalist sales role at a start-up to two or more defined roles to manage acquisition and account retention. When you face a change like this, my hope is that the various chapters in this book help you to think through and implement the needed changes that knit together well.

If all elements of your system point in the same direction, then it is likely your sales staff will head in that direction.

New product launches

A very common situation where the sales approach will need to be revisited is when you launch a new product. It is worth stepping back at this point to ask: how should a product/

DOI: 10.4324/9781003449614-18

service like this be sold? Thus, revisiting Chapter 3 and cross-checking your assumptions about the type of sales process needed will pay dividends. From here, all the linked sales organisation elements might need to be adjusted:

- Metrics
- Sales methodology
- Training and coaching
- Value proposition design
- Pricing
- Structures/roles
- Sales management routines

Paying attention to your sales system is no different from looking after your physical well-being. If you want to get fitter, you might need to do more gym work, improve flexibility, nutrition, sleep and so on. Working on one element alone is unlikely to lead to the success you are searching for.

The future of sales management

One thing I love about sales management is the highly dynamic nature of the profession. Because of strong competition in many industries, there is a continual need to evolve and adapt to stay relevant to customers.

At this point in history, we are facing two huge drivers of change for sales: technology and business model innovation. Both have the potential to massively disrupt the way we sell today.

The case has been made for why technology is so vital in sales in Chapter 12. Why is business model innovation important to consider? An example would be the introduction of 'freemium' models for apps, where consumers can have a free basic version of a software (think LinkedIn) or pay extra for a bells-and-whistles version (think LinkedIn Navigator).

This model is a relatively new one in the world of commerce. Previously, the zeitgeist was that product/services were paid for. This new business model enables companies to reach enormous scale (the so-called network effect[2]) before monetising this advantage. Investment capital is always attracted to industry disruptors who can scale very fast, so they rapidly reap the rewards of their investment.

This market force rewards entrepreneurs who can think of faster ways to grow, and asking the existential question of "how can we sell without selling", I believe, help us to think outside the box and be open to disruptive ways of trading that do not involve sales organisations.

So, the challenge for SMEs and start-ups, nimble and agile as they are, is to keep one eye on building a world-class sales engine and, at the same time, think innovatively of new ways to grow that customers will love.

With this in mind, can you imagine a more exciting role to have than the one you have now?

Notes

1 N. Lee "Evaluating and solving problems" *The International Journal of Sales Transformation* Issue 3.4 2017
2 J. McGee et al *Strategy: Analysis and practice* p473 McGraw Hill 2005

Index

Note: **Bold** page numbers refer to tables; *italic* page numbers refer to figures.